# The Emotions in the Classics of Sociology

*The Emotions in the Classics of Sociology* stands as an innovative sociological research that introduces the study of emotions through a detailed examination of the theories and concepts of the classical authors of discipline.

Sociology plays a crucial role emphasizing how much emotional expressions affect social dynamics, thus focusing on the ways in which subjects show (or decide to show) a specific emotional behaviour based on the social and historical context in which they act. This book focuses the attention on the individual emotions that are theorized and studied as forms of communication between subjects as well as magnifying glasses to understand the processes of change in the communities. This volume, therefore, guides the readers through an in-depth overview of the main turning points in the social theory of the classical authors of sociology highlighting the constant interaction between emotional, social and cultural elements. Thus, demonstrating how the attention of the emotional way of acting of the single subject was already present in the classics of the discipline.

The book is suitable for an audience of undergraduate, postgraduate students and researchers in sociology, sociology of emotions, sociology of culture, social theory and other related fields.

**Massimo Cerulo** is Associate Professor of Sociology at the Department of Political Sciences of the University of Perugia, Italy, and *chercheur associé* at the CERLIS Laboratory, University of Paris, France. His research interests include the sociology of emotions, the social theory, and the sociology of culture. He has introduced in Italy parts of the social theory of some classics of sociology such as Pierre Bourdieu, Gabriel Tarde, and Arlie R. Hochschild. He is the author of the first Italian handbook about the sociology of emotions: *Sociologia delle emozioni* (2018). His latest book is: *Émotions et dynamiques sociales* (2021).

**Adrian Scribano** is Director of the Centre for Sociological Research and Studies (CIES) and a Principal Researcher at the National Council for Scientific and Technical Research of Argentina. He is also the Director of the *Latin American Journal of Studies on Bodies, Emotions and Society* and leads the Study Group on Sociology of Emotions and Bodies in the Gino Germani Research Institute, Faculty of Social Sciences, University of Buenos Aires. He also serves as a Coordinator of the 26 Working Group on Bodies and Emotions of the Latin American Association of Sociology (ALAS) and as Vice-President of the Thematic Group 08 Society and Emotions of the International Sociological Association (ISA).

# Routledge Advances in Sociology

316 **Anxiety in Middle-Class America**
Sociology of Emotional Insecurity in Late Modernity
*Valérie de Courville Nicol*

317 **Boredom and Academic Work**
*Mariusz Finkielsztein*

318 **The Emotions in the Classics of Sociology**
A Study in Social Theory
*Edited by Massimo Cerulo and Adrian Scribano*

319 **Emotions and Belonging in Forced Migration**
Syrian Refugees and Asylum Seekers
*Basem Mahmud*

320 **Languages and Social Cohesion**
A Transdisciplinary Literature Review
*Gabriela Meier and Simone Smala*

321 **The Social Construction of the US Academic Elite**
A Mixed Methods Study of Two Disciplines
*Stephanie Buyer*

322 **Domestic Economic Abuse**
The Violence of Money
*Supriya Singh*

For more information about this series, please visit: www.routledge.com/Routledge-Advances-in-Sociology/book-series/SE0511

# The Emotions in the Classics of Sociology

A Study in Social Theory

Edited by Massimo Cerulo
and Adrian Scribano

LONDON AND NEW YORK

First published 2022
by Routledge
2 Park Square, Milton Park, Abingdon, Oxon OX14 4RN

and by Routledge
605 Third Avenue, New York, NY 10158

*Routledge is an imprint of the Taylor & Francis Group, an informa business*

© 2022 selection and editorial matter, Massimo Cerulo and Adrian Scribano; individual chapters, the contributors

The right of Massimo Cerulo and Adrian Scribano to be identified as the authors of the editorial material, and of the authors for their individual chapters, has been asserted in accordance with sections 77 and 78 of the Copyright, Designs and Patents Act 1988.

All rights reserved. No part of this book may be reprinted or reproduced or utilised in any form or by any electronic, mechanical, or other means, now known or hereafter invented, including photocopying and recording, or in any information storage or retrieval system, without permission in writing from the publishers.

*Trademark notice*: Product or corporate names may be trademarks or registered trademarks, and are used only for identification and explanation without intent to infringe.

*British Library Cataloguing-in-Publication Data*
A catalogue record for this book is available from the British Library

*Library of Congress Cataloging-in-Publication Data*
Names: Cerulo, Massimo, editor. | Scribano, Adrián, editor.
Title: The emotions in the classics of sociology : a study in
social theory / edited by Massimo Cerulo and Adrian Scribano.
Description: Abingdon, Oxon ; New York, NY : Routledge, [2021] |
Series: Routledge advances in sociology |
Includes bibliographical references and index.
Identifiers: LCCN 2021014111 (print) | LCCN 2021014112 (ebook) |
ISBN 9780367542566 (hbk) | ISBN 9780367542580 (pbk) |
ISBN 9781003088363 (ebk)
Subjects: LCSH: Emotions–Sociological aspects. |
Emotions–Social aspects. | Social structure. | Sociology.
Classification: LCC HM1033 .E532 2021 (print) |
LCC HM1033 (ebook) | DDC 301–dc23
LC record available at https://lccn.loc.gov/2021014111
LC ebook record available at https://lccn.loc.gov/2021014112

ISBN: 978-0-367-54256-6 (hbk)
ISBN: 978-0-367-54258-0 (pbk)
ISBN: 978-1-003-08836-3 (ebk)

DOI: 10.4324/9781003088363

Typeset in Times New Roman
by Newgen Publishing UK

To our families.

# Contents

|  |  |
|---|---|
| *List of contributors* | ix |
| *Acknowledgements* | xii |
| Introduction<br>MASSIMO CERULO AND ADRIAN SCRIBANO | 1 |
| 1  Harriet Martineau<br>ANGÉLICA DE SENA | 5 |
| 2  Karl Marx<br>ADRIAN SCRIBANO | 23 |
| 3  Gabriel Tarde<br>MASSIMO CERULO | 39 |
| 4  Émile Durkheim<br>JUAN PABLO VÁZQUEZ GUTIÉRREZ | 54 |
| 5  Max Weber<br>GREGOR FITZI | 68 |
| 6  Georg Simmel<br>MASSIMO CERULO AND ANTONIO RAFELE | 81 |
| 7  Vilfredo Pareto<br>VINCENZO ROMANIA | 96 |
| 8  Charles Horton Cooley<br>MARIANO LONGO | 113 |
| 9  George Herbert Mead<br>LORENZO BRUNI | 134 |

10  Norbert Elias                                          152
    GABRIELA VERGARA

11  Ibn Khaldun                                            168
    ADRIAN SCRIBANO

    *Index*                                                185

# Contributors

**Lorenzo Bruni** is a senior researcher in Sociology at the University of Perugia. His research topics, to which he has devoted many national and international publications, concern social recognition, emotions, shame, critical theory, solidarity and classical sociological theory. He is member of international research networks, including the Working Group "Society and Emotions" of ISA - International Sociological Association and the Research Group "REDISS - Red Internacional de Sociología de las Sensibilidades".

**Massimo Cerulo** is Associate Professor of Sociology at the Department of Political Sciences of the University of Perugia (IT), and *chercheur associé* at the CERLIS Laboratory, University of Paris (FR). He has introduced in Italy parts of the social theory of some classics of sociology such as Pierre Bourdieu, Gabriel Tarde, and Arlie R. Hochschild. He is the author of the first Italian handbook about the sociology of emotions: *Sociologia delle emozioni* (il Mulino 2018). His latest book is: *Émotions et dynamiques sociales* (PULM, 2021).

**Angélica De Sena** is Independent Researcher by CONICET-UNLaM and the Gino Germani Research Institute (FCS-UBA). She coordinates the Study Group on Social Policies and Emotions at CIES (GEPSE). She was visiting professor at University Cambridge, Universitá di Milano-Bicocca, Shanghai International Studies University. She is the director of the Latin American Journal of Social Research Methodology (ReLMIS). She is the Coordinator of the UNLaM Regional Node in the Latin American Network of Social Sciences Methodology (RedMet). She is the Coordinator of the CLACSO Working Group: "Sensitivities, subjectivities and poverty". She is co-coordinator of the ISA Working Group "Society and Emotions".

**Gregor Fitzi** is associate researcher at the Centre Georg Simmel, École des Hautes Études en Sciences Sociales, Paris. After his PhD in Sociology at the University of Bielefeld, he was assistant professor at the Institute of

Sociology, University of Heidelberg, Interim Full Professor of Sociological Theory at the University of Bielefeld and Co-Director of the Centre for Citizenship, Social Pluralism and Religious Diversity, at University of Potsdam. Among his recent publications are: *The Challenge of Modernity. Simmel's Sociological Theory*, (2019) and with Bryan S. Turner. 'Max Weber's Politics as a Profession'. Special Issue of *the Journal of Classical Sociology*, 4/2019.

**Mariano Longo** is Full Professor of Sociology at the University of Salento, where he teaches History of Sociology and Qualitative Methods for the Social Sciences. His main research interests are social theory, narratives and the sociology of emotions. Recent publication in these fields are *Fiction and Social Reality. Literature and Narrative as Sociological Resource* (Routledge, 2015) *and Emotions through Literature. Fictional Narrative, Society and the Emotional Self* (Routledge, 2019).

**Antonio Rafele** is Professor of Communication at the University of Naples Federico II and Research Fellow at the CEAQ, University of Paris Descartes La Sorbonne. His research focuses on media and culture theory problems that have given rise to several publications, including two monographs: *Representations of Fashion* (San Diego University Press, 2013) and *Replay. Calcio, vetrine e choc* (Luca Sossella, 2018).

**Vincenzo Romania** is Associate Professor in Sociology at the University of Padua and invited professor at the Venice International University. He has been editor of different sociological journals and secretary (2017–2020) at the AIS (Italian Sociological Association) Section in Sociological Theory and Social Transformations. He has published and edited several books and articles on sociological theory, identity studies and multiculturalism.

**Adrian Scribano** is Director of the Centre for Sociological Research and Studies (CIES estudiosociologicos.org) and a Principal Researcher at the National Council for Scientific and Technical Research of Argentina. He is also the Director of the *Latin American Journal of Studies on Bodies, Emotions and Society* and the Study Group on Sociology of Emotions and Bodies, in the Gino Germani Research Institute, University of Buenos Aires. He also serves as Coordinator of the 26 Working Group on Bodies and Emotions of the Latin American Association of Sociology (ALAS) and as Vice-President of the Thematic Group 08 Society and Emotions of the ISA.

**Juan Pablo Vazquez Gutiérrez** is Full-Time Professor and Researcher in Social Theory, Culture and Emotions at the Social and Political Sciences Department of the Universidad Iberoamericana, Mexico City. He is member of the National System of Researchers, CONACYT, Level I,

He is also member of the Group on Bodies and Emotions of the Latin American Association of Sociology (ALAS).

**Gabriela Vergara** is Associate Researcher at the National Scientific and Technological Research Council, Argentina and Associate Professor at the National University of Rafaela. She is also researcher of the Centre for Sociological Research and Studies (CIES estudiosociologicos.org) and co-director of Social Studies Group about Subjectivities and Conflict (gessyco.com.ar). She also serves as Program Coordinator of the Thematic Group 08 Society and Emotions for the Forum ISA 2021-Porto Alegre of the International Sociological Association (ISA).

# Acknowledgements

We want to thank Mary Holmes and Emily Briggs for trusting on this project. We also want to thank Lakshita Joshi for the editorial assistance, and Majid Yar for his valuable assistance. The proofreading has been financed by the Department of Political Sciences, University of Perugia: "Progetto di ricerca di base, TITOLO: 'LE TRASFORMAZIONI DELLA SFERA PUBBLICA E L'EVOLUZIONE DELLE MIGRAZIONI INTERNAZIONALI. DUE PROSPETTIVE DI ANALISI', finanziato con il Fondo Ricerca di Base, 2017".

# Introduction

*Massimo Cerulo and Adrian Scribano*

This book stands as an innovative sociological study that introduces the study of emotions through a detailed examination of the theories and concepts of the classical authors. This study leads both to a discovery of "forgotten" sociological theories, and to an updating of classical texts in the light of the dynamics of contemporary society. Through a revised study of the theories of the classical authors of sociology – who represent an unlimited source of knowledge due to the depth of their analysis – the main objective is to study the emotions from a sociological perspective, consistent with the emotional expressions produced by their subjects.

Sociology plays a crucial role in emphasizing how emotional expressions affect social dynamics, thus focusing on the ways in which subjects show or decide to show a specific emotional behaviour based on the social and historical context in which they act. In particular, emotions are considered to be endowed with a visibility and a weight to be considered external to the inner reality of the subject: they can be shaped, copied and managed differently over time, based on the cultural context (Hochschild, 1979; see Stets, Turner, 2014; 2007; Turner, Stets, 2005; Bolton, 2005; Francis, 1994).

This book, therefore, aims to guide the reader to an in-depth understanding of social reality through the interpretative lens of emotional manifestations, through an analysis of the very first sociology studies, thus demonstrating how attention to the subject's emotional forms of action was already present in the classics of the discipline.

This is the first volume of its kind in the world in English. No other book on the international market combines an accessible introduction to the topics and historical perspective for the first sociological studies about the emotions in society together with a narrative about the modernity of these theories.

It is a research endeavour that demonstrates how critical emotions have always been for sociology since its birth (as will be shown by the chapters dedicated to the first sociologists: Martineau, Marx, Tarde, etc.). This certainly does not mean that only a few studies in the sociology of emotions are available today. But it is also true that the sociology of emotions is characterized by an ambivalent nature: on the one hand, it is configured as a consolidated current of study, born in the USA in the 1970s, with much of autonomous teaching available today in most American universities and with sections dedicated to it in the two main world associations of sociology (the International Sociological Association and the European Sociological Association); on the other hand, it is a porous field of study, since its analysis often intersects with those relating to sexuality (cf. Piazzesi, 2017; Piazzesi et al., 2020; Hakim, 2011) and to intimate relationships (cf. Kaufmann, 2017; 2007; 2002; De Singly, 2016; Bauman, 2003; Plummer, 2003; Swidler, 2001; Jamesion, 1998; Giddens, 1992; Beck, Beck-Gernsheim, 1990), as well as with gender studies (see Stets, Turner, 2014, ch. 19; Fisher, 2000) and with those about the body (see. Le Breton, 2016; Elliot, Lemert, 2006).

However it is still possible to state that, nowadays, the sociology of emotions finally enjoys a sociological prestige, not only in the USA, but also in Latin America (see: De Sena, Scribano, 2019; Scribano, 2019; 2018; 2017) and, in particular, in Europe (Kleres, 2009), where specialized textbooks are produced (see: Cerulo, 2018a; Harris, 2015; Stets, Turner, 2014; 2007; Flam, 2002), along with collected volumes (see, among others: Cerulo, 2018b; Greco, Stenner, 2009), and focused analysis (see, among others: Cerulo, 2021; Demertzis, 2020; Kahl, 2019; Illouz, 2019; 2006; Jeantet, 2018; Le Bart, 2018; Bernard, 2017; 2015; Martuccelli, 2016; Ferréol, 2015; Flam, Kleres, 2015; von Scheve, 2014; Paperman, 2013; Maffesoli, 2012; Turner, 2011; Hopkins et al., 2009; Rimé, 2005; Turner, Stets, 2005).

Among the main objectives of the volume are to:

- provide the readers with an updated overview of the main sociological theories produced by classical authors;
- re-build, even historically, the theoretical path that led to defining emotions as objects of social and sociological (and not exclusively psychological) studies; and
- enrich the scientific community with new analytical tools to study the social micro-macro processes (see Barbalet, 1998), as well as provide readers with the possibility to read their own behaviours with greater emotional expertise.

## References

Barbalet, J.M. (1998) *Emotion, Social Theory, and Social Structure. A Macrosociological Approach.* Cambridge: Cambridge University Press.
Bauman, Z. (2003) *Liquid Love. On the Frailty of Human Bonds.* Cambridge: Polity Press.
Beck, U., Beck-Gernsheim, E. (1990) *Das ganz normale Chaos der Liebe.* Frankfurt am Main: Suhrkamp.
Bernard, J. (ed.) (2015) Émotion/Émotions. *Terrains Théories*, 2.
Bernard, J. (2017) *La concurrence des sentiments. Une sociologie des émotions.* Paris : Mètaillé.

Bolton, S.C. (2005) *Emotion Management in the Workplace*. Basingstoke: Palgrave.
Cerulo, M. (2018a) *Sociologia delle emozioni. Autori, teorie, concetti*. Bologna: il Mulino.
Cerulo, M. (2018b) L'étude sociologique des émotions dans la société du capitalisme. Dialogue avec Eva Illouz. *Rassegna Italiana di Sociologia*, LIX, 4, 815–830.
Cerulo, M. (2021) *Émotions et dynamiques sociales*. Montpellier: PULM.
De Sena, A., Scribano, A. (2019) *Social Policies and Emotions: A Look from the Global South*. London: Palgrave.
De Singly, F. (2017) *Sociologie de la famille contemporaine*. Paris: Armand Colin.
De Singly, F. (2016) *Le soi, la couple, la famille*. Paris: Armand Colin.
Demertzis, N. (2020) *The Political Sociology of Emotions: Essays on Trauma and Ressentiment*. Abingdon and New York: Routledge.
Elliot, A., Lemert, C. (2006) *The New Individualism. The Emotional Costs of Globalization*. London and New York: Routledge.
Ferréol, G. (ed.) (2015) *Sentiments et émotions*. Bruxelles: EME.
Fischer, A. (2000) *Gender and Emotion. Social Psychological Perspectives*. Cambridge: Cambridge University Press.
Flam, H. (2002) *Soziologie der Emotionen: eine Einführung*. Konstanz: UVK Verlagsgesellschaft mbH.
Flam, H., Kleres, J. (eds). (2015) *Methods of Exploring Emotions*. Abingdon and New York: Routledge.
Francis, L.E. (1994) Laughter, the Best Mediator: Humor as Emotion Management in Interaction. *Symbolic Interaction*, 17, 147–163.
Giddens, A. (1992) *The Transformation of Intimacy. Sexuality, Love and Eroticism in Modern Societies*. Cambridge: Polity.
Greco, M., Stenner, P. (eds). (2009) *Emotions. A Social Science Reader*. London and New York: Routledge.
Hakim, C. (2011) *Erotic Capital*. New York: Basic Books.
Harré, R. (ed.) (1986) *The Social Construction of Emotions*. Oxford: Blackwell.
Harris, S. (2015) *An Invitation to the Sociology of Emotions*. Abingdon and New York: Routledge.
Hochschild, A.R. (1979) Emotion Work, Feeling Rules and Social Structure. *American Journal of Sociology*. 85(3) 551–575.
Hochschild, A.R. (1983) *The Managed Heart: The Commercialization of Feeling*. Berkeley, CA: University of California Press.
Hopkins, D., Kleres, J., Flam, H., Kuzmics, H. (eds.) (2009) *Theorizing Emotions. Sociological Explorations and Applications*. Chicago: University of Chicago Press.
Illouz, E. (2006) *Gefühle in Zeiten des Kapitalismus*, Frankfurt am Main: Suhrkamp Verlag.
Illouz E. (ed.) (2019) *Emotions as Commodities. Capitalism, Consumption and Authenticity*. Abingdon and New York: Routledge.
Jamesion, L. (1998) *Intimacy: Personal Relationships in Modern Societies*. Cambridge: Polity.
Jeantet, A. (2018) *Les émotions au travail*. Paris: CNRS.
Kahl, A. (2019) *Analyzing Affective Societies: Methods and Methodologies*. Abingdon and New York: Routledge.
Kaufmann, J.-C. (2002) *Premier matin*. Paris: Armand Colin.

Kaufmann, J.-C. (2007) *Agacements. Les petites guerres du couple*. Paris: Armand Colin.
Kaufmann, J.-C. (2017), *Sociologie du couple*. Paris: Presses Universitaires de France.
Kleres, J. (2009) *Preface: Notes on the Sociology of Emotions in Europe*. In D. Hopkins, J. Kleres, H. Flam, H. Kuzmics (eds). *Theorizing Emotions. Sociological Explorations and Applications*. Frankfurt am Main: Campus Verlag, 7–27.
Le Bart, C. (2018) *Les émotions du pouvoir. Larmes, rires, colères des politiques*. Paris: Armand Colin.
Le Breton, D. (2016) *Sociologie du corps*. Paris: PUF.
Maffesoli, M. (2012) *Homo eroticus. Des communions émotionnelles*. Paris: CNRS Éditions.
Martuccelli, D. (2016) L'affectivité implicative et la vie en société. *Quaderni di Teoria Sociale*, 1, 9–28.
Paperman, P. (2013) *Care et sentiments*. Paris: PUF.
Piazzesi, C. (2017) *Vers une sociologie de l'intime: éros et socialisation*. Paris: Hermann.
Piazzesi, C., Blais, M., Lavigne, J., Lavoie Mongrain, C. (eds). (2020) *Intimités et sexualités contemporaines*. Montréal : Les Presses de l'Université de Montréal.
Plummer, K. (2003) *Intimate Citizenship: Private Decisions and Public Dialogues*. Washington, DC: Washington University Press.
Rimé, B. (2005) *Le partage social des émotions*. Paris: PUF.
Scribano, A. (2017) *Normalization, Enjoyment and Bodies/Emotions: Argentine Sensibilities*. New York: Nova Science Publishers.
Scribano, A. (2018) *Politics as Emotions*. Devon: Studium Press.
Scribano, A. (2019) *Love as a Collective Action: Latin America, Emotions and Interstitial Practices*. Abingdon and New York: Routledge.
Stets, J. E., Turner, J.H. (eds). (2007) *Handbook of the Sociology of Emotions*. New York: Springer.
Stets, J., Turner, J.H. (eds). (2014) *Handbook of the Sociology of Emotions: Volume II*. New York: Springer.
Swidler, A. (2001) *Talk of Love. How Culture Matters*. Chicago: University of Chicago Press.
Turner, J.H. (2011) *The Problem of Emotions in Societies*. London and New York: Routledge.
Turner, J.H., Stets, J.E. (2005) *The Sociology of Emotions*. Cambridge: Cambridge University Press.
Von Scheve, C. (2014) *Emotion and Social Structures. The Affective Foundations of Social Order*. London and New York: Routledge.

Chapter 1

# Harriet Martineau

Angélica De Sena

## 1.1 Introduction

Harriet Martineau (1802–1876) was a founder of social criticism in the UK. Feminist, sociologist, economist, and writer are just some of the characteristics of a woman who fought against loneliness, illnesses, and misunderstanding.

This chapter seeks to emphasize Harriet Martineau's role as the founding mother of sociology and a classic contributor to the study of emotions and sensibilities as axes of social analysis.

> This is a book [chapter] about social theory and about the history of sociology. It makes three claims: that women have always been significantly involved in creating sociology; that women have always made distinctive and important contributions to social theory; and that women's contributions to sociology and social theory have been written out of the record of the discipline's history.
> (Madoo Lengermann and Niebrugge, 1998)

Harriet Martineau's work was a tribute to the Victorian moral context, to the critical situation of the "social question" in the United Kingdom, and the new movements and ideas such as anti-slavery, feminism, and social criticism in general. This is the context from which it is not possible to forget the emergence of the "autonomy" of the social sciences, especially political economy, and sociology.

The chapter is organized in the following way: first, a schematic biography of the author will be presented; second, it is pointed out how emotions play a preponderant role in her most recognized texts; third, fourth and fifth place emphasis is placed in the importance of emotions and sensibilities in three of her most influential books. The chapter ends by reconstructing the arguments used to show the centrality of the author for sociology in general, as well as the sociology of emotions in particular.

## 1.2 Harriet Martineau: An introductory biography

Harriet Martineau (1802–1876), born in Norwich into a middle-class family and attending a Unitarian school for girls, was one of the most outstanding intellectuals of her time. A tireless writer, she made the figure of the traveller the starting point to investigate, describe, and explain the social world, making important contributions to political economy, sociological theory, and political analysis.

She was interested in the question of the "condition of England" and the debates on the question of women in the Victorian era. Martineau received a better formal education than most women of her time and, after the death of her father, a textile manufacturer, she decided to pursue a career as a writer, one of the few legitimate occupations open to women in Victorian England.

Martineau, who endured a series of physical ailments, became deaf at the age of 12 and had to use a trumpet for the rest of her life. She also suffered from a loss of taste and smell. At thirty she was bed-bound for more than five years; when doctors described her illness as incurable, she decided to opt for mesmerism. Despite all the prognoses, after a few months she managed to improve and described her case in "Life in the Sick Room: Essays by an Invalid" (1844) and "Letters on Mesmerism" (1845). She openly discussed her own illnesses and started a public debate about illness, cures, and the status of the disabled in society.

Towards the end of the 1820s, she wrote a series of educational treatises, dealing with industrial development, anticipating her most popular publication, *Illustrations of Political Economy*. After her initial success as a journalist and social commentator, Martineau moved to London, where she met the most eminent writers, intellectuals, and scholars of her time, including William Wordsworth, John Stuart Mill, Thomas Carlyle, Thomas Malthus, Robert Owen, and Charles Babbage.

Martineau's popularity crossed the Atlantic and in 1832–1834 she visited the United States. After her return, she published *Society in America* (1837) and two novels, *Deerbrook* (1839) and *The Hour and Man* (1841).

She propped up the Radical Reform Movement because she believed its members advocated economic and social progress. Martineau exerted a great influence on social thought in England through her critical analyses, her views on current affairs, and her fictional narratives.

Our author was in favour of a deterministic doctrine of causality, derived from John Locke and popularized by Joseph Priestley (1733–1804), who held that everything was a consequence of what had preceded it. There is no free will or free human action; a person is a creature of circumstances. She argued that the universe, in general, and society, in particular, operate according to certain natural laws that can be understood through science and education. In this context, she sought to convince both capitalists and workers that they should accept economic laws and work in harmony with them in an ordinary way.

When visiting the United States, she met some abolitionist leaders with whom she shared some common causes (e.g. the end of slavery), becoming a fervent defender of this movement, when it was still unpopular. Martineau wrote anti-slavery diatribes in the *Daily News*, stimulating the radical and progressive thinking of her day. She ironically argued that the slaveholders appreciated their horses more than their slaves since they did not sexually abuse them. And she, at the same time, explained that the abuse of the slaves was not only due to physical passion, but also due to the economic gains that the children who were born through said abuse implied.

It is in this context that Martineau asks the now-well-known question: "Why would a man pay for a woman every time he goes to bed with her when he can buy her for life, sleep with her whenever he wants …?". For our author, women and slaves suffered similar domination. In both cases, condescension was practiced as a substitute for justice, and she concluded that both are key factors in defining the moral condition of North American society.

As she herself argued:

> In discussing the subject of Female Education, it is not so much my object to inquire whether the natural powers of women be equal to those men, as to shew the expediency of giving proper scope and employment to the powers which they do possess.
>
> (in Yates, 1985: 88)

Martineau has been nominated as "the first female sociologist". Martineau's writings on political economy and scientific methods, her comparative study of American societies, and her knowledge of the subordination of women in American society in the 1830s has received unanimous recognition. Martineau's main achievements can be recognized as follows: (1) writing the first book on sociological methodology, (2) completing an in-depth and methodologically advanced analysis of American society, and (3) translating and condensing Comte's fundamental work (Deegan, 2003). In this context, it should be noted that Martineau wrote *The Rules of the Sociological Method* sixty years before Durkheim with similar content.

Martineau criticizes the popular notion of the moral sense, the view that moral principles are "fixed and immutable" so everyone must agree on what counts as sin and virtue in every case. The moral adherent to a rigid doctrine sees "sin" where there is only "difference" and suffers the "agitation of being shocked and alarmed" at strange sights instead of preserving "calm", "hope" and "sympathy". The problem with the moral sense, for Martineau, is that, in proposing a universal and absolute system of moral principles, it does not take into account the wide range of differences across historical ages and cultures, thus blinding the observer by forcing him to disapprove of behaviour that is alien to his experience rather than trying to understand it (Pace Vetter, 2008).

For Shulamit Reinharz (1992) the work done by Harriet Martineau in *Society in America* is the clear beginning of a feminist ethnography. In her Introduction, she explains that the duty of the researcher is to provide detailed observations and data so that readers can make their own judgements.

It is within the framework of this life of commitment and reflection that we see Harriet Martineau's journey from journalism, through social criticism, to her status as the 'founding mother' of sociology in a combination of social conscience and scientific rigor.

In the next section we will briefly review how sensations, emotions, and sensibilities are a crucial element in her most outstanding works.

## 1.3 Emotions, senses, and sensibilities as a starting point

Our author's work was deeply connected to her interest in having emotions, senses, and sensibilities at the center of her analyses. Her book *Household Education* begins with reflection on happiness and the importance of it for relations with others as the constitutive axis of society:

> Household Education is a subject so important in its bearings on every one's happiness, and so inexhaustible in itself, that I do not see how any person whatever can undertake to lecture upon it authoritatively, as if it was a matter completely known and entirely settled. It seems to me that all that we can do is to reflect, and say what we think, and learn of one another. This is, at least, all that I venture to offer. I propose to say, in a series of chapters, what I have observed and thought on the subject of Life at Home, during upwards of twenty years' study of domestic life in great variety.
>
> (Martineau, 1843: 1)

In her famous book *Morals and Manners*, considered one of the founding books on the methodology of social research, she first considers the sensations:

> There is no department of inquiry in which it is not full as easy to miss truth as to find it, even when the materials from which truth is to be drawn are actually present to our senses. A child does not catch a goldfish in water at the first trial, however good his eyes may be, and however clear the water; knowledge and method are necessary to enable him to take what is actually before his eyes and under his hand.
>
> (Martineau, 1838: 1)

It is clear that, for our author, political economy is structured around the enjoyment of life, giving rise to comfort, pleasure, and harmony:

> Political Economy treats of the Production, Distribution and Consumption of Wealth; by which term is meant whatever material objects contribute to the support and enjoyment of life. Domestic economy is an interesting subject to those who view it as a whole; who observe how, by good management in every department, all the members of a family have their proper business appointed them, their portion of leisure secured to them, their wants supplied, their comforts promoted, their pleasures cared for; how harmony is preserved within doors by the absence of all causes of jealousy; how good will prevail towards all abroad through the absence of all causes of quarrel.
> 
> (Martineau, 1832: a3)

In the Preface to the book, while discussing the observations made on her trip to the United States, she clearly states her criticism of a science erected as a measure of a policy of specific sensibilities and following what she prescribed in *Moral and Manners*:

> I am not finding fault with the Americans, as for falling behind the English, or the French, or any other nation. I decline the office of censor altogether. I dare not undertake it. Nor will my readers, I trust, regard the subject otherwise than as a compound of philosophy and fact. If we can all, for once, allay our personal feelings, dismiss our too great regard to mutual opinion, and put praise and blame as nearly as possible out of the question, more that is advantageous to us may perhaps be learned than by any invidious comparisons and proud judgments that were ever instituted and pronounced.
>
> (Martineau 1837: V)

In her famous book *Society in America*, where she narrates and reconstructs the observations made on her trip through the United States on a journey very similar to that made by Tocqueville, since it has the same Introduction, it is possible to notice her interest in making evident the politics of the sensibilities of that country:

> I am sure, I have seen much more of domestic life than could possibly have been exhibited to any gentleman travelling through the country. The nursery, the boudoir, the kitchen, are all excellent schools in which to learn the morals and manners of a people: and, as for public and professional affairs—those may always gain full information upon such matters, who really feel an interest in them—be they men or women. No people in the world can be more frank, confiding and affectionate, or

more skilful and liberal in communicating information, than I have ever found the Americans to be. I never asked in vain; and I seldom had to ask at all; so carefully were my inquiries anticipated, and my aims so completely understood. I doubt whether a single fact that I wished to learn, or any doctrine that I desired to comprehend, was ever kept from me because I was a woman.

(Martineau, 1837: xii–xiii)

In her defence of the equality of women to access the information necessary to reconstruct the morals and manners of all forms of society, our author points out daily life as a special area for elaborating a picture of the world of a given society. The kitchen, the dressing table, and the school are presented as places where the confidence necessary to express the life lived is revealed.

With this first approximation of some of the texts of Martineau, it is possible to observe the central place of emotions in her view of the world. From the beginning of each of the books referred to, our author establishes an important place for sensations, emotions, and sensibilities in the sociology that she is founding.

The next section deals with the place of emotions in her iconic book on the methodology of social research.

## 1.4 Morals and manners

*How to Observe. Morals and Manners* (1838) is perhaps the first book on the methodology of social research that was systematically prepared to make explicit the observation modality of a nascent science such as sociology and as a guide to carrying out the systematic and critical record of the aforementioned observation. A pioneer in its genre, *Morals and Manners*, was written several years before Émile Durkheim's *The Rules of the Sociological Method* (1895) and provides a detailed framework of sociological procedures for reconstructing the social world. Our author carries out an epistemic and methodological practice rarely seen in sociology. She writes a systematic guide on how she observes, including the philosophical, theoretical, and practical foundations from which others can make, analyse, and evaluate their own observations.

*Morals and Manners* is not only a pioneering book on the rules of social research methodology, but it is also a preview of an epistemology that considers and includes the connection between sensations, perceptions and analysis; it is thus a manual on the one hand, but on the other hand, it is a fundamental explanation of the epistemic values of the author.

### 1.4.1 The prerequisites

The book opens with the exposition of three types of prerequisites for the systematic observation of social reality: philosophical, moral, and mechanical, where the answers to three basic questions of social inquiry are discusses: what, how, and with whom. Martineau thus produces a conceptual-ontological leap that is still not sufficiently valued today: she includes observed subjects in her research rules.

Our author imagines philosophers and theorists drawing conclusions from what is observed and recorded under the slogan that no "fact" lacks analytical utility and that recording and observing has a specific function. From the beginning of the book, she advises that the observer should be considered "the servant instead of the lord of science".

In this sense, the selection of the position of traveller as a constitutive trait of the observer leads her to postulate:

> There are two parties to the work of observation on Morals and Manners—the observer and the observed. This is an important fact which the traveller seldom dwells upon as he ought; yet a moment's consideration shows that the mind of the observer—the instrument by which the work is done, is as essential as the material to be wrought. If the instrument be in bad order, it will furnish a bad product, be the material what it may. In this chapter I shall point out what requisites the traveller ought to make sure that he is possessed of before he undertakes to offer observations on the Morals and Manners of a people.
> (11)

In this context, Martineau organizes philosophical prerequisites into four sections that begin with the certainty of what the traveller wants to observe and ends with the problematization of what she calls "universal feelings":

a   "He must have made up his mind as to what it is that he wants to know" (11).

b   "Being provided with a conviction of what it is that he wants to know, the traveller must be furthermore furnished with the means of gaining the knowledge he wants. The universal summary notions of Morals may serve a common traveller in his judgments as to whether he would like to live in any foreign country, and as to whether the people there are as agreeable to him as his own nation" (14).

c   "As an instance of the advantage which a philosophical traveller has over an unprepared one, look at the difference which will enter into a man's judgment of nations, according as he carries about with him the vague popular notion of a Moral Sense, or has investigated the laws under which feelings of right and wrong grow up in all men. It is worth while to dwell a little on this important point" (21).

d   "The traveller having satisfied himself that there are some universal feelings about right and wrong, and that in consequence some parts of human conduct are guided by general rules, must next give his attention to modes of conduct, which seem to him good or bad, prevalent in a nation, or district, or society of smaller limits. His first general principle is, that the law of nature is the only one by which mankind at large can be judged. His second must be, that every prevalent virtue or vice is the result of the particular circumstances amidst which the society exists."

The architecture of these philosophical prerequisites shows how, for our author, the articulation between what one wants to know by capturing the moral senses in force in the observed societies is a fundamental condition of the development of social science. The next set of prerequisites for the investigation consigned by our author are rightly nominated as Morals.

For Martineau, a good observer is someone who abandons all prejudice, moral perversion, and anything that can distort her gaze; that is why the traveller, after following the philosophical prerequisites, must also have the following moral ones:

> 1stly. With a certainty of what it is that he wants to know, 2ndly. With principles which may serve as a railing point and test of his observations, 3rdly. With, for instance, a philosophical and definite, instead of a popular and vague, notion about the origin of human feelings of right and wrong, 4thly. And with a settled conviction that prevalent virtues and vices are the result of gigantic general in- fluences, —is yet not fitted for his object if certain moral requisites be wanting in him.
>
> (40)

The recommendations are clear and very "advanced" for her time: the researcher must perform a pre-reflective action that allows him to critically analyse his emotions and sensibilities and understand the "moral framing" to which he travels. It is in this context that our author clearly points out the centrality of empathy as a resource, and also as an epistemic and methodological objective:

> The observer must have sympathy; and his sympathy must be untrammeled and unreserved. If a traveller be a geological inquirer, he may have a heart as hard as the rocks he shivers, and yet succeed in his immediate objects: if he be a student of the fine arts, he may be as silent as a picture, and yet gain his ends: if he be a statistical investigator, he may be as abstract as a column of figures, and yet learn what he wants to know: but an observer of morals and manners will be liable to deception at every turn, if he does not find his way to hearts and minds. Nothing was ever more true than that "as face answers to face in water, so is the heart of man".
>
> (41)

It is very clear that both the philosophical and moral prerequisites are woven into the material of the position and disposition of the researcher in the face of sensations and sensibilities.

Finally, what Martineau calls mechanical prerequisites, refers to a set of recommendations on travel, ways of travelling, languages and their particularity. Seeing, recording and analysing seems to be the cadence of observation that our author strongly recommends; this question is reinforced in the final section of the book entitled "Mechanical Methods". Each and every one of these mechanical guidelines is based on achieving a fluid conversation where the information to be remembered.

Only the reconstruction of these prerequisites reveals how Martineau is undoubtedly the founder of an inquiry strategy based on the observation and analysis of accepted and acceptable sensibilities. This issue becomes clearer and more solid as the book progresses.

### 1.4.2 Research and feelings

What to investigate concerns both what the traveller wants to do and what is relevant to understanding societies, an issue that is not possible to ascertain without talking to people and treating them as the "first connoisseurs of the world". Knowledge of things is mediated by the discourse of agents since they are the first to know what to comment on about the things of the social world:

> The grand secret of wise inquiry into Morals and Manners is to begin with the study of THINGS, using the DISCOURSE OF PERSONS as a commentary upon them.
>
> (63)

The feelings associated with objects, things, institutions and nature expressed in conversations by people who live the day-to-day life of societies and countries are the guides to rebuild the acceptable and accepted sense and experience in those times and spaces. That is why Martineau states with regard to the potential information of the observable:

> The voice of a whole people goes up in the silent workings of an institution; the condition of the masses is reflected from the surface of a record. The Institutions of a nation—political, religious, or social—put evidence into the observer's hands as to its capabilities and wants which the study of individuals could not yield in the course of a life-time. The Records of any society, be they what they may, whether architectural remains, epitaphs, civic registers, national music, or any other of the thousand manifestations of the common mind which may be found among every

people, afford more information on Morals in a day than converse with individuals in a year.

(64)

Among the many facets that places Martineau at the forefront of her field is her awareness of the amalgamation between the cognitive and the affective, the emotional and rational, which occupies a place of privilege, even more so if, as she suggests, among other things, studying the songs generated by politics as a way to ascertain ideas and feelings:

> Under representative governments, where politics are the chief expression of morals, the songs of the people cannot but be an instructive study to the observer; and scarcely less so in countries where, politics being forbidden, the domestic and friendly relations must be the topics through which the most general ideas and feelings will flow out.
>
> (137)

It is obvious to Martineau that the aesthetic productions of societies involve the feelings that people experience and that such artistic works then serve to help us know societies through those feelings:

> All have Fiction (other than dramatic); and this must be one of the observer's high points of view. There is no need to spend words upon this proposition. It requires no proof that the popular fictions of a people, representing them in their daily doings and common feelings, must be a mirror of their moral sentiments and convictions, and of their social habits and manners.
>
> (142)

For Harriet Martineau, feelings are also a cement of society as the basis of a collaborative encounter:

> The need of mutual aid, the habit of co-operation caused by interest in social objects, has a good effect upon men's feelings and manners towards each other; and out of this grows the mutual regard which naturally strengthens into the fraternal spirit.
>
> (219)

Aesthetics, politics, economics, and education, according to our author, should be observed through the comments of people emerging from conversations and objects produced by a particular society. In this vein, religion becomes a very important part of every society being observed, because it lets us see the feelings that join the subjects to one another:

> The rules by which men live are chiefly drawn from the universal convictions about right and wrong which I have mentioned as being formed everywhere, under strong general influences. When sentiment is connected with these rules, they become religion; and this religion is the animating spirit of all that is said and done. If the stranger cannot sympathize in the sentiment, he cannot understand the religion; and without understanding the religion, he cannot appreciate the spirit of words and acts.
>
> (44)

Undoubtedly, according to what we have already argued in the context of this monumental work of Methodology of Social Research, this is enough to justify Harriet Martineau's position as the founding mother of the sociology of emotions; but this will only be fully complete when we consider the analysis carried out in two of her other fundamental works.

## 1.5 Household education

*Household Education* is an exemplary view of how Harriet Martineau's sociological gaze includes and uses a special sociology of emotions, masterfully analysing the politics of sensibilities. The book begins by stating the author's clear intention of influencing the course of daily life by making people who inhabit a house take each other's actions into account. Our author states that she has a strong desire for household partners to consult together about their path of action towards others.

The book consists of 26 chapters where the author presents her ideas about the skills, virtues, and values to be cultivated in an education that empowers men and women. Between chapters 8 and 14 our author develops hope, fear, patience and love as powers of the human to structure personal and interpersonal emotions within the framework of the exercise of will, truth, veneration and scrupulousness; these become the axes of an education for autonomy. Martineau's intention is very clear: to provide a guide that facilitates the reconstruction of the accepted and acceptable politics of sensibilities.

> And having once remembered, it will remember more every day. Every day it will give signs of Hope and Desire. Will shows itself very early. Fear has to be guarded against, and Love to be cherished, from the first days that mind appears. It is the highest possible privilege to the child if the parents know how to exercise its power of Conscience soon enough, so as to make it sweet and natural to the young creature to do right from its earliest days.
>
> (70)

### 1.5.1 Hope

For our author, hope is one of the central components of the empowerment of the human being that must be provided in household education to provide a better life:

> This great power of Hope must determine the leading features of the character of the man or woman; determine them for good or evil according to the training of the power from this day forward. Shall the man continue a child, or sink into the brute by his objects of hope continuing to be what they are now—food or drink? Shall his frame be always put into commotion by the prospect of pleasant bodily sensations from eating and drinking, and other animal gratifications?
>
> (79)

Hope must be appreciated in life as a whole, not just as an expectation of a particular benefit, but as a hopeful sensibility in general. For Martineau, hope must be continually valued as a faculty for life acquired and used step-by-step, as conditioning towards autonomy. Hope is a source of personal development linked to the goals of gratification, happiness, and transcendence: eating and drinking, entertainment, performing tasks, commitment to others. Hope is the sensibility on which personal improvement, growth and development are based.

### 1.5.2 Fear

The administration of fear, the management of worries, and the regulation of ghosts is one of the axes of the formation of children according to Martineau:

> There is nothing in which children differ more than in their capacity for Fear. But every child has it more or less—or ought to have it: for nothing can be made of a human being who has never experienced it. A child who has never known any kind of fear can have no power of Imagination; can feel no wonder, no impulse of life, no awe or veneration.
>
> (89)

Fear blocks, prevents, makes impossible the development of human faculties and that is why it is one of the central components in the education of children. In Martineau's eyes, a good father will never wish to create fear in his son, knowing what torment and suffering fear causes. Our author categorically asserts that a truly loving parent is aware that it would be less cruel to physically hurt their child than to plant feelings of torture in their mind. Martineau affirms that the most effective way, for all intents and purposes, is to discover the fear that is already there and to alleviate it, thus transforming this weakness into a source of strength and comfort.

### 1.5.3 Patience

Martineau includes patience among the basic sensibilities of every good education for the empowerment and autonomous life of human beings:

> Some may be surprised to find Patience spoken of among the Powers of Man. They have been accustomed to consider it a passive quality, and not as involving action of the mind. They do not find it in any catalogue of the organs of the brain, and have always supposed it a mere negation of the action of those organs. But patience is no negation. It is the vigorous and sustained action, amidst outward stillness, of some of the most powerful faculties with which the human being is endowed; and primarily of its powers of Firmness and Resistance.
> (103)

In what is awfully close to what, in contemporary language, is often called resilience, our author connects the ability to persist with goals and tolerance for failure as being one of the basic elements for children's education. For our author, the first milestone on the road to self-government, as the goal of all human life, is patience. Patience is both a social practice and includes a strong action of the mind: that is why there is nothing further away from patience than passivity.

### 1.5.4 Love

In the context of strongly pointing out the place of love in the home and in the development of human beings, Martineau has dedicated a chapter to reflecting on it. She analyses love as a platform of autonomy and growth for human beings, and as one of the most important faculties to develop. She identifies three kinds of love: passion, idolatry, and benevolence.

> This benevolence is the third form in which we have already seen what is called love. Can any tiling be more clearly marked than the difference between these three—the love that leads to marriage; fondness for objects which can be idolized; and benevolence which has no fondness in it, but desires the diffusion of happiness, and acts independently of personal regards? None of these yield the sort of affection which the heart of the parent desires and which is essential to family happiness.
> (142)

Our author warns that the saddest thing is the existence of unloved children, pointing out the centrality of the power of attachment and the exceptionality of a hermit life in the midst of the multitude of human life. In this way, it is possible to observe how emotions play a fundamental role in *Household Education* as an essay aimed at exposing the components of the development of autonomous and socially conscious lives. Hope, fear, patience, and love are the four components of the formation of children which are vital to create a better life.

## 1.6 Political economy

Martineau's proposed *Political Economy* is an interesting example of two features of her work that transform her into a founding mother: an awareness of generating new knowledge and her conviction of the urgency of "massifying it." The argumentative strategy chosen in the *Illustrations'* narratives, involving dialogue and problems, is a good example of these two traits. For our author, the purpose of the knowledge of political economy was happiness, general well-being and the diminution of inequality:

> It is certain, however, that sciences are only valuable in as far as they involve the interests of mankind at large, and that nothing can prevent their sooner or later influencing general happiness.
>
> (X)

It is in this context that in the book's own Preface, Martineau clearly explains her perspective on wealth and inequality using a narrative about a stranger's visit to a castle during feudalism:

> If it has been interesting to watch and assist the improvement of domestic economy from the days of feudal chiefs till now, can it be uninteresting to observe the corresponding changes of a state? If it has been an important service to equalize the lot of the hundred members of a great man's family, it must be incalculably more so to achieve the same benefit for the many million* of our population, and for other nations through them. This benefit cannot, of course, be achieved till the errors of our national management are traced to their source, and the principles of a better economy are established. It is the duty of the people to do this.
>
> (VI)

Clearly it is part of the political economy of morality and political sensibilities to associate economic order and collective benefits:

> If a stranger had entered the castle of a nobleman, eight hundred years ago, and, grieved at what he saw, had endeavoured to put matters on a

better footing, how ought he to set about it, and in what temper should he be listened to?

(VI)

First, Martineau points out the distance between waste and hatred as a sensibility of the "old regime" altering the balance of an economy for all:

> If he had the opportunity of addressing the entire household at once, he would say, " I have been in your splendid halls, and I saw vast sums squandered in gaming, while hungry creditors were looking on from without with rage in their countenances".

(VI)

Martineau points out how the the injustice between the lords who have an excess of food while their servants are treated no better than animals, is a landscape of sickness and conflict:

> I have been in your banqueting room, and I saw riot and drunkenness to-day where there will be disease and remorse to morrow. I have been in your kitchens, and I saw as much waste below as there had been excess above, while the under servants were driven into a cold corner to eat the broken food which was not good enough for their masters' dogs.

(VII)

Our author denounces the punitive system as miserable, idle, and melancholy which warns us of her interest in connecting the insidia of unjust prisons and the generation of wealth with their associated emotions:

> I have been in your dungeons, and I saw prisoners who would fain have laboured for themselves or their fellow-captives, condemned to converse in idleness with their own melancholy thoughts, or with companions more criminal and miserable than themselves.

(VII)

In the same way, Martineau describes the inequality produced by a system that does not allow human beings to connect and exchange goods freely, and which even forces them to give up their profits, which draws our attention to the importance she attached to building free social relations:

> I have been among the abodes of those who hew your wood and draw your water, and till your fields, and weave your garments; and I find that they are not allowed to exchange the produce of their labour as they will, but that artificial prices are set upon it, and that gifts are added to the profits of some which are taken out of the earnings of others.

(VII)

Oppressed and troubled, perplexed and disgruntled, the polar tensions our author uses to describe the poor and the rich, the rulers and the governed, the message is clear— a system that pays no attention to the principles of political economy generates a policy of unjust and disturbing sensibility:

> I hear complaints from all in turn, from the highest to the lowest; complaints which I cannot call unreasonable, since it is equally true that the poor among you are oppressed, and that the rich are troubled; that the rulers are perplexed and the governed discontented.
>
> (VII)

Harriet Martineau wrote a treatment of political economy aimed at motivating the citizens of her country to be aware of their principles and to seek good and safe government for all:

> These things need not be. There are methods of governing a family which will secure the good of all. I invite you to join me in discovering what these methods are.
>
> (VII)

Food, exchange, credit, and the punitive system, are some of the traits that colour the painting of the world that our author selects to point out how political economy implies a policy of sensibilities.

### 1.6.1 Openings to "re-start"

Without a doubt, Harriet Martineau's vibrant personality, her struggles as a social critic, and her intellectual legacy make her the founding mother of sociology in the United Kingdom and Europe, which encourages us not only to rethink her work, but also to take note of the problems with which it was concerned. Her feminism, her criticism of an unjust economic and social systems, her anti-slavery views, her commitment to the situation of the sick, and her interest in education, transforms our author's analytical perspective into an excellent map with which to explore the central problems of our century.

Neither objects, animals nor servants would be a good trilogy to synthesise the radical criticism raised by Harriet Martineau towards the model of patriarchal submission of the Victorian era, all components of the current feminist actions against the persistence of said model despite the "advances" that may have occurred.

The lives of girls and boys in poverty, the misery of the workers, the precariousness of the habitat, the lack of decent work, the ignorance of the laws of social structuring by common people and poor medical care, were all objects of concern for her. Harriet Martineau's analytics, in various ways, continue to be a valuable focus of the denunciation in critical thinking to today.

In keeping with the above, her journalistic work and her narrative style were always connected with what she identified as one of the axes of the reforms of her time: letting more people understand how and why society was constituted in one way and not in another. The context shown here allows us to better understand how Harriet Martineau's concern for emotions, sensations and sensibilities also cements her position as the founding mother of the sociology of emotions.

First, because of the centrality of sensations and emotions in the methodology of social research as essential components of what today we call the necessary double hermeneutics in the inquiry of the social. For Harriet Martineau, making immersion in "what people feel" becomes a central starting point for all research.

Second, because of the special position that love, hope, fear, and patience occupy in the education of girls, understanding that the experience within the family has a cognitive, affective, and moral impact on their formation.

Third, due to the emphasis on the sensibilities and feelings that she notes in her recording, narration, and analysis during her trips to the USA and the Islamic world, her acute observation is combined, with a neat application of her own rules elaborated in *Morals and Manners*. She also demonstrates a singular hermeneutical mastery in the analysis of the politics of sensibilities of both peoples and nations.

Within the framework of the horizon that the impetus and genius of Harriet Martineau painted more than a century ago, the legacy of this founding mother is undoubtedly to continue deepening the journey of the sociology of emotions as a critical academic practice that seeks the construction of a better world.

## References

Madoo Lengermann, P. and Niebrugge, G. (1998) *The Women Founders: Sociology and Social Theory 1830–1930*. Waveland. EEUU Press.
Pace Vetter, L. (2008) Harriet Martineau on the Theory and Practice of Democracy in America. *Political Theory*, 36(3), 424–455.
Reinharz, S. (1992). *Feminist Methods in Social Research*. New York: Oxford University Press.
Deegan. M. (2003) *Textbooks, the History of Sociology, and the Sociological Stock of Knowledge. Sociological Theory*, 21(3), 298–305.
Martineau, H. (1832) *Illustrations of Political Economy*. Vol. I. London. Charles Fox.
—— (1837) *Society in America*. 2nd edn. New York. Saunders and Otley.

—— (1838) *How to Observe. Morals and Manners*. London: Charles Knight.
—— (1843) *Household Education*. London: Edward Moxon.
Yates, Gayle Graham, ed. (1985) *Harriet Martineau on Women*. New Brunswick: Rutgers University Press.

# Chapter 2
# Karl Marx

*Adrian Scribano*

## 2.1 Introduction

Marx is undoubtedly a classic of the social sciences, and paradigms, theories, and revolutions have originated from his writings (Scribano, 1997, 2010). The question that this chapter seeks to clear up is: is Karl Marx a classic of the sociology of emotions? The answer is obvious: yes.

Elsewhere we have extensively considered why Marx is a classic contributor to the sociology of emotions, carrying out an analysis, in particular, of *The 1844 Manuscripts* (1974), *The Grundrisse* (1973), the Theory of Surplus Value, and, in general, a good part of his works since his Doctoral Thesis, The 18th Brumaire, The Class Struggles in France, etc. (Scribano, 2016, 2018). A synthetic version that includes the two aforementioned views was offered in 2018 in my article "Sociology of Bodies/Emotions: The Perspective of Karl Marx". Very recently I published a chapter on "The Other as radical intersubjectivity in Karl Marx", addressing the issue of intersubjectivity, alterity, the place of the other and sensibilities (Scribano, 2020). As we have already addressed on two occasions in three different ways, we have also demarcated what "being" a classic implies, and this applies to Marx because he shares the following characteristics with the rest of the "founding fathers" of the social sciences:

1   The work is taken as a conceptual and ontological source.
2   Like all classics, it is understood as an initiator and starting point for the development of images of the world and a specific way of understanding social relations.
3   It founds a genealogy of social knowledge, a field of theoretical and methodological belonging.
4   It produces one of the great metaphors that is later used as architecture, as the structure of different worldviews and analytical approaches of the social sciences.
5   Finally, it constitutes a horizon from which particular methodological structures of knowledge can be elaborated.

It is in this framework that this chapter seeks to make evident that Marx is a classic of the sociology of emotions from the reading of *Capital*, to expose this synthetically by pointing out the connections between senses, muscles, brain and flesh, and cruelty as a specific component of the politics of sensibilities of capitalism.

For the purposes of identifying Marx's contribution to the sociology of emotions, elsewhere we have constructed[1] five models/perspectives:

a  *Macro or micro*: This dichotomy privileges the individual/subjective or the collective/social as the "space" and source of emotions.
b  *Management or "significance"*: The differences come about by understanding emotions as "experiential" processes managed by the subjects or as processes that mark/signify the experiences of the subjects.
c  *Constructed or biological*: One side emphasizes the physiological/organic character of emotions (and bodies), and the other the fact that they are the result of the processes of construction by individuals.
d  *Basic emotions or emotions "as evaluations"*: The distance is established by either highlighting the existence of fundamental (anger, fear, happiness) emotions (linked to corporal reactions), or understanding emotions as the product of the subjects' appreciations of their surroundings.
e  *Social constructionist or social interactionist*: Interactionists claim that emotions "pass" through the processes of inter-relation between subjects, whereas constructionists uphold that emotions have a high cognitive content and are socially "elaborated" by individuals.

It becomes clear in the above table and in Marx's ideas as presented here, that he not only establishes a set of clear guidelines for the construction of a sociology of bodies/emotions, but also offers an important epistemic contribution to such a construction.

As I will show in this chapter, these features can be found, not only in the *Manuscripts*, in Marx's Doctoral Thesis, or in *The Grundrisse*, but also, specifically, in *Capital*. Marx explores in his main work the connections between bodies, sensations and constitutions of the real and the perceptions of the world and time and gives more than solid cues for analysing the politics of sensibilities involved in the political economy of morality. It is important to emphasize that in this chapter we have chosen to analyse *Capital* from the standpoint of sensations as an organizing vector of capitalist sensibility, and cruelty as a practice of feeling that makes up the emotional ecology of capitalism. In this context we can argue that Marx established the main milestones of a sociology of bodies/emotions as a social critique, and in this chapter, we will highlight some features in his most important book as evidence of this.

Karl Marx 25

Table 2.1 Marx's rupture of the classification criteria of contemporary perspectives

| Models/perspectives | Marx's perspective in the manuscripts |
| --- | --- |
| 1. Macro or Micro | The definition of the senses as resulting from human existence and regulated by the political economy of morality dissolves the pair individual/society as an aporia. |
| 2. Management or "significance" | The connections between having the other as an object of enjoyment and the substitutions of material/sensible potentialities in, and through, money are a clear rupture of this pair. |
| 3. Constructed or Biological | The fact that the formation of the five senses is the result of the eternal historical process deconstructs the aporetic situation between social and physiological construction as an explanation of sensations and emotions. |
| 4. Basic Emotions or Emotions "as Evaluations" | The statement on the relations between objects, needs, and human senses overruns this "epistemological pair". |
| 5. Social Constructionist or Social Interactionist | The analyses of the constitution of the political economy of morality as "linking" practices of expropriation turned into moral imperatives breaches the aporia of these perspectives. |

Source: Own elaboration.

## 2.2 Senses, muscles, brain and flesh

Based on the folding and unfolding of various Mobesian bands around what is organic/social in the body, Marx elaborates a look at the starting and finishing points of the constitution of the capitalist system anchored in the bodies/emotions.

One of the nodes in the plot of Marx's gaze on the place of bodies/emotions in the structuring of capitalism is configured around the senses. The social history of the senses opens the door to understanding the place of human being in the development of the various social formations that he builds. Another node is built around the clues that our author gives regarding the weight of the muscles and the brain when analysing salaried work. Among the folds of life/death that the system of social relations established by capitalism involve, Marx finds and refers to the tension between senses/muscles/brain as an indicator of the social structuring that said social system implies.

### 2.2.1 Senses

The senses of the human being are favourably associated with the intervention of the (over) human organism and its functions in the construction of society. The senses are also connected to the notion of corporeal materiality that takes on value as "put-at-work" appears for others and the Other:

> As we can see, the mystical character of the merchandise does not arise from its use value. But neither does it spring from the content of their value determinations. In the first place, because however much useful work or productive activities differ, it is an truth physiological incontrovertible that all these activities are functions of the organism human and that each of them, whatever its content and its form, represents an expense. Essential brain human, nerves, muscles, senses, etc.
>
> (Marx, 1909: 49)

> This indifference of the merchandise with respect to what is concrete in the corporeal materiality of another, is supplemented by its possessor with his five and more senses.
>
> (Idem 4)

It is important to note that (as in *The Manuscripts*) for Marx, the human begins his connection with the world in and through his senses, configuring his perceptions of the social forms among which the one he has a privileged position, in the capitalist system, with money.

> Between the circulation of money as capital and its circulation as money purely and simply, it mediates, then, as can be seen, **a perceptible difference through the senses.**
>
> (ibid. 105, emphasis ours)

It should be noted how Marx sees the proximity/distances between the body, the machine and the social senses of the human being as a key to understanding productive activities and modes of exploitation:

> This mechanical device does not come to supply a specific instrument, **but the human hand itself, in the operations in which it gives the worked material,** iron for example, a specific shape, handling various cutting instruments in different directions. In this way, it is possible to produce the geometric shapes of the different pieces of machinery, "with a degree of ease, precision and speed that no accumulated experience could lend to the hand of the most skilled worker".
>
> (ibid. 314–15, emphasis ours)

Working conditions are part of the conditions of existence insofar as they alter all the senses by putting/exposing the worker's body for exploitation. Marx's view of exploitation implies a direct connection between the means of production as "nature" (resources) and variable capital (human nature), both as objects to be exploited and depredated:

> Here we will only allude slightly to the material conditions under which work is performed in factories. All senses are disturbed by the artificial elevation of the temperature, the atmosphere laden with material waste, the deafening noise, etc. And let's not talk about the danger of having to work and circulate among the crammed machinery, which produces its industrial battle parts with the periodicity of the seasons. The tendency to economize the social means of production, a tendency that under the factory system, matures as a stove plant, becomes, in the hands of capital, a systematic plunder against the living conditions of the worker during work, an organized robbery of space, light, air and personal means of protection against unhealthy production processes, and let's not talk about the devices and facilities for the comfort of the worker. Is Fourier right or wrong when he calls factories "attenuated prisons"?
>
> (Idem 352–53)

Nose, ears, eyes altered, shocked, dispossessed of their "qualities" in and through a looting that involves heat, noise, the smell of a place thought to "steal organized" space, light, air: Marx clearly sees that capitalism is a factory for the naturalization and construction of sensations arranged for exploitation. That makes work an experience that modifies bodies.

> They were true experiments in corpore vili, such as those made in anatomy labs with frogs. Although I have pointed out – says Inspector Redgrave – the real income of workers in many factories, it is not believed that they receive the same sums week after week. Workers are subject to the greatest fluctuations, due to the constant experimenting ("experimentalizing") of manufacturers ....
>
> (Idem 381)

It is very interesting that Marx has selected the Latin expression "in corpore vili" since it makes clear that in capitalism there is no body without emotions in dialectical tension with the senses: workers are treated as vile, worthless, wasteful bodies. The exploited body of the worker is already in itself the "incarnation" of a sensibility: vileness. The workers are animalized, like frogs in the laboratory, they are the objects of someone else's experiences; they are subjected to experiments.

The identification, description and explanation of the "state-of-the-senses" is a fundamental key to explaining wage labour. The five senses, as the inscription surface of the exploitation and organic conditions of the worker, are analysed in two complementary directions: (a) as part of the politics of the bodies/emotions characteristic of capitalism, and (b) as a theoretical–critical instrument.

### 2.2.2 Muscles/brain

There is a constant in Marx: he describes and "represents" the human organism using the brain and muscles. Both play a central role in referring to different social practices, but especially to work. Whether by denial or affirmation, according to the development of the productive forces, the organic/cognitive/affective elements that link the living force of the muscles with the creative/productive potential of the brain and their connections are seen as central in social structuring. One of Marx's permanent references when he refers to the brain and the muscles refers to the connection between energy expenditure, livelihoods and work. Therefore, it is evident that the human body is a priority for making a critique of political economy:

> However, the workforce is only realized by exercising, and it is only exercised by working. When exercising, when working, a certain number of muscles, nerves, human brain, etc., are used, which must be replaced. As this expenditure intensifies, income must also intensify. After having worked today, the owner of the workforce has to repeat the same process tomorrow, in identical conditions of strength and health. Therefore, the sum of food and means of life must necessarily be sufficient to maintain the working individual in his normal state of life and work.
>
> (Idem 124)

It is easy to see how Marx emphasizes the view of the body as a complex totality that is not just a "set of parts" but a network of relationships with the aim of procuring life. The expenditure/income connection that our author maintains is a sample of his conviction about the existence of a flow that must be permanently rebuilt and that capitalism has had the cunning to subdue for the sole purpose of perpetuating its profits:

> Disregarding some other singularities. We do not believe that it is, for example, the price of bread that reappears in the form of new forms infused into man, but his food substances. And what reappears as the value of these forces is not precisely the food itself, but its value. **If these supplies only cost half, they will produce exactly the same amount of muscles, bones, etc., in sum the same force, but not a force of the same value.**
>
> (ibid., 157, note 7, emphasis ours)

There is a clear relationship between expenditure on the body and accumulation of wealth, between muscles, workforce and surplus value. In this context, it is important to highlight that when the situation of the working class must be described, reference is made immediately to the body, the means necessary for its reproduction and the sensibilities associated with it. It is evident that the corporeal anchorage of capitalism is in direct relation to industrialism and machinism and with its consequences for the body of the worker. One of the keys to the factory system is the supplantation of the energy and capacity of the muscles as a metaphor for bodily energy:

> In the factory, a dead mechanism exists above them, to which they are incorporated as living appendages. "That sad routine of endless torture of work, in which the same mechanical process is continually repeated, is like the torment of Sisyphus; the burden of work constantly rolls over the exhausted worker, like the rock of the fable." **Mechanical work greatly affects the nervous system, stifles the varied play of the muscles, and confiscates all free physical and spiritual activity of the worker.** Even the measures that tend to facilitate work become means of torture, since the machine does not free the worker from work, but rather deprives it of its content.
>
> (Idem 340, emphasis ours)

Capitalism is primarily a body/emotion-confiscating apparatus. The factory is a device for the dispossession of energies to which bodies are grafted. Marx clearly sees that there is a systemic relationship between a body politics based on torture, drowning and death involving wage labour and factory discipline.

> Machinery, by rendering muscle power useless, makes it possible to employ workers without muscular strength or without full physical development, who, on the other hand, have great flexibility in their limbs. The work of women and children was, therefore, the first cry of the capitalist application of machinery. In this way, that gigantic instrument created to eliminate work and workers, immediately became a means of multiplying the number of wage earners, placing all the individuals of the working family, without distinction of age or sex, under the immediate dependence of capital. Forced labor at the service of the capitalist came to invade and usurp, not only the place reserved for children's games, but also the place of free labor within the domestic sphere and, to break with moral barriers, invading the orbit reserved even for the same home.
>
> (Idem 323)

In the displacement of the need for large volumes of muscular strength, Marx sees the emergence of new moral regimes: the factory reconstructs the rules and familiar spaces, weak bodies are more apt to produce profit, and muscular flexibility becomes a metaphor for adaptability as an experiential parameter to survive.

> The capital that is given away in exchange for labor power is converted into means of life, **the consumption of which is used to reproduce the muscles, nerves, bones, and brains of today's workers and to procreate those to come**. Thus, within the limits of what is absolutely necessary, the individual consumption of the working class once again converts the capital paid in exchange for labor power into new labor power exploitable by capital.
>
> (Idem 481, emphasis ours)

Capital produces "bodies-for-the-future" where they will have a place in exploitation and productive work: muscles/brains depend on the consumption levels of livelihoods directly associated with the nutrients/food/hunger of a certain time/space. Marx emphasizes the role of the politics of bodies/emotions as a politics of hunger that combines a special grammar between instinct/hunger/energy in such a way that this relationship becomes a condition of the possibility of exploitation.

### 2.2.3 The "flesh" as analytic of the politics of the bodies/emotions

The flesh as a metaphor/indicator of the positions of the bodies/emotions in capitalist society is taken up again and again by Marx in *Capital*. The flesh becomes the inscription surface of the religion of capital, of the forms of exploitation and of the geometries of the bodies that are involved in the politics of the bodies/emotions of capitalism. In *Capital*, Marx repeatedly returns to the idea of society made flesh, the worker's flesh turned into merchandise and a space for obtaining surplus value; the limiting flesh and possibility of sensibilities, thus delineating Marx's sociology of bodies/emotions.

> The system, as described in rev. Montagu Valpy, is a system of unbridled slavery in all senses, in the social, in the physical, in the moral and in the intellectual ... What to think of a city in which a public assembly is held to ask that the men's work day is reduced to 18 hours a day!? ... We have had enough of crying out against the planters of Virginia and the Carolinas. But is it that its black markets, even with all the horrors of the whip and the trafficking in men's flesh, are more abominable than this slow human slaughter that has mounted here to manufacture veils and lace collars for the benefit of the capitalist?
>
> (Idem 189)

The wage labor regime is described as "trafficking in the flesh of men" given the conditions of expropriation of bodily energies that it demands, the states of unconditional subjection that it entails and its similarity to slavery as a politics of bodies/emotions.

It is "a human carnage": human beings who sell themselves as flesh, and the indiscriminate slaughter of humans. Human beings are trafficked like cattle and slaughtered like animals. There is an impudence that is woven with the aestheticization of death through the objects that will be sold thanks to their aforementioned sacrifice.

> (...) Since the enormous demand for work was encountering a depopulation movement in Ireland and in the agricultural districts of England and Scotland with an unprecedented flow of emigration towards Australia and America, and also with the positive decline of the population in some English agricultural districts, a decline caused, in part, **by those who had managed to destroy the vital energies of the people, and in part by the earlier depletion of the available population thanks to traffickers in human flesh.**
> 
> (Idem 210, note 78, emphasis ours)

It is precisely the use of the expression "vital energies of the people", associated with the trafficking of human flesh, that clearly indicates how Marx thought of the system of expropriation of bodily energies as one of the axes of the modality of capitalist exploitation. The trafficking of flesh linked to population movements and the variation of available bodily energies indicates in the direction of the geometries of the bodies the development that capitalism implies. It is the embodied collective energies that sustain capitalist expropriation on a systemic scale.

> Once the deal is closed, it is discovered that the worker is not "no free agent", that the moment in which he is released to sell his labor power is precisely the moment in which he is forced to sell it and that his vampire does not give up in their endeavor "as long as there is a muscle, a tendon, a drop of blood to suck". To 'defend themselves' against the serpent of its torments, the workers have no choice but to tighten the fence and uproot, as a class, a state law, an insurmountable social obstacle, that prevents them from selling themselves and selling their offspring as meat of death and slavery through a free contract with capital.
> 
> (Idem 241)

The politics of the bodies/emotions that the free labor contract implies as "defence" of the workers' rights is pointed out by Marx as that which prevents the sale of their offspring "as flesh of death".

The analogical use of the character of the vampire to describe the behaviour of the capitalist with respect to the worker leads us to identify the conviction of our author about the parasitic nature of the structure of the sensibilities of capitalism as a system. A parasite that, by intervening, "condemns" the other to occupy the place of host by which it comes to life, a parasite that makes and becomes the body through what the body, the blood, nourishes and which lives off the death of the flesh. The vampire analogy is an analogy of flesh that dies when it is sold.

> The character of capital is the same everywhere, both in its primitive and rudimentary forms and in its more progressive manifestations. In the Code that imposed the influence of the slavers on the New Mexico territory, shortly before the Civil War broke out, it is said: the worker, during the time that the capitalist has bought his labor power 'is his money' (the capitalist) (The labourer is bis (the capitalist's) money.) It is the same idea that the Roman patricians professed. The money lent by them to the commoners became, through the provisions bought with it, into the flesh and blood of the debtor. Therefore, "this flesh and this blood" was "his money." Hence the Shylockian law of the XII Tables. Linguet's hypothesis, according to which patrician creditors organized from time to time, on the other side of the Tiber, banquets of debtor's roast meat, is as questionable as Daumer's hypothesis about the Last Supper of Christ.
>
> (Idem 228)

The flesh and blood of the worker carries the means of life acquired with the salary paid by the capitalist who operates a politics of bodies in at least two senses: (a) transubstantializes the worker and leaves him in a condition to be eaten, and makes it the guarantor with its flesh of what is "won" here on earth, and (b) transforms life into a religious continuity of a life lived as repetition.

Marx ironically polemicizes with the literary/mythical/religious readings transformed into a hermeneutics of "capitalist profit", pointing out that the limit of cannibalism is transgressed as that exploitation becomes flesh. In the flesh and blood of the worker there is a clear indicator of three key phenomena for the development of capitalism: the limits of the production of labour power, the visibility of the exploitation regime, and the management of the population.

Senses, muscles/brain, and flesh elaborate special geometries of the bodies in capitalist exploitation that are knotted and tensed with enjoyment, pleasure and cruelty as axes of capitalist sensibility.

### 2.2.4 Cruelty as a feature of the worker's life

Among the many practices of feeling associated with the lives lived by workers in the framework of capitalist exploitation, cruelty stands out for its persistence and depth. It is used by Marx as a tool to describe the daily experience of the forms of work that configure sociabilities, experiences and sensibilities associated with death. The material conditions of existence are precisely the experiences of a system that, in weaving an acceptable/accepted sociability, elaborates sensibilities that naturalizes dispossession. From food and the politics of hunger, through working conditions to the initial education of the workers' children, they institutionally instantiate cruelty as a couple in solidarity with enjoyment/abstinence as a mandate for the capitalist.

The feeling practices that we have characterized in the complex webs between enjoyment and jouissance as axes of the state of sensibilities associated with accumulation and exploitation are intertwined with cruelty as a form of sociability and experience embodied by the capitalist in his personification of capital.

The cruelty of the conditions of existence and sale of its labour power for the worker represents/actualizes the ghostly forces of fatality that prevent us from perceiving any other way than the actualization of this said sale. For the worker, his situation is a "cruel fatality". The cruelties of capital are entangled with various forms of abuse and plunder that make the situation of the workers similar to that of the slaves and the Indians of the colonies; it is in this context that the law should have come to the aid of the capitalist by setting "limits" on exploitation.

The structure of cruelty in factories leads Marx to maintain that, in these workplaces, Dante would find his most cruel infernal fantasies overcome, and it is possible to realize that cruelty, as a bourgeois form of sensibility, implies the naturalization of torments and spoils worthy of hell. "Punishments" that when taking shape in the sociability of capitalism become part of that religion. In consonance with what we have already explored, Marx associates the cruel exploitation of the worker with the conditions of the slaves, transferring the colonial excesses to the situation of the working classes in the metropolises; something that makes us think again about the feature of coloniality of all capitalist action.

> No; who says work capacity does not say work, in the same way that the capacity to digest is not the same as digestion. To digest, it is certainly not enough to have a good stomach. When we say work capacity, we do not ignore the means of life necessary to feed it. Far from it, we express the value of these in the value of the former. And if he cannot sell it, it is of no use to the worker; On the contrary, he considers it a cruel fatality that his capacity for work requires a certain amount of means of life for its production and continues to constantly demand them for its reproduction.
>
> (Idem 126)

There is, in cruelty, a fate of perpetual acceptance and resignation that leaves the worker at the mercy of his individual fears: cruelty is an experiential experience that, turned against sensibility, sacralizes collective exploitation. Cruelty is also a class deterrence strategy.

> So far, we have observed the instinct to prolong the working day, the insatiable hunger for surplus labor, in a field where excessive abuses, not outweighed, as a bourgeois economist in England puts it, by the cruelties of the Spanish against the Indians in America, finally forced capital to be tied to the chains of law. Let us now turn to some branches of production in which the crushing of the worker's labor power is still, or was until recently, free of all hindrance.
>
> (Idem 188)

The connections between cruelty, cannibalism and sociability are evident here as points that draw one of the triangles that imply exploitation: cruelty and the law as an ordering power look at each other in a Faustian sense.

> Let us now see how capital, for its part, conceives this 24-hour system. It goes without saying that capital silently passes on the excesses of the system and its abuses of **"prolongation cruel and implausible" of the working day**.
>
> (Idem, 203, emphasis ours)

The conditions of exploitation are such that the cruelty that they imply become for Marx implausible: they go beyond all rational understanding. The degrees of cruelty are processed as excesses by keeping them "silent": the pornography of cruelty speaks for itself.

> To this, the author of the Essay on Trade and Commerce replies: 'If it is considered a divine institution to sanctify the seventh day of the week, it follows that the remaining six days are due to work (that is, as immediately it will be seen, capital), and whoever imposes this divine precept cannot be called cruel ... That humanity in general tends, by nature, to comfort and inertia, is a fatal experience that we can see verified in the behavior of the mob of our manufactures ...'.
>
> (Idem 216, our emphasis)

The religiosity of cruelty as a nodal part of political economy is one of the features that Marx highlights in his critique of bourgeois practices. For Marx there is a root of cruelty in capitalist production "methods" that do not diminish with machinery and the supposed reduction of the working day.

> The real facts, which the optimism of certain economists tries to disguise, are these: the workers displaced by the machinery from the workshop to the labor market, where they will increase the census of the labor forces

available for capitalist exploitation. In the seventh section, we will see that this effect of the machinery, which is to be presented as compensation for the working class, is, on the contrary, **the most cruel whip that lashes the workers.**

(Idem, 265–266, emphasis ours)

Machinism hits the body, marks the worker and, far from being a benefit, subjects him to greater cruelty. The whip and the whipping are metaphors for a trait that we have already advanced (that is, whipping the servants and the slave): cruelty is exemplary, it is part of a sensibility.

> The logical effect of this was appalling cruelty … In many factory districts, especially in Lancashire, these innocent and wretched creatures, consigned to the manufacturer, were subjected to the most hideous torture, they were killed on the job … whipped, loaded with chains, and tormented with the finest refinements of cruelty; In many factories, they were starving and made to work by whipping ….
> 
> (Idem 645, emphasis ours)

Cruelty is not a collateral result of the system of exploitation, it is the key to the processes of elaboration of the policies of the bodies/emotions that draw the religious face of capitalism and constitute one of the centres of the political economy of morality.

> If money, according to Augier, "is born with natural blood stains on a cheek", capital comes into the world dripping blood and mud from every pore, from head to toe.
> 
> (Idem 646)

Cruelty is not an "effect", it is not a "consequence", it is the making-body-the-system; there is no capitalist exploitation without the acceptance of cruelty, without a forced resignation to the fate of the "cruelty that is life".

## 2.3 Some final emphasis

In the context of the above, it is interesting to synthetically systematize the features of Marx's analytics that mark him as one of the founders of the sociology of emotions, trying to elaborate a framework in which to inscribe what will be analysed later in this chapter.

Marx's sociology of emotions can be summarized in three central axes: (a) a sociology of sensibilities, (b) a sociology of pain/oppression, and (c) a sociology of empathy.

Each of these sociological views of the world, in turn, can be captured by a set of vectors that, dialectically, allow us to observe the constitution of capitalist society. These vectors are, for various reasons, the outstanding features of the politics of sensibilities analysed by our author. In this chapter we have provided some of the evidence to guarantee the first two axes presented here; it is in this context that we offer empathy as a hypothesis that we have already explored, with some profundity, in Marx's ideas about his view of otherness (Scribano, 2020).

a   From the perspective of sensibility, it is possible to observe the centrality of sensibility in three elements: science, the senses, and the objectification of life. The history of human beings, other living beings, and the planet can be understood by the special place of sensibilities as the "beginning" of all science. For Marx, science is made, it is elaborated starting from a critical relationship with what is perceived and through the sensible grasp of the world.

However, for our author, the processes of the social construction of the senses are traces of how social history becomes a body. The eye, arms, and ears become human qualities in so many socially constructed senses, the situation of proximity and distance of the senses (marked in particular times/spaces) with the potentialities of the human being to feel and mark their identity. The third vector is constituted by the senses as a fetishistic object of the commodification of the world. For Marx, it is through the senses that the objects become, under the rules of things, capricious forms of fantasized relationships.

b   For Marx the everyday life of capitalism can be understood as alienation and cruelty, as sources of pain from the commodification of bodies/emotions. The separation of objects, the separation from oneself, and the separation from the collective are the sources of the alienation of workers as an experience of social pain. The separation that is radically experienced in the reconstruction that our author carries out on the cruelty of a system that elaborates the unnoticed insensibility of the acceptance of the cruel as destiny.

There is also social pain which forms the basis of social accumulation mandates. Marx also finds, in the tension between ascetic saving and waste, the axes of the politics of the sensibilities of capitalist accumulation. The rules are abstention or excess according to time/space that one or the other favours accumulation as the central gear of capitalist society.

The third vector of Marx's sociology of social pain is his analysis of the conditions of existence of exploited children and women that are the basis for the constitution and reproduction of capitalism. One of the most innovative facets of Marx, in this sense, is his analysis of the link between the unequal distribution of nutrients, conditions of habitability, and social pain.

c    It is clear that beyond all possible contention, Marx offers a classic analysis of empathy between workers as a class, as a collective, and as a common project. For Marx, communism was a utopian form of empathy where "each and everyone" would live happily. The critique of capitalist ideology is based on the modalities of existing (being/consciousness): creating new existences is the objective of the proletariat as a class in struggle. Utopia consists of the possibility of feeling in material conditions of existence similar/egalitarian with others. The community configuration as an intersubjective encounter is a radical act of class empathy as the beginning of a new society. Marx is dedicated to identifying the obstacles that the system has to avoid in such an encounter and points out the ways for its suppression.

Finally, our author promotes feeling one with others as a break from alienation and this involves the experience of being part of a collective. With these three axes made up of three vectors each, it is possible to elaborate the geometry of a classic sociology of emotions in Marx.

## Note

1   These models/perspectives are based on: Gross, and Feldman Barrett (2011); Smith and Schenider (2009), Hochsild (1990, 2003) and Kemper (1981, 1987, 1990).

## References

Gross, J. J. and Feldman Barrett, L. (2011) Emotion Generation and Emotion Regulation: One or Two Depends on Your Point of View. *Emotion Review*, 3(1), 8–16.
Hochschild, A. R. (1990) Ideology and Emotion Management: A Perspective and Path for Future Research in: T.D. Kemper (ed.) *Research Agenda in the Sociology of Emotions*. New York: University of New York Press.
―――― (2003) *The Managed Heart. Commercialization of Human Feeling*. New York: Twentieth Anniversary Edition.
Kemper, T. D. (1981) Social Constructionist and Positivist Approaches to the Sociology of Emotions. *American Journal of Sociology*, 87(2), 336–362.
―――― (1987) How Many Emotions Are There? Wedding the Social and the Autonomic Components. *American Journal of Sociology*, 93(2), 263–289.
―――― (1990) Social Relations and Emotions: A Structural Approach in Theodore D. Kemper, *Research Agendas in the Sociology of Emotions*. New York: State University of New York Press, 207–237.
Marx, K. (1909) *Capital: A Critique of Political Economy. Volume I: The Process of Capitalist Production*, Trans. from the 3rd German edition, by Samuel Moore and Edward Aveling, (eds). *Frederick Engels. Revised and amplified according to the 4th German ed. by Ernest Untermann*. Chicago: Charles H. Kerr.
Marx, K. (1973) *Grundrisse*. Harmondsworth: Penguin.

Marx, K. (1974 [1844]) *Manuscripts: Economics and Philosophy*. Madrid: Alianza Editorial.Online. Available at: www.marxists.org/archive/marx/works/1844-epm/3rd.htm. Accessed 23/08/2000.

Scribano, A. (1997) El Problema de la Acumulación de Conocimiento en las Ciencias Sociales. *Estudios Sociológicos*, 15(45), 857–869.

Scribano, A. (2010) Cuerpo, Emociones y Teoría Social Clásica. Hacia una sociología del conocimiento de los estudios sociales sobre los cuerpos y las emociones in José Luis Grosso and María Eugenia Boito (eds) *Cuerpos y Emociones desde América Latina*. CEA-CONICET. Doctorado en Ciencias Humanas. UNCa., 15–38.

Scribano, A. (2016) *La sociología de las emociones en Carlos Marx*. Raleigh, NC: Editorial A Contracorriente.

Scribano, A. (2018) Sociology of Bodies/Emotions: The Perspective of Karl Marx. *Quaderni di Teoria Sociale*, 149–172.

Scribano, A. (2020) The Other as Radical Intersubjectivity in Karl Marx in Scribano, A. and Korstanje, M. E. *Imagining the Alterity: The Position of the Other in the Classic Sociology and Anthropology*. New York: Nova Science Publishers.

Smith, H. and Schneider, A. (2009) Critiquing Models of Emotions. *Sociological Methods & Research*, 37(4), 560–589.

# Chapter 3

# Gabriel Tarde

*Massimo Cerulo*

## 3.1 Introduction

Gabriel Tarde (1843–1904) is a fully fledged classic of sociology, a keen observer of individual and historical-social peculiarities who theorized sociological laws and devised new methods for the analysis of social reality. An eclectic researcher, endowed with boundless culture, who took part in the scientific debate which, in the last decades of the nineteenth century, focused on the relationship between society and the individual, and tried to identify rules and dynamics that govern this relationship (cf. Candea, 2010; Davis, 2009; Mucchielli, 2000, 1998; Milet, 1970).

The French sociologist represents a real "case" for what concerns the history of sociological thought: forgotten for decades by European sociology, he was treated in France after his death as a "minor" author compared to the (presumed) substance of the Durkheimian school (see Niezen, 2014; Bergson, 1909). But Tarde's course of study is interdisciplinary. If we read his resumé, we notice a scientific path that characterizes the approach of a social theorist. Trained in legal studies, he first became a judge (substitute) and then deputy prosecutor, and he collaborated actively with the French Ministry of Justice until he became, in the last years of his life (1900), professor of modern philosophy and moral psychology at the Collège de France, (at that time, the position of Chair of Sociology did not exist the first would be that of Durkheim at the Sorbonne in 1913). In this time period, he was considered a prestigious researcher as well as a precursor of sociological studies, but a few years after his death, with the advent of Durkheim and the affirmation of his "School", Tarde had almost been forgotten in sociological circles (the commitment of Georg Simmel is not enough to obviate this forgetfulness although, in 1891, he reviewed the volume *Les lois de l'imitation*, showing a wide appreciation for the work of the French sociologist, and thus damaging his personal relationship with Durkheim (Simmel, 1891)).

Especially if we consider the scientific period in which he worked, this looks like a an accusation without scientific substance, i.e., he was perceived as being too devoted to spiritualism and psychologism (see Latour, 2002; Borlandi,

1994). Overlooking the validity of this accusation, the point is that this ostracism cost a lot to the diffusion of Tarde's scientific production, both in terms of obscurantism towards his studies – his sociological production has almost been forgotten: for many years, in France he was cited exclusively as a legal expert – and for a confusion pertinent to his main field of reference. In the United States, for example, it has been well received both through the urban studies of Robert Park and, in general, by the Chicago School (see Joseph, 2001; Hughes, 1961), as well as through Lazarsfeld's profound diffusion work. Lazarsfeld favours Tarde as a researcher of two specific concepts: social communication (according to Lazarsfeld, the French sociologist was the first to use the concept of conversation, several decades before the studies of Sacks on the subject) and opinion (see Tarde, 1969; Katz, Lazarsfeld, 1955).

Although, therefore, he has been little considered by many sociologists due to the lack of empiricism in his research, his scientific production has manifested itself in various fields. Even if the beginning of his professional career has a legal imprint, immediately after the age of thirty – around 1875 – he began writing about criminology, social psychology and sociology, clearly manifesting his tendency towards the study of society in a broad sense, rather than a prolonged interest in the field of law. When, at the end of the 1870, he published the volume *Contes et poèmes*, we understood how the turning point towards the human and social sciences was taking place. After this, he simultaneously became involved in studies on crime (in later years he came into contact with Cesare Lombroso) and on moods, collaborating actively with prestigious scientific journals and contributing – thanks to the diffusion of his work *La criminalité comparée* – to the creation of what has been defined as the "French school", that is a movement of criminology researchers who related the causes of deviance to mainly social reasons (Tarde, 1885).

But the scientific field in which he declares himself to be more at ease is sociology, as his more mature works amply demonstrate. In particular, *Les lois de l'imitation* (1890), *La logique sociale* (1895) and *Les lois sociales* (1898), attest that the main object of study for Tarde is the relationship between the individual and society: with the aim of trying to identify general laws and behaviours, both individual and collective, that influence and regulate it (Tarde, 1884).

## 3.2 The first sociologist of emotions: *La logique sociale des sentiments*

Within a study on the contribution of the classics to sociological theories on emotions, in our opinion, Tarde can be considered, in historical terms, as the "first" sociologist of emotions: the first to have written an entire text on the sociology of emotions: *La logique sociale des sentiments* (Tarde, 1893). He focused on emotions as a "social emerging" (according to the well-known definition of Mead found in this book), meaning tools that, by emerging from the psychological and philosophical study in which they had been locked up until then, allowed the birth of social interaction which proved to be decisive for maintaining social balance. In this text, Tarde is the first sociologist to provide us with an analysis of the diffusion of emotions from the individual to the group, through a process based on forms of imitation and contagion of expressions, attitudes and behaviours (see Abrutyn, Mueller, 2014).

The French sociologist, placing himself on a line of thought similar to that of Feuerbach (who considered the senses as the main tools for investigating and analysing social reality, according to the theorem "feeling leads to truth"), considers emotional-sentimental states and their manifestation as crucial elements for the analysis of social reality, equal to the behaviours defined as rational. In addition – and this is a fundamental point of Tarde's theory – he highlights a "logic" in the social manifestation of emotions, describing the latter not only as tools of social integration and encounter with the other (and therefore as the social glue which holds society together) but also identifying the signs of a social construction of emotions implemented by charismatic leaders (*meneur*, in Tarde's original terms) or dominant groups, who would use it as a tool of power (Tarde, 1893; see Citton, 2010).

In the text *La logique sociale des sentiments*, an essay on social theory that saw the light for the first time in 1893, published within the *Revue Philosophique*, Tarde writes and theorizes emotional-sentimental states from a sociological perspective: the latter are, in fact, intended as tools for meeting, communication and social integration. They are used to analyse the relationship between individuals and society without anchoring to "oppressive" sociological categories such as individualism or holism, action and structure, but trying to analyse the details of human behaviours, interpreting them through the emotional-rational interpretation. We could therefore consider Tarde as the founder of a "microsociology" (see Tonkonoff, 2017; Latour et al., 2012) as argued, in particular, by Gilles Deleuze who, commenting on the innovation of the French researcher's sociological approach, puts it this way:

> It is completely wrong to reduce Tarde's sociology to a psychologism or even an interpsychology. Tarde criticizes Durkheim for assuming what must be explained – namely, "the similarity of thousands of men". For the alternative – impersonal givens or the Ideas of great men – he substitutes the little ideas of little men, the little inventions and interferences between imitative currents. What Tarde inaugurates is a microsociology, which is not necessarily concerned with what happens between individuals but with what happens within a single individual: for example, hesitation understood as "infinitesimal social opposition", or invention as "infinitesimal social adaptation". (…) All of Tarde's philosophy may be presented in this light: as a dialectic of difference and repetition which founds the possibility of a micro sociology upon a whole cosmology.
>
> (Deleuze, 1968: 314, Eng edn 1994)

In terms of a sociology of emotions, from an historical perspective it is already evident that Tarde is an innovator and a forerunner of theories that will be structured in the years to come. Before the other classics of sociology, he focused on the role of emotional-sentimental states, considering them as means of social integration and therefore subjects of sociological investigation (Tarde, like his other colleagues of that time – Durkheim, Weber, Simmel – did not provide hermeneutic and etymological distinctions between the terms emotion, sentiment, passion: thus, states of feeling very different from each other in intensity and duration are catalogued indifferently in the type feeling states). All this nineteen years before Durkheim's *Les formes élémentaires de la vie religieuse*, fifteen years before Simmel's *Große Soziologie* (in our opinion, the sociologist of emotions *par excellence*), eleven years before Weber's *Die protestantische Ethik und der Geist des Kapitalismus*. This is fully eighty years before the appearance in the United States of the first scientific articles on the sociology of emotions and the consequent creation of ad hoc university chairs (see Kemper, 1978; Hochschild, 1975).

For Tarde, a profound reader and connoisseur of Auguste Comte's works, the social relationship arises mainly thanks to two moods or impulses, as he himself defines them, which would characterize and guide the behavioural choices of the vast majority of members of a society: *desire* and *belief* (see Tarde, 1880). The sociologist's task is to decipher the different ways in which these two moods combine, giving place to different forms of social relationship. The researcher's gaze must turn to the perspective of social actors and to the way in which a social phenomenon changes according to the perspective of the latter. It is therefore necessary to use a sociological method that explains the history of societies with the ideas of its actors and not with those of the social scientist (Tarde, 1890). In other words, it is not a question of reasoning about the cause-effect relationship of a social phenomenon (otherwise sociology would become a sort of metaphysics or ontology), but of identifying the social laws of which it is composed and, through them, explaining the phenomenon itself by interpreting it in the light of those laws. And by proceeding, moreover, to an historical-social comparison with similar phenomena observed in other societies or in other epochs: analysing and linking similarities and repetitions to which these social phenomena give place (see Tarde, 1904). Social science must, therefore, be comparative, elementary and inter-psychological: studying the multiplicity of actions/reactions of a social action and of a feeling about another person or another feeling. We could therefore say that, in general, for Tarde, "doing sociology" means studying the concatenation of short flows of action from one subject to another: it is the problem of the micro-sociological construction of reality implemented by individual subjects or social groups in the course of history:

> (My) conception is, in fact, almost the exact opposite of the unilinear evolutionists' notion and of M. Durkheim's. Instead of explaining

everything by the supposed supremacy of a law of evolution, which compels collective phenomena to reproduce and repeat themselves indefinitely in a certain order, – instead of thus explaining lesser facts by greater, and the part by the whole, – I explain collective resemblances of the whole by the massing together of minute elementary acts – the greater by the lesser and the whole by the part. This way of regarding phenomena is destined to work a transformation in sociology similar to that brought about in mathematics by the introduction of the infinitesimal calculus.

(Tarde, 1898, Eng edn 1899: 35)

To implement such methodological practices, the sociologist must resort to two sciences: social logic and social teleology, which are the basis of general sociology. On the one hand, social logic aims to identify the right mix between the beliefs in vogue in a given society, in order to guarantee a peaceful balance between its members. Social logic must indicate the changes which the subdivision of affirmative or negative belief will have to undergo, in order to achieve its main social objective, namely to avoid contradiction and to obtain an agreement for the welfare of society. On the other hand, social teleology, studies desire and must analyse how to distribute desire, both in terms of its valence, meaning a desire transformed into repulsion, and in terms of intensity, to maximize the convergence of social desires and to minimize their opposition (Tarde, 1895: 13–14):

> But it is then true that, within feelings, something that corresponds to the social or individual systems of ideas and beliefs; to the social or individual systems of intentions or desires exists? Absolutely yes. There is, in the public heart as well as in the private one, a close solidarity between certain sympathies which suppose certain antipathies, between certain prides which presume certain contempts, etc. These systems, which play a huge role throughout history, are the solution provided by social logic to our first problem. Feelings, we know, have a double face: belief on the one hand, desire on the other. They are judgments and wills combined into original impressions, into feelings of a higher level which have as their object ideas, actions and impressions of other individuals. Their possible agreement is therefore of two types, logical or teleological, or one and the other at the same time. In other words, the different coexisting feelings owe their cohesion to: (1) that for which they confirm each other or which, by the way, do not contradict each other; (2) that for which they help each other or for which, by the way, they do not hinder each other.
>
> (Tarde, 1893: 563, French edn).

## 3.3 Emotional contagion and leaders

Let's deepen the analysis from the point of view of the sociology of emotions. According to the French sociologist, many of the most common social behaviours are actually created by only a few individuals: those with greater personality, spirit of initiative, enterprise; the rest of the subjects do nothing but *wish* to be like those individuals, *believing* that the behaviour of the latter is the best and the more desirable in a given social circumstance (Tarde, 1890). This belief is based on a process of imitation that spreads from one individual to another until it reaches the mass (see Borch, Stäheli 2009, Borch 2005). Therefore, there would be fewer subjects, leaders, to create social actions, attitudes, behaviours and morals. The rest of the members of a society would do nothing but follow this example above all for the good of society and its balance: to avoid social conflicts and discussions. This process would also shape public opinion or at least a large part of it. A path of imitation would, therefore, take place, with the aim of copying the dominant perspective, which would entail various advantages: among them, social integration and low mental fatigue for those who imitate others (Tarde, 1901).

Distancing himself from Spencer's theories on the evolution of society (Spencer, 1885; 1865) Tarde identifies, in individual socio-psychological processes, the engine of the formation of emotions, opinions, trends, attitudes, and interaction practices: more than interest or utilitarian calculation, it would be the beliefs and actions of a few individuals that guide the behaviour of the group (Tarde, 1907; see also Mubi Brighenti, 2010). The social being, therefore, does nothing but behave like a sleep-walker: he/she deludes him/herself and believes he/she has his own ideas and feelings, when instead the latter are suggested and "imposed" by others through a sort of emotional contagion:

> An assembly or an association, a crowd or a sect, has no other idea than the one that is blown into it, and this idea, this more or less intelligible trace of an aim to pursue, a means to employ, may well diffuse from one's brain to the brains of all, remains the same; he who blows the idea is therefore accountable of its direct effects. But the emotion that comes with this idea and diffuses with it, does not remain the same, rather it intensifies through a sort of mathematical progression, so that what was moderate desire or hesitant opinion in the mind of the author of such propagation, for instance the first inspirer of a suspicion about a certain category of citizens, swiftly turns into passion and belief, hate and fanaticism, in the fermentable mass where such germ is brought.
> (Tarde, 1901: 165–166, French edn)

In particular, when in his studies he analyses what he calls "extra-logic influences" (Tarde, 1890; 1893), the French sociologist, speaking of emotional contagion, uses concepts such as "sleep-walking" and "magnetism" to explain the process of imitation of the subordinate towards the superior, of the crowd towards the leaders (*meneur*). The latter, therefore, represent the inventors, those who would spread their inventions to the masses through the prestige held in the eyes of the latter, in a process whose success is directly proportional to the intensity of the emotions that the leader is able to arouse in the public. A sort of emotional entrainment (Abrutyn, Mueller, 2014: 708):

> Now many great men from Rameses to Alexander, from Alexander to Mahomet, from Mahomet to Napoleon, have thus polarised the soul of their people! How often has a prolonged gaze upon the brilliant point of one man's glory or genius thrown a whole people into a state of catalepsy! The torpor that appears in somnambulism is, as we know, only superficial; it masks an intense excitement. This is the reason why the somnambulist does not hesitate to perform great feats of strength and skill.
> (Tarde, 1890, Eng edn 1903: 83)

We have therefore clarified the role played by emotions in this process of imitation and contagion. But are these emotions then manifested in an unconscious and unthinking way, without any rationality on the part of the one who shows them? To answer this question, it is appropriate to recall Tarde's characteristic theoretical perspective, as well as his vision of social action.

He lines up social theorists, those who do not have to do with numbers and statistics, choosing a theme to which the economy does not pay attention: emotional-sentimental states, actions that start and take impulse directly from the heart, which play a decisive role in human life. The latter hold social life together (Tarde, 1893). Sanctioning from the Kantian vision that theorized them as "cancers" of reason and carriers of individual and social madness and imbalance, Tarde theorizes (at first glance paradoxically) a logic within them, a sort of strategy in the manifestation of emotional-sentimental states. If the social relationship arises mainly through desires and beliefs, if there are few individuals who create social action, who "invent", according to Tarde's terminology, new behaviours to be then imitated by the crowds, in that case this should also be valid for emotions and for the feelings through which members of a society come into contact. The individual cannot simply be prey to his emotional states, so "suffering" without any power over them: there must be a channel to address them, an object to which they can be directed, a social procedure to manage them. There is, therefore, a social logic in the manifestation of emotions, precisely because it is society that "imposes" it: it pushes its members to be emotionally cautious with respect to the behaviours put in place in order to maintain the social balance necessary for peaceful relations between the subjects (see Tarde, 1895).

This result, however, is an achievement of modernity. This is a fundamental point. As the French sociologist demonstrates through a series of diachronic analysis, in fact, several conflicts have broken out in the history of humanity because individuals have not been able to analyse and contain their emotions, privileging the negative ones – carriers of imbalance – to the detriment of those positive – vehicles of peace and social harmony (think of the wars of primitive, ancient and medieval societies). During the process of social aggregation typical of modern states, however, individuals are forced to share their emotions with those of foreign individuals: it is the only way to build integration and collaboration. In this process, positive emotions play a main role within the nascent states, as they allow social collaboration, a peaceful life and, consequently, the survival of an enlarged society. Modern individuals are therefore required to analyse their feelings, to reason about the most suitable forms of emotional manifestations to be used, based on the circumstances in which they find themselves and the person in front of them.

According to Tarde, therefore, emotions and feelings and the way in which they are manifested hold social life together: a stable society is, first of all, an "intertwining of feelings of sympathy" (Tarde, 1893: 561), of positive emotions harmonized with each other. But how can society transmit one emotion rather than another? And how do individuals adapt to the feeling rules imposed by society?

Tarde distances himself from the Durkheimian vision of a *sui generis society* (which in the early twentieth century would become dominant in France and beyond) and aims to privilege the role played by the individual in creating social integration. It is not society that binds and manages individual relationships, but rather the hearts of individuals that allow social relations and, therefore, create society (because of this theory, some late-twentieth-century analyses paint Tarde as the theorist of the end of the social sphere (Latour, 2002; see also King, 2016;Toews 2003).

## 3.4 The Logic of Social Sphere, Emotions and Morals

To answer the two previous questions, it is necessary to focus on the French sociologist's study on sexual morality (Tarde, 1907). Tarde studies its changeable traits, relying on the processes of imitation and the desire-belief flows, not limiting himself to reconstructing the changes that have occurred during the course of history (for example, the main stages of the evolution of marriage in the various eras) nor to listing the social causes responsible for these changes. His objective is indeed to analyse the social laws that produce changes in the public and private manifestation of emotional states and, consequently, the change in sexual morality. The latter, in turn, will produce changes in the law, in religion, in the behaviour of individual societies.

To produce this study, he reconstructs the history and geography of sexual unions, analysing their evolution in a comparative perspective. To this end, Tarde notes that monogamy has historically been the most widespread sexual practice, both in "savage" and in more civilized populations. The explanation can only derive from propagation and repetition of both male and female customs and the habits of different populations. Monogamy (and the consequent emotional behaviours between partners, both public and private), is therefore the originating practice of sexual relations because it is the most widespread practice.

To analyse the variations of sexual morality, Tarde then studies the degree of civilization reached by specific societies through the diffusion of religious practices, civil interaction, conversation and *divertissement* (theatres, newspapers, etc.). These elements influence and shape the emotional behaviours put in place by the subjects and, consequently, are the causes of the changes in sexual morality in different societies and eras. The propagation of these emotional behaviours always occurs through forms of imitation and emotional contagion:

> Sometimes it is a *sculptor*, sometimes a *painter*, sometimes a *tailor*, who dares something a bit *risky*. A slightly more realistic nudity, a more open bodice, from which the bust of a graceful woman emerges (…). Once acquired and legitimized, this progress becomes intangible and serves as a starting point for a new progress, which, starting in the rich classes of the big cities, spreads slowly from here to the rest of the population (…).
> (Tarde, 1907: 18, French edn)

However, do not forget that, in order for this movement not to clash with any decisive and reactive resistance from the public, it is first needed that the feelings and moral habits, shaped under the weight of tradition and religious beliefs, have lost strength before collapsing completely. There is a continuous alternation, which must never be forgotten, of action and reaction, between beliefs and desires (Tarde, 1907: 18, French edn).

When old beliefs, related to tradition or religion, lose importance in terms of sources from which to learn emotional behaviours and sexual practices, small individual initiatives intervene, those that Tarde calls "inventions". They can become models to follow when they are repeated, imitated and propagated (that is, when the crowd is infected by such models through the manifestation of specific emotions that accompany certain behaviours).

Changes in morality based on the affirmation of such inventions through repetition, which propagates, remember, through a form of emotional contagion that spreads from the individual to the group. Note the difference between Durkheim's normative and coercive view of morality compared to Tarde's spiritualistic and vital one. For the latter, the shaping of emotions and behaviours always comes from an imitation: a subject influences the desires and beliefs of others, based on specific social conditions: wealth, class, culture, religion, etc.

The emotions faced by Tarde – this is the key point of his theory – are born in the heart of each subject; later, they become intertwined with those experienced by other individuals and can change shape or manifestation. But the social relationship takes shape thanks to the action carried out by the individual subject, who comes into contact with a fellow through the sharing of an emotion. Subsequently, the individual endowed with greater personality or charisma has the task of harmonizing this encounter, ensuring that this intertwining extends and lasts for the survival of society: to ensure that other positive emotions and feelings arise, those that make life in common possible and affable through forms of mutual solidarity and collaboration. This is why, according to Tarde, social groups are born, within which many subjects imitate the emotion felt and shared by the first individual/s. The role of these leaders (*meneurs*) (that is, those who invent behaviours and share emotions) is fundamental for the maintenance of society.

However, Tarde knows well that social life is not only intertwined with positive emotions: there is also a mixture of sympathy and antipathy, love and hate, joy and sadness. This happens in every society, regardless of the historical era. The role of individuals (the leaders mentioned above) lies precisely in being able to create and maintain that emotional-sentimental balance that allows every society to live harmoniously and according to a stable form. It is, therefore, very important that the opposite emotions generated within a group or a society (or of several groups or societies in relation to each other), find a *teleological* agreement (not just one that is logical), to guarantee the survival of the society itself. If this harmony is not achieved, the balance shatters and the society is forced to renew itself: through new elections or electoral consultations (in democratic societies), or through wars and conflicts when there is no harmony between societies or nations (Tarde, 1893).

In summary: Gabriel Tarde can therefore be considered as the first sociologist of emotions. He argued that emotions are conveyed and modelled by individual actions according to the historical-social context in which they are implemented. This means that they become tools of integration and social balance, thus anticipating the theory that, in the second half of the twentieth century, was thematized as a "social construction of emotions". This identified a line of sociological studies on emotional-sentimental states that arose a few decades ago in the United States and considered emotions as elements existing in the human organism – exactly like Tarde's view: they are born in the heart of each subject – but which take shape exclusively thanks to social relationships and the symbols through which these relationships acquire meaning in a specific social context (see Cerulo, 2019). Yet, for Tarde, they form at the same time of their interpretation and of the consciousness of the subject located in a determined and specific social context as well as of his interactions with other individuals. The social construction of emotions is one with the manifestation of the emotion itself and, as such, it is constantly changing: emotions change following changes in social rules of behaviour and in relationships between individuals (Tarde, 1907).

Tarde would be part of, clearly unconsciously due to the years in which he writes, this scientific of of the sociology of emotions We could say that it generates the prodromes. Better, it represents the initiator, the one who first sees what will be, the forerunner of a line of studies that would flourish, institutionally and academically, almost eighty years later.

## 3.5 Emotions as a social glue

Tarde clarifies that emotions are social constructions and directly depend on the interactions that take shape between individuals, and does this also when he addresses the relationship between them and religion, which plays the dual role of imitative assimilation between human beings of the same civilization and of differentiation between human beings of different civilizations:

> After all, Religion exercises such a powerful action on the public heart because it is the most energetic means of both imitative assimilation between humans of the same civilization, and of differentiation (parallel imitative) between humans of different civilizations. It is therefore to the laws of Imitation (...) that we must ask for the ultimate explanation of vicissitudes of feeling. The final work of Imitation, as for Religion, seem to me to be the development of sympathy; but the former, like the latter, very often debuts through a reverse effect. The moment in which two populations, hitherto indifferent to each other, begin to feel a mutual dislike is when they begin to imitate each other.
> (Tarde, 1893: 37–38, French edn)

Through religious rites, emotions and their manifestations are "domesticated", made malleable and manageable, transformed into that social glue that holds together the members of a community (including both those who are born there, and foreigners or migrants).

According to Tarde, religions have understood the need to control and to address what one naturally feels. They focused on the issue of social harmony: to have peace and social integration, it is necessary to transform natural emotions into what we have defined as social constructions: common habits, collective rites, in order to homologate individuals to a "controlled" manifestation of their own feelings.

According to Tarde's analysis, religion is a "form of cement" among people, in the sense that, through religious rites, the emotional-sentimental states experienced by a few individuals spread to others. Even better, they are imitated by others. Feeling the same emotion – or being convinced to do so – creates strength, transmits self-esteem and generates that social cohesion of which Durkheim would prove to be a master, but from a different perspective. It is not society that, through the religious ritual, "creates" the individuals, but it is the latter who participate (and, ultimately, constitute) the ritual by sharing their emotional-sentimental states and, from this experience, they build more. The previously expressed concept of emotional entrainment is back again.

Through his analysis of the relationship between religion and emotions, Tarde theorizes how the latter are a kind of cultural artefact that directly depend on the socio-historical context in which they take shape. If it is true that leaders experience an inner feeling which, following social rules, they manifest according to forms and modalities dependent on their will, it is equally true that most of the subjects belonging to the same circle will tend to imitate such behaviours: they will be convinced that they feel the same emotions, they will build social representations based on what Tarde calls "the law of imitation" and will implement behaviours directly dependent on the intensity of the emotion built in common. In this sense, among the examples most often cited by Tarde in his works there is racism, meant as a mixture of feelings of hatred and contempt felt by one or more individuals towards others, which is not natural but which has been constructed by historical-social context.

Taking part in a religious rite, practicing a creed, inevitably means manifesting the emotions that religion spreads: imitating the priests, the leaders, who provide subjects with the behavioural indications to be expressed in the rite. To support this thesis, Tarde often uses the example of Christianity: it has favored the spread of positive feelings (of sympathy and affection) among believers and practitioners.

In other words, religion is a generating force of both positive and negative emotions. Unlike Durkheim, who theorized that collective consciousness or effervescence remains suspended and indistinct in the empty, devoid of a clear differentiation in terms of emotions, feelings, affects or passions, in Tarde's analysis, the feelings begin to have a name (sympathy, antipathy, affection, joy, envy, etc.) and disclose as a picklock of social action through a practice that has logic and rationality.

Contrary to what Durkheim will affirm, these are not individuals who during a religious rite are seized by electricity that leads them to exaltation, nor do emotions resemble an avalanche that increases as we advance (Durkheim, 1912). When leaders participate in the ritual and share their emotions (or better: they invent or spread specific forms of emotional manifestation), they do so with a rational awareness that is necessary for the survival of society (emotions will be positive or negative based on the objective to be achieved for the good of the group itself).

In Tarde, therefore, the individual-religion relationship is bijective: if, on the one hand, it is the individual who acts, building and putting into practice the rite, imitating and letting himself be emotionally infected by other peers; then, on the other hand, it is from this sharing that new emotions are born in a process of social construction (generated by an individual action) that never ends (otherwise we would live a society without relationships).

The reflections produced by Tarde on the relationship between emotional-sentimental states and modernity are also interesting in this sense (Tarde, 1893). Even before Simmel – who in the 1903 text *Die Großstädte und das Geistesleben* tackled the theme in great depth – Tarde grasps the ambivalence that modern life brings to the manifestation of emotional-sentimental states.

The freedom from family and neighbourhood ties and the cosmopolitanism that can be breathed in the cities of the late nineteenth century translate, on the one hand, into a wide choice of subjects to attend and who direct emotions and feelings (a relationship is undertaken by choice and not as an obligation, as was the case in rural areas and in past ages); on the other hand, however, these states of mind are no longer as strong as in past times but are fleeting and not very deep, as they are subject to the modern social need for the continuous satisfaction of new relationships.

## 3.6 Conclusion

For Tarde, what every human being keeps in his or her interiority is a private and public treasure at the same time. It is an individual and social resource. An engine that, if used well, allows individuals (and therefore the societies they live and act in) to progress and grow over time. After all, as the French sociologist explains:

> the social life is a long, obscure, and tortuous transition from a state of elementary diversity to one marked by the possession of personal physiognomy. It appears as a mysterious alembic of numberless spiral curves where one thing is sublimated in another, where out of an infinite number of dements that have been bent and crushed and despoiled of their distinct characteristics is mental and fleeting attributes of personality, its idiosynextracted an essential and volatile principle, the fundacrasies, its ways of thinking and feeling, here today, vanished tomorrow.
> (Tarde, 1890: 393, Eng edn 1903)

The social analysis on emotions carried out by Tarde is remarkable, especially if we consider the time in which was written. In a nutshell, it represents an intuition that will prove fruitful in the future for numerous generations of social researchers: emotional and rational action are nothing more than two sides of the same coin, that is the social action that from the mind and heart of each individual simultaneously draws his own existential oxygen.

It is, therefore, worthwhile, in conclusion, to underline the two sociological "discoveries" of Tarde: he theorizes that emotions are often socially constructed, shared and domesticated through a process of social imitation and emotional contagion that starts from one or more leaders and gets to the mass; and he also provides us with an anticipation of the role of social glue that emotions can play within a specific group.

## References

Abrutyn, S., Mueller, A.S. (2014) Reconsidering Durkheim's Assessment of Tarde: Formalizing a Tardian Theory of Imitation, Contagion, and Suicide. *Sociological Forum*, 29(3), 698–719.

Bergson, H. (1909) Lettre. In G. Tarde, *Discours prononcés le 12 septembre 1909 à Sarlat à l'inauguration de son monument*. Sarlat: Michelet.
Borch, C. (2005) Urban Imitations: Tarde's Sociology Revisited. *Theory, Culture & Society*, 22(3), 81–100.
Borch, C., Stäheli, U. (eds) (2009) *Soziologie der Nachahmung und des Begehrens. Materialien zu Gabriel Tarde*. Frankfurt: Suhrkamp.
Borlandi, M. (1994) Informations sur la rédaction du Suicide et sur l'état du conflit entre Durkheim et Tarde de 1895 à 1897. *Durkheimian Studies*, 6, 4–13.
Candea, M. (2010) *The Social after Gabriel Tarde. Debates and Assessments*. London and New York: Routledge.
Cerulo, M. (2019) The Sociological Study of Emotions: Interactionist Analysis Lines, *Italian Sociological Review*, 9(2), 183–194.
Citton, Y. (2010) *Mythocratie. Storytelling et immaginaire de gauche*. Paris: Éditions de Amsterdam.
Davis, M.M. (2009) *Gabriel Tarde, An Essay in Sociological Theory*. Charleston: Bibliobazaar.
Deleuze, G. (1968) *Différence et répétition*. Paris: PUF. English edn: *Difference and repetition*, trans Paul Patton. New York: Columbia University Press, 1994.
Durkheim, È (1912) *Les formes élémentaires de la vie religieuse*. Paris: PUF.
Hochschild, A.R. (1975), The Sociology of Feeling and Emotion: Selected Possibilities. In M. Millman and R.M. Kantor (eds), *Another Voice: Feminist Perspectives on Social Life and Social Science*. New York: Anchor, 208–237.
Hughes, E.C. (1961) Tarde's Psychologie économique: An Unknown Classic by a Forgotten Sociologist. *American Journal of Sociology*, 66(6), 553–559.
Joseph, I. (2001) Tarde avec Park: À quoi servent les foules?. *Multitudes*, 7. Available at: http://multitudes.samizdat.net/Tarde-avec-Park.
Katz, E., Lazarsfeld, P.F. (1955) *Personal Influence*. Glencoe: Free Press.
Kemper, T.D. (1978), *A Social Interaction Theory of Emotions*. New York: Wiley.
King, A. (2016) Gabriel Tarde and Contemporary Social Theory. *Sociological Theory*, 34(1), 45–61.
Latour, B (2002) Gabriel Tarde and the End of the Social. In P. Joyce (ed.) *The Social in Question: New Bearings in History and the Social Sciences*. London, New York: Routledge, 117–133.
Latour, B., Jensen, P., Venturini, T., Grauwin, S. and D. Boullier, (2012) The Whole Is Always Smaller Than the Parts. A Digital Test of Gabriel Tarde' s Monads. *British Journal of Sociology*, 63(3), 590–615.
Milet, J. (1970) *Gabriel Tarde et la philosphie de l'histoire*. Paris: Vrin.
Mubi Brighenti, A. (2010) Tarde, Canetti, and Deleuze on Crowds and Packs. *Journal of Classical Sociology*, 10(4), 291–314.
Mucchielli, L. (1998) *La Découverte du social. Naissance de la sociologie en France*. Paris: La Découverte.
Mucchielli, L. (2000) Tardomania? Réflexions sur les usages contemporaines de Tarde. *Revue d'histoire des sciences humaines*, 2(3), 161–184.
Niezen, R. (2014) Gabriel Tarde's publics. *History of the Human Sciences*, 27(2), 41–59.
Simmel, G. (1891) Book review to G. Tarde, *Les lois de l'imitation*. Paris: Alcan, 1890. *Zeitschrift für Psychologie und Physiologie der Sinnesorgane*, 2, 141–142.
Spencer, H. (1865) *Social Statics*. New York: Appleton.
Spencer, H. (1885) *The Study of Sociology*. London: Kegan Paul, Trench.

Tarde, G. (1880) La croyance et le désir. La possibilité de leur mesure. *Revue philosophique*, XX, 150–180.
Tarde, G. (1884) Qu'est-ce qu'une société? *Revue philosophique*, XVIII, 489–510.
Tarde, G. (1885) Le type criminel. *Revue philosophique*, XIX, 593–627.
Tarde, G (1890) *Les lois de l'imitation*. Paris: Alcan. English edn: *The Laws of Imitation*, trans Parsons EC. New York: Holt, 1903.
Tarde, G. (1893) La logique sociale des sentiments. *Revue philosophique*, XXXVI, 561–594.
Tarde, G. (1895) *La logique sociale*, Paris: Félix Alcan.
Tarde, G. (1898) *Les lois sociales: Esquisse d'une sociologie*. Paris: Alcan. English edn: *Social Laws: An Outline of Sociology*, trans Warren HC. New York: Macmillan, 1899.
Tarde, G. (1901) *L'opinion et la foule*. Paris: Alcan. Partial English translation: *The opinion and the crowd*. In: T.N. Clark (ed.) *Gabriel Tarde: On Communication and Social Influence: Selected Papers*. Chicago: University of Chicago Press, 1969, 277–294.
Tarde, G. (1904) La sociologie et les sciences sociales. *Revue Internationale de Sociologie*, XII, 86.
Tarde, G. (1907) La morale sexuelle. *Archive de l'Anthropologie criminelle, de criminologie et psychologie normale et pathologique*, XXII, 5–40.
Tarde, G. (1969) *On Communication and Social Influence. Selected Papers*. Chicago: University of Chicago Press.
Toews, D. (2003) The new Tarde: Sociology after the End of the Social. *Theory, Culture & Society*, 20(5), 81–98.
Tonkonoff, S. (2017) *Tarde and the Infinitesimal Sociology*. In S. Tonkonoff, *From Tarde to Deleuze and Foucault. The Infinitesimal Revolution*. London: Palgrave, 25–43.

# Chapter 4

# Émile Durkheim

*Juan Pablo Vázquez Gutiérrez[1]*

## 4.1 Introduction

The goal of this chapter is to offer a general overview of Durkheim's approach to emotions and affections.[2] Although this goal may seem simple and descriptive, in reality it entails a series of difficulties that must be explained.

Strictly speaking, Durkheim's work was not dedicated to the analysis of emotions. Yet it is possible to reconstruct his view of them by considering the references he makes to them. In an exercise of this type, we must stress the highly selective nature of the vision presented. The criteria for the selective process entail finding passages related to the emotional dimension, linked particularly to a key component found in all of Durkheim's work – his diagnosis of the moral integration of modern societies. In this sense, our review has a dual purpose – to reconstruct the trajectory of Durkheimian thinking on moral integration, and at the same time to show its connections to the topic of emotions.

The argument we are defending is that, even though the author did not directly cover the emotional component, it is not an irrelevant or fringe issue in his work, instead representing an essential piece of his thought. It is seen in the foundations of his thinking on the normative construction of social life, integration, and social change.

Considering these points, this chapter is divided into three sections. The first refers to the Durkheimian analysis of the emotional foundations of the normative world, through a review of three aspects – the interiorization of norms, the control of emotions, and the desirability of the ideal. The second section summarizes a reconstruction of the main aspects of the Durkheimian diagnosis of modern societies, highlighting his explanation of the emergence of the emotional regime within them, as well as the main collective affections exposed by their crises – anomie and selfishness. The third considers Durkheim's analysis of the symbolic institution of society and the role of the sacred in processes of integration and social change, reviewing his emotional expression in processes of collective effervescence.

Finally, we must note the format of this text, which in theory has been conceived as a *preliminary outline* for the purpose of identifying the main topics and problems linked to Durkheim's view of the emotional dimension. Once this point has been clarified, the goal of this text is to situate and pinpoint the issues that are relevant to our topic, and to establish lines of thought by which to reflect on them.[3]

## 4.2 The emotional foundations of the normative word

We can identify within Durkheim's theory some important points of continuity that underpin his thinking on modern societies. In this sense, far from a series of dispersed topics that seem to lead him through many different non-interconnected ideas (from the division of work to suicide, from law to education, from family to religion), it is possible to identify in his works some recurring concerns about one object considered from several angles – the topic of social integration and the weight of the moral and emotional aspects present in this process.

As we move towards an understanding of this central problem that gives meaning to his work, it is convenient to recall some key topics and concepts that are crucial to his theory – an inquiry into the conditions that make possible the integration of a differentiated social order; the identification of the new role of individualism and of organic solidarity; the need to diagnose the moral malaise of modern European societies, made clear in its increasing suicide rates; and the search for symbolic mechanisms to face the main problems of social integration. The listing of these topics reveals a progressive course toward an understanding of the moral dimension. This course begins with asking about the mechanisms that make social order possible. We shall reconstruct the main terms of his thinking on this topic, placing special emphasis on their link with the emotional dimension.

1.1 In *The Rules of the Sociological Method* (1895), Durkheim defines social facts as collective ways of doing, thinking, and feeling that are *imposed on us* and which we would not have reached by following our own inclinations (Durkheim, 1982: 59).

The definition in Chapter 1 of *The Rules of the Sociological Method* first presents social facts as,

> ways of acting, thinking, and feeling which possess the remarkable property of existing outside the consciousness of the individual. Not only are these types of behaviour and thinking external to the individual, but they are endured with a compelling and coercive power by virtue of which, whether he wishes it or not, they impose themselves upon him.

A few pages later, the definition is expanded with the words,

> A social fact is any way of acting, whether fixed or not, capable of exerting over the individual an external constraint; or which is *general* over the whole of a given society whilst having an existence of its own *independent* of its individual manifestations.
> (Durkheim, 1982: 51 and 59, italics added)

The identification of this *imperative* nature leads us to an important implicit conclusion in Durkheim's perspective – the social world has a moral nature. What does this claim mean? Strictly speaking, it means that the social world is made up of collective representations, values, and feelings with the coercive power and prestige needed to be imposed upon individuals.

1.2. Through what process is this constrictive social world put into place, a world that emphasizes obligations and behaviour patterns, when they did not exist naturally? Why does the agent accept the determinations imposed by society, to the detriment of the free expression of his nature? The typically social power of coercion, assumed to be a moral obligation, refers to an act of *obedience with informed consent*. According to Durkheim, such an act is possible due to a subject's internal willingness – the *spirit of discipline* (Durkheim, 1982: 178). This is the name given to the process by which the principle of duty is interiorized. In Durkheim's view, the moral act is unthinkable without this faculty, accepted as a basic disposition that must be constructed throughout the socialization process. As such, for our author, society imposes upon us, but in doing so it socializes us and creates in us the mechanisms that make us accept and require it. Durkheim certainly recognizes that there is no social conformism that does not at the same time suppose relative margins of individual autonomy (Durkheim, 1982: 46, note 6). Yet even within these margins of freedom, the will itself constitutes a social product; it is always a will determined socially and compelled by conditions that lead to action in the indicated social sense in virtue of the respect imposed by these conditions. As we can see, the heart of the problem behind these ideas is none other than an explanation of the collective order by means of a theory of social regulation. This work presents an outline of Durkheim's sociopolitical perspective, where we find a first explanation of the conditions that guarantee the institution and maintenance of social life, based on its *normative dimensions*.

1.3. According to Durkheim, social acts constitute a *patterned* behaviour. In this sense, there is a direct correlation between the Durkheimian characterization of the moral act and his definition of social facts as *moulds* into which action is poured (Durkheim, 1982: 58). With this basis, the Durkheimian perspective leads us to the configuration of a social world regulated by moral guidelines, such that society becomes a *moral power* that, as an object of respect and a source of shared ideas, sets *normative frameworks within which action is inscribed*. In this way, it is possible to assert that Durkheim's point of view establishes a tradition that assumes that social action is a process engraved in *normative frameworks*; "The dominant models in the field of the theory of social action can be differentiated by the image of their anthropological case. There are three dominant ones. One of them is *homo moralis*, which came from Durkheim and Kant's sociologization and was revisited and enhanced by Parsons and structural functionalism. This image is of a moral subject who has interiorized a normative universe that applies in his different situations of action, a disciplined reader of all-inclusive codes who knows what is prescribed for himself and for others in each possible situation" (Ramos, 1999b: 236).

1.4. In the arena of emotions and affections, this compulsory determination supposes an ongoing labour of control and emotional management geared toward limiting, transforming, or displacing natural inclinations, in an attempt to adjust them to the requirements of social life. The collective guidelines established for what is socially expected, demand ways of feeling and make up a normative framework that is continuously in place, explicitly or implicitly, affirming the accepted emotional expressions and sanctioning feelings considered to be *inappropriate*. This normative configuration regarding the emotional dimension has been subsequently developed, for instance, by authors such as Arlie Hochschild, in his analysis of "feeling rules," and by William Reddy, with his concept of "emotional regime." Among Spanish speakers, this concept has been developed and enhanced from a Foucauldian angle by Federico Besserer, considering the term "regimes of feelings" to refer to the dimension of normative control that regulates the field of the emotions (Cf. Bericat, 2000; Pampler, 2014; Besserer, 2014).

1.5. According to *The Rules of the Sociological Method*, that which makes it possible to comply with a normative order is society's transcendence and moral authority. In this sense, the subject takes on the norm as legitimate, in that it represents a *superior* power that is at the same time a *desirable* value. Society thus seems to the individual to be a principle that imposes compliance with the normativity in virtue of its *transcendence* (Durkheim, 1982: 176–178). This transcendent reality is made up of two dimensions. Along with Duty, social life entails a less-visible dimension – the Good (Durkheim, 1982: 48, note).

1.6. Social life, as Durkheim established, is not simply a constricting world, at least not *only that*. It is also, and above all, an order that is taken as *legitimate*, as well as a *desired* order, in that it is underpinned by social ideas from which the individual affirms his social condition and transcends beyond himself. Coercion is assumed *only and to the degree to which* the society is a *regulatory power* as well as a *desired good*. In this sense, no regulation can be established without a basis of value; there is no way to demand respect for the norm if this norm does not have values that make this compliance acceptable. Meanwhile, this value is fed by appropriate *feelings* that lead to the required action being carried out. It is this union between Good and Duty that characterizes social acts, that makes it possible for them to be imposed upon us.

## 4.3 Durkheim's diagnosis of modern societies: social order, individualism, and normative crises

2.1. In *The Division of Labour in Society* (1893), a book based on his doctoral thesis, Durkheim develops a quite comprehensive exercise to explain how traditional societies become modern societies. The text posits a theory of social differentiation that explains, through the development of the division of labour, the passage from a mechanical solidarity (founded in similarities) to an organic one (based on functional inter-independence). He thus describes not a process of dissolving but of *transformation* in social integration mechanisms. The value of this type of explanation when considering the emotional aspect rests in the fact that social solidarity is made up of collective feelings.

2.2. In *The Division of Labour in Society*, Durkheim deals with the topic of moral integration, analysing the transformation of the mechanisms of solidarity. His main question centres on relations between the individual personality and social solidarity, in the framework of differentiation and assuming that the division of labour has a moral dimension (Durkheim, 1984: XXX, 6).

2.3. The work attempts to cover progressively these three main objectives:
   (a) To explain the nature of social solidarity and its historical expressions, reflected in the types of mechanical and organic solidarity. They each represent different models of social cohesion, with emotional and value regimes that are also different.
   (b) To develop an evolutionary theory of society that explains these transformation processes through changes in the material conditions of the social environment (an increase in moral volume and density) (Durkheim, 1984: 208–211). This point is relevant for our review, because it presents a hypothesis of *correspondence* between *social mediums* and *emotional regimes with value*.
   (c) To elucidate – in the framework of this process of differentiation and the type of solidarity it entails – the moral and emotional mechanisms that make integration possible, or at least that lead to crisis conditions.

2.4. The main thesis of *The Division of Labour in Society* establishes an historical convergence between the emergence of a cooperative society and the development of the individual personality. It is possible for Durkheim in that the cooperation derived from the division of labour produces *simultaneously* conditions for personalization and for increasing moral bonds among individuals. Durkheim envisions organic solidarity as a platform for social integration, open to a diversity of functions and values, but integrated in the end by a series of common beliefs and feelings articulated around respect for the individual personality. Regarding the affective aspect, this process supposes the emergence of a *new emotional regime* linked to these beliefs and values (Durkheim, 1984: 283).

However, the cult of the individual takes on an exceptional and, in the end, paradoxical form within the argumentative framework of *The Division of Labour in Society*. Even though he recognizes the relevance that this cult has acquired in modern societies, Durkheim remains uniquely reserved about it. To him, respect for the individual personality is *insufficient* on its own to guarantee social integration. In fact, its unilateral development may lead to a certain type of social entropy, when its development is incapable of producing the altruism required for social life. According to Durkheim, the cult of the individual refers to a private goal, not to a true social bond (Durkheim, 1984: 332).

If the cult of the individual cannot be taken as a cornerstone of social integration, what does social integration depend on? The answer given by Durkheim once again refers to the moral function of the division of labour. In traditional societies, the collective consciousness made up the main integrating factor. This role is taken on in modern societies by the division of labour (Durkheim, 1984: 332). Since the cult of the individual is shown to be an insufficient regulatory mechanism, Durkheim believes that the moral effects of the division of labour (expressed in the multiplication of bonds and regulatory groups in each professional sphere) can promote the integration of a differentiated social order. Yet this answer is provisional and is clearly insufficient, in light of the considerations in the latter part of the book.

In the third and final part of *The Division of Labour in Society*, we find for the first time a systematic expression of the concept of *anomie* to allude to "abnormal" types of labour division characterized by serious regulatory-type problems, where the rules are not complied with, are inexistent, or are being adjusted to new or changing conditions. Even though these anomic types of crises are considered here as provisional, in that they express processes of rapid transition in the economic and social order, their introduction is relevant because they announce concerns and problems that Durkheim will cover more rigorously in his subsequent writings. It is relevant that these aspects are mentioned because they foreshadow a first version of the Durkheimian diagnosis of modern societies, characterized by the identification of normative-type crises. In our analysis, their consideration is doubly meaningful with regard to the identification of emotional expressions of the implicated anomic disruptions.

### 4.3.1 Collective affections and moral malaise: emotional expressions of egoism and anomie

2.5. In his next book, *Suicide* (1897), Durkheim abandons his initial optimistic tone that considered the evils of the modern society to be transitory. While *The Division of Labour in Society* shows a society disrupted by the effect of strong, yet temporary transformations, in *Suicide* the problems analysed refer to a broader *structural condition*. In this sense, the problems covered are conceived as a *symptom* of a profound moral crisis that puts on display the breakdown of social bonds and the need for profound reforms in the societies analysed. The topic of suicide is taken as part of a deeper issue, yet is in no way a temporary one; general conditions of social cohesion are analysed here as part of a framework where the emotional and value-laden aspect will take on a more prominent role (Durkheim, 2002: 353–359).

2.6. The analysis in *Suicide* offers a new vein of interpretation of the links between the individual and society. The increase in suicides expresses not only the increasing state of individuals incapable of dealing with modern life, but also, and above all, the general crisis of the societies to which they belong (Durkheim, 2002: 221, 307). In this sense, the book looks at progress through a sceptical lens, taking its object of study (the growth in suicide rates with regard to cohesion and social health) as a *symptom* of the moral malaise of modern society (Durkheim, 2002: 167, 328–336). Durkheim points it out in these terms: "Thence are formed currents of depression and disillusionment emanating from no particular individual but expressing society's state of disintegration. They reflect the relaxation of social bonds, a sort of collective asthenia, or social malaise, just as individual sadness, when chronic, in its way reflects the poor organic state of the individual" (Durkheim, 2002: 172).

2.7. The diagnosis made in *Suicide* adds a profound, critical evaluation of society's ability to regulate the conduct of individuals and make them a part of groups that offer support and meaning to their existence. Thus, society is seen as a power that *regulates* and a moral means that *integrates* "… society is not only something attracting the sentiments and activities of individuals with unequal force. It is also a power controlling them" (Durkheim, 2002: 201).

This perspective introduces an important watershed moment, the incorporation of a new analytical dimension. The framework applied initially to explain social life (centred on coercion and regulation) is extended to incorporate the role of *integration* as a mechanism of social cohesion (Ramos, 1998: 25–31). The implications of this incorporation are likewise on display in Durkheim's explanation of the basic mechanisms of social cohesion – no social institution, on its own, produces integration without the series of shared values or the role of institutions that offer cohesion (the family, religion, etc.). No normative order can be sustained without ideals, in other words, without the concurrence of a common framework of values that act as a base. Thus, obedience with informed consent (which was discussed in the first section) requires at least an emotional and value-centred foundation to back it up.

2.8. The explanatory framework developed in *Suicide* also represents an important step on the path toward a more profound theory of limits, tensions, and contradictions in the modern order. Based on this new approach, problems associated with social cohesion derive from an insufficient or excessive presence of regulatory (R) and integration (I) mechanisms. This operational defect results in different types of fractures in the social order, and consequently, in different types of suicide, depending on the mechanism to which they refer. Based on this new interpretation, the analysis of the different types of suicide can be linked to the creation of *collective affections* and *emotional structures* where the regulatory or integration processes, or both, show different types of failures.

Based on this classification, problems derived from a *regulation insufficiency* (-R) lead to what Durkheim calls *anomic suicide*. On the other hand, *excessive regulation* provokes perturbations categorized as *fatalistic* suicide (R+). Meanwhile, problems derived from *insufficient integration* (-I) lead to *egoistic* suicide, while cases of excessive integration (I+) lead to *altruistic* suicide (Durkheim, 2002: 332). From this framework a diagnosis is derived that conceives of modernity as subjugated to a *constitutively selfish and anomic* logic whose sources and expressions are significantly reflected in the emotional dimension (Durkheim, 2002: 330–332; Ramos, 1998: 39).

2.9. The perspective presented in *Suicide* had repercussions and resonance in the texts that Durkheim would develop in the following years, particularly regarding morality, education, and religion. For the latter two, there are clear connections with the emotional dimension. The regulation and integration crises reflected in the growing suicide rates prove the need to construct new models to stimulate social cohesion, based on values and collective emotions that can reconstruct moral unity.

Within this framework, education plays a key role, as we can see in texts such as *Education and Sociology* (Durkheim, 1968), *The Evolution educational thought: lectures on the formation and development of secondary education in*

*France* (Durkheim, 2006), and *Moral Education* (Durkheim, 1961). In the latter text in particular, moral education becomes strategic, since it is a means of fighting against anomie (forming in the individual the spirit of discipline) and of dealing with egotism (by fostering group membership). It requires as a foundation a framework of values that offer freedom and are not taken on merely out of tradition or imposition (moral autonomy). The *subtext* surrounding all these reflections is clearly emotional, since it deals with the management of, work with, and control of emotions, as well as the reconversion, transformation, or sublimation of desires in terms of the requirements raised by problems of integration in contexts and conditions of crisis.

## 4.4 Religion, symbolic integration and collective effervescence

In a well-known autobiographical reference from 1907, Durkheim recognizes retrospectively the moment in which what he classifies as a *crucial change in direction* came about in his thinking, based on the comprehension of the role of religion in social life:

> It was only in 1895 that I had a clear view of the capital role played by religion in social life. It was in that year that, for the first time, I found a means of tackling sociologically the study of religion. It was a revelation to me. That lecture course of 1895 marks a watershed in my thinking, so much so that all my previous research had to be started all over again so as to be harmonized with these new views. The *Ethik of Wundt*, which I had read eight years previously played no part in this change of direction. It was due entirely to the studies of religious history which I had just embarked upon, and in particular to the works of Robertson Smith and his school.
>
> (Durkheim, 1907/1982: 259–260)

Finding this new approach to religion would allow him to enhance his thesis on social facts, moving toward the approach used by the Good/Duty duo. This dual-dimension approach would come about by means of analytical instruments that would allow him to capture their profound dimension. In this sense, *The Elementary Forms of the Religious Life* (1912), which crowned his work regarding this approach to the study of religion, continues with the reflections first introduced in *Suicide*. As we shall we, the role of emotions and affections takes on a progressively greater weight in this stage.

4.1. In the final stage of his life, Durkheim assigned a relevant role to the analysis of religion. Yet his reflections on the topic do not make up an isolated chapter within his comprehensive perspective of society; rather they should be taken as the result of a deeper analysis and pinpointing of questions closely linked to the understanding of the mechanisms that make the integration of modern societies possible.

4.2. Durkheim's analysis of religion moves from an initial definition in which religion is taken only formally according to its obligatory nature, to a progressive approach to its origins and integrative functions. The definition of religion given in *The Elementary Forms* is wide-ranging, based on the notion of the *sacred* and modelled on the topic of social regulation and integration (Durkheim, 1995: 44).

4.3. Religion is a phenomenon of origins, since it represents the basis on which a first type of distinction and hierarchal creation is instituted in the world – the distinction between sacred and profane, the origin of all subsequent distinctions (Durkheim, 1995: 36–37, 224). The sacred does not represent a physical reality but rather a *distinction* that includes two dichotomous spheres of the world – the sacred and the profane (a distinction that gives way to the separation between permitted/restricted worlds; everyday life/eminent sacred sphere, etc.).

4.4. Durkheim establishes a mutual relationship between the social and the sacred. What is sacred (eminent collective reality) has a social origin, since society constructs the source of all authority. On the other hand, what is sacred (at the mercy of the influence of its authority and transcendence) contributes to the *constitution* of what is social. The transcendence assigned to society (and with it to the values and practices it expresses) is an attribution constructed not in individual solitude but in *association*. Durkheim introduces here an important thesis, regarding the construction of social aspects based on moments of *effervescence*, in which collective ideals are periodically updated so as to maintain among the members of the group the principles of social unity. These moments of effervescence have a significant emotional aspect (Durkheim, 1995: 213–214).

4.5. The symbolic institution of society is thus set in an *emotional* assumption. The creation of shared ideals makes up the basis of social integration, from which is in turn derived all attachment to normative criteria. Moral authority refers to Duty; it institutes and maintains it, but at the same time, this authority is not maintained without an attribution to *shared values and feelings*. Values and emotions are needed that legitimize the restriction and sacrifices that moral life and the acceptance of a governed life demands. Even though society is structured on norms, this structure gets its strength from an emotional factor, derived from the experience of the sacred, which Durkheim classifies as the *dynamogenic power* of religion (Durkheim, "Durkheim, E. (1975). Le problème religieux et la dualité de la nature humaine. Extrait du Bulletin de la Société française de philosophie, 1913, 13, pp. 63-100. In Émile Durkheim, Textes. 2. "1975, T. 2:24). This force is recreated in ceremonies, cults, and ways of reactivating the moral ideal. Religion (or more precisely, the sacred) is thus seen not only as a ritual marking of a mythical social beginning, but as a series of practices through which the collective identity is constructed and social bonds are constantly maintained. Upon this foundation, the institution of what is social is possible since it is taken as an expression of a moral and emotional community of values and beliefs. In this way, Giddens (1995: 129) notes that the main objective of *The Elementary Forms* is not, as has often been believed, to show that religion produces society, but rather that the collective representations incorporated in religion express the self-creating capability of what is social. Based on this characterization, Durkheim introduces the role of ideals in the constitution of society. His argumentation contemplates two fundamental pillars: (1) Even though everything sacred is social, *not everything social is sacred* (distinction between moments of atony/effervescence); (2) What is sacred expresses *characteristic* social experience that leads the individual to transcend himself, according to collective values (see Durkheim, 1975, T. 2:87).

4.6. Religion is not merely false consciousness; it expresses real feelings. The faithful are not deceiving themselves by feeling a power that transcends them. That power is real, since it derives from the collective force that the community of believers produces through ceremonies, rites, or events, which, no matter what form they may take, create emotional energies through the association and production of practices that produce a community of emotions and beliefs. The representations produced by religion are not an invention; they have a practical efficacy and *their consequences are real*. In this profound sense, *the idea is a builder of reality* (Durkheim, 1995: 229).

4.7. If the sacred principle is nothing more than the expression of society itself as a concrete reality, ritual life can be interpreted in secular, rational terms. Society consecrates men, things, and even ideas such as freedom, reason, or homeland (Durkheim, 1995: 215). Thus, even revolutions can be understood as experiences of social effervescence full of *emotional life*, where shared beliefs originate and strengthen, emotions circulate and are enhanced, and values are promoted or fought for, in the interest of producing new collective ideals (Durkheim, 1995: 220–221).

## 4.5 Some closing thoughts

Before ending this chapter, we would like to incorporate two ideas that we believe may suggest other veins of interpretation to establish links between the latest results on Durkheim's sociology of religion and the proposal of a theory of knowledge and of social action, set in emotional foundations.

5.1. In the text "Systems of Primitive Classification" (1902), Durkheim shows that the emotional aspect is found *at the base of systems of classification*. In fact, the material and symbolic organization of the world produced from these classification systems *comes from an emotional orientation* (Durkheim and Mauss, 1963: 47). This idea includes significant capital for our analysis, highlighting the *practical, emotional nature* of processes by which reality is organized, knowledge is presented, and forms of intervention are produced (Durkheim and Mauss, 1963: 83–86).

5.2. In the text "The Religious Problem and the Dualism of Human Nature" (Durkheim, 1913/1975), Durkheim underscores the practical nature of religion. Its main value does not consist in offering conceptions of the world, but in offering *practical principles of faith*. Religion is, above all, a *power*. Its dynamogenic virtue resides in this *energetic component*, linked to the ritual action in which social life is originally produced, in moments characterized by elevated levels of collective effervescence. The descriptors of collective effervescence in this text are the concepts of *emotion* and *collective energy*. What is more, in the development of this text, as Eva Illouz (2007: 15) has suggestively noted, emotions are shown as *the energetic component of action*. This thesis offers interesting lines of thought, especially when related to claims made in the course *Pragmatism and Sociology* (Durkheim, 1983), where the practical aspect of knowledge and its implications for understanding a theory of action and of truth are covered. In all these considerations, the process of producing collective representations about the world, and the systems of classifications to which these representations belong, include a significant emotional component.

## Notes

1 Full-time professor. Social and Political Sciences Department, Universidad Iberoamericana, Mexico.
2 In writing this chapter we have considered the current development in the fields of sociology and emotions, affections, and sensibilities. Even though we recognize the differences in these approaches, for this chapter we have considered both emotions and affections, covering them based on the notion of *emotional dimension*. For a general overview of these topics, see García & Sabido, 2014:20–22; Ariza, 2016:11–12; Clough, 2008; Clough & Halley, 2008; Gregg & Seigworth, 2010; Scribano, 2012; Calderón, 2014.
3 Some relevant works on the study of emotions in Durkheim include those by Barnwell, 2018; Bericat, 2001; Cuin, 2001; Chahbenderian, 2013; Fish, 2016; Fischer & Chong, 1989. For a complete biographical review of his works, cf. Fournier, 2013; Lukes, 1973; Ramos, 1999a. For a systematic overview of his work in recent years, see Datta, 2008; Gane, 2002; Pearce, 1989; Poggi, 2000; Ramos, 1999a, 2011; Scribano, 2020; Stedman, 2001.

## References

Ariza, M. (ed.) (2016). *Emociones, Afectos y Sociología: Diálogos desde la Investigación Social y la Interdisciplina*. México: Instituto de Investigaciones Sociales, Universidad Nacional Autónoma de México.

Barnwell, A. (2018). Durkheim as Affect Theorist. *Journal of Classical Sociology*, 18(1), 21–35

Bericat, Eduardo. (2000). La Sociología de la Emoción y la Emoción en la sociología. *Papers: Revista de Sociología*, 62, 145–176.

Besserer, F. (2014). Regímenes de Sentimientos y la Subversión del Orden Sentimental. Hacia una Economía Política de los Afectos. *Nueva Antropología*, XXVII (81), 55–76.

Calderón, E. (2014). Universos emocionales y Subjetividad. *Nueva Antropología*, XXVII (julio-diciembre), 11–32.

Chahbenderian, Florencia (2013). 'Disciplina, ¿estás ahí? Algunas reflexiones del amor a las reglas en torno a Emile Durkheim.' In Scribano, A. (ed.). 2013. *Teoría social, cuerpo y emociones*. ESE (Editora Estudios Sociológicos), Buenos Aires, 71–86.

Clough, P. (2008). The Affective Turn: Political Economy, Biomedia and Bodies. *Theory, Culture & Society*, 25(1), 1–22. Available at: https://doi.org/10.1177/0263276407085156.

Clough, P., & Halley, J. O. (2008). The affective turn: Theorizing the social. Available at: https://doi.org/10.1215/9780822389606

Cuin, C. (2001). Émotion et rationalité dans la sociologie classique: les cas de Weber et Durkheim. *Revue Européene des Sciences Sociales*, XXXIX–120.

Datta, R. (2008). Politics and Existence: Totems, Dispositifs and Some Striking Parallels between Durkheim and Foucault. *Journal of Classic Sociology*, 8(2), 283–305.

Durkheim, E. (1961). *Moral Education: A Study in the Theory and Application of the Sociology of Education*. New York: Free Press.

––––––– (1968). *Education and Sociology*. New York: Free Press.

––––––– (1913/1975). *Le problème religieux et la dualité de la nature humaine*. Extrait du Bulletin de la Société française de philosophie, 1913, 13, pp. 63–100. In Émile Durkheim, *Textes*. 2. "Religion, morale, anomie", pp. 23 à 59. Paris: Éditions de Minuit.

––––––– (1982). *The Rules of Sociological Method and Selected Texts on Sociology and Its Method*. (Edited by Steven Lukes; translated by W.D. Halls). New York: The Free Press.

––––––– (1983). *Pragmatism and Sociology*. New York: Cambridge University Press.

––––––– (1984). *The Division of Labour in Society*. New York: Palgrave Macmillan.

––––––– (1995). *The Elementary Forms of the Religious Life*. New York: The Free Press.

––––––– (1907/1982). Influences upon Durkheim's View of Sociology [Two letters to the director, *Revue néo-scolastique* (Louvain)]. Translated by W. D. Halls. In S. Lukes (ed.), (1982). *The Rules of the Sociological Method and Selected Texts on Sociology and Its Method*. (Ed. by Steven Lukes; trans. by W.D. Halls). New York: Free Press, 259–260.

––––––– (2002). *Suicide. A Study in Sociology*. London: Routledge.

––––––– (2006). *The Evolution of Educational Thought: Lectures on the Formation and Development of Secondary Education in France*. Edited by W. S. F. Pickering. London: Routledge, 2006.

Durkheim, E. and Mauss, M. (1963). *Primitive classification*. Translated by Rodney Needham. Chicago: University of Chicago.

Fish, J. (2016). *Defending the Durkheimian Tradition. Religion, Emotion and Morality*. New York: Routledge.

Fischer, G. A., & Chon, K. K. (1989). Durkheim and the Social Construction of Emotions. *Social Psychology Quarterly*, 52(1), 1–9.
Fournier, M. (2013). *Émile Durkheim: A Biography*. Cambridge: Polity Press.
Gane, M. (2002). *The Radical Sociology of Durkheim and Mauss*. London: Routledge.
Garcia, A., & Sabido, O. (eds). (2014). *Cuerpo y Afectividad en la Sociedad Contemporánea. Algunas Rutas del Amor y la Experiencia Sensible en las Ciencias Sociales*. México: CONACYT – UAM Azcapotzalco.
Giddens, A. (1995). Durkheim and the Question of Individualism. *Politics, Sociology and Social Theory. Encounters with Classical and Contemporary Social* Thought. Stanford University Press, 116–135.
Gregg, M., & Seigworth, G. J. (eds). (2010). *The Affect Theory Reader*. Durham, NC: Duke University Press.
Illouz, E. (2007). *Cold Intimacies. The Making of Emotional Capitalism*. Cambridge: Polity Press.
Lukes, S. (1973). *Emile Durkheim, his Life and Work: A Historical and Critical Study*. Harmondsworth, England: Penguin Books.
Pampler, J. (2014). Historia de las Emociones: Caminos y Retos. *Cuadernos de Historia Contemporánea*, (36), 17–29. Available at: https://doi.org/10.5209/rev_CHCO.2014.v36.46680
Pearce, F. (1989). *The Radical Durkheim*. New York: Oxford University Press.
Poggi, G. (2000). *Durkheim*. Oxford: Oxford University Press.
Ramos, R. (1998). Un tótem frágil: aproximación a la estructura teórica de El Suicidio. REIS N° 81. Enero-marzo 1998. Monográfico: cien años de la publicación de un clásico, *El suicidio*, de Emile Durkheim.
—––––– (1999a) *La sociología de Émile Durkheim. Patología social, tiempo, religión*. Centro de Investigaciones Sociológicas/ Siglo XXI de España, Madrid
—––––– (1999b). "Homo tragicus." *Política y Sociedad, 30*, 213.
—––––– (2011) "La sociología de Durkheim y la política" Prefacio a *Emile Durkheim. Escritos políticos*. Barcelona: Gedisa.
Scribano, A. (2012). Sociología de los Cuerpos/Emociones. *Revista Latinoamericana de Estudios sobre Cuerpos, Emociones y Sociedad*, 4(10), 91–111.
—––––– (2020). Durkheim´s Vision of the Individual and Corporations. The Prelude of Another Management. In: Scribano, A., and M. Korstanje (2020). *Imagining the Alterity. The position of the Other in the Classic Sociology and Anthropology*. Nova Science Publisher: New York, 35–58.
Stedman, J. (2001). *Durkheim Reconsidered*. Cambridge: Polity Press.

Chapter 5

# Max Weber

*Gregor Fitzi*

## 5.1 Introduction

Max Weber (1864–1920) is considered today as 'the classic' of sociology par excellence, its grounding father and most influential author. The historical-critical edition of his work was concluded in 2020 (Weber 1984–2020; here cited as MWG). Thus, his complete oeuvre is now at the disposal of the scientific community. Yet, rather surprisingly, there is less scientific debate about his sociological theory than expected. The mainstream of sociological research is somehow convinced that his work is outdated. Paraphrasing the motto of medieval scholasticism, one commentator states that it can be read at least 'because it is useless'. Accordingly, the widespread knowledge about Weber's classical sociology is more the product of an 'oral vulgate' than of a scientific assessment of his texts. This also concerns Weber's relationship to the issue of emotional behaviour. The most accredited variation of the narrative suggests that Weber is possessed by substantial rationalist prejudice and disregards the world of passions in his scientific work. The modern age would witness the fulfilment of the process of 'disenchantment' that dominates reality through the rational means of science and technology. The modern individual would be forced to bow to social change and live in an emotionless reality. Weber's alleged extreme methodological and existential rationalism is then interpreted as the origin of the many accidents of his biography: his nationalism and his nervous breakdown; or his sexual malaise and his extramarital adventures.

That these hypotheses do not match the complexity of Weber's life and work is highlighted by Jaspers' illuminating portrait of Weber as the most multifaceted intellectual of his age (Jaspers, 1989). Nevertheless, the phantasmagoria of the demonic Weber offers a classical plot of literature that is intriguing for any novelist. Weber is depicted as the Faust of the turn of the century. He banishes the spirits of passion from his laboratory during the day and summons them again at night. The result is his political and sexual irrationalism. The most atavistic chords of the German spirit would play through in Weber's oeuvre and thus determine the reasons for a fatal attraction or an absolute refusal of his viewpoints. There is, of course, some serious scientific research on Weber's biography (Kaesler, 2014; Kaube, 2014; Radkau, 2005). Yet, at the end of the day, an image emerges that discourages the scientific assessment of his sociological theory building.

The predominant neoliberal worldview derives a crucial advantage from this irrational approach to sociological classics because social critique must cope without the analytical means that interpretative sociology could provide it with. Yet, if despite all the bans on reading that one encounters in the sociological vulgate and elsewhere, some brave researchers finally decide to read Weber's texts, they rapidly note how his Faustian image is misleading. Weber's sociology offers a far more differentiated appreciation for the meaning of emotions in both ancient and modern societies. This foundation encourages a systematic reconstruction of Weber's unlabelled sociology of emotions that is nonetheless present in all domains of his sociological work from the 'Basic Sociological Terms' (MWG I/23, 147–215) to the 'Sociology of Domination' (MWG I/23, 449–497). Yet, the analysis of the role of emotions also plays a central role in Weber's sociological-historical work. Thus, a reconstruction of Weber's sociology of ascetic Protestantism will show how, somewhat unexpectedly, the emotional residue of the 'rationalism of world domination' represents for Weber the architect both of its material success and its decline as a 'religious conduct of life' (MWG I/18).

## 5.2 The sociological dignity of non-rational choice

Max Weber has often been accused of rationalist prejudice. Yet, his focus on the rational aspects of action is dictated by purely epistemological reasons (MWG I/23, 147–215). 'Interpretative sociology' is a scientific critique of everyday life experience as well as of established social knowledge. Its methodological procedure consists in reconstructing the development of social action and starts with the aspects that are most evident from the viewpoint of its scientific observer. Among these, the modalities of social action based on rational calculation, especially economic calculation, play a fundamental role. They offer the highest degree of evidence to the observer and can thus be more easily understood intellectually. Based on this assumption, sociology can explain the rational stratum of social action, by reconstructing 'rational ideal-types' that can be applied to the analysis of social reality. If the observed social action deviates from what could be predicted on the basis of this knowledge, it is necessary to understand which other ideal-types of action come into play that have lesser degree of intellectual evidence. By such means, interpretative sociology can develop a scale of theoretical models that serve as a framework of interpretation to understand the observed social reality, starting from the easiest explanatory frames of rational action and penetrating subsequently into the non-rational ones.

The 'rational choice' which, in particular, characterizes economic action – Weber's 'purposive rationality' – thus represents a fundamental dimension of social action, yet it is neither the only nor the main one, if one considers social reality in its complexity. Furthermore, the concept of rationality needs to be critically reflected upon. Different historical periods and cultural regions generated very different forms of rationality. Weber devoted his study of the 'economic ethics of world religions' to this issue (MWG I/19–21), which unfortunately remained unfinished (Schluchter, 1991). The historical form of social action that comes closest to the ideal-typical model of purposive rationality, the 'rationalism of world domination' through science and technology, must be regarded as the product of the historical development of the modern Occident since the Protestant Reformation (MWG I/18). Yet, the greatest part of human history is grounded either on other forms of rationality, e.g., on Confucianism as in contemporary China (Bell, 2010), or on non-rational modalities of social action. Sociological theory must, therefore, be capable of taking into account not only 'voluntary, interest-driven and rational action', on which the paradigm of the theory of rational choice today insists (Becker, 1976; Coleman, 1990; Norkus 2001). Furthermore, interpretative sociology must contemplate the forms of passive and irrational action that have come to the fore. In addition, for Weber there are also limitations for the faculty of sociology to comprehend human behaviour. Thus, he draws a clear distinction between sociology and social psychology that excludes from the domain of sociological comprehension the phenomena that characterized the work of French mass psychology. The reason for this is that, for Weber, the precondition for sociological analysis is determined by the meaningful reference of social action to 'other social actors', so that he denies the presence of this reference in mass behaviour or pure imitation of others' behaviour (Le Bon, 1898; Tarde, 1890). This definition of the limits of interpretative sociology is a matter of debate. Yet, what is certain is the fact that Weber postulates emotionally driven action with reference to the actions of others as a constituent part of the research domain of sociology. This theoretical option of Weber's sociological research project confronts the interpreter with the question of what status he, at the end of the day, grants to emotional action.

The quadripartite typology of social action proposed by Weber stems from the attempt to found the epistemological autonomy of sociology on the capacity of explaining economic as well as religious and political behaviour, by integrating their ideal-types into two great conceptual dichotomies. It is to Schluchter's credit that he highlights the often-ignored meaning of the first of these dichotomies, between 'purposive rationality' and 'value-rational social action' (Schluchter, 2005: 28). Its meaning lies in the contrast between a 'success-oriented' (*Erfolgshandeln*) and a 'validity-oriented' (*Geltungshandeln*) form of social action. Rational action with regard to values, therefore, is not a variant of purposive rationality, in which the material goal is replaced by a value. Here, the focus is not on the endpoint, but on the unfolding of action, because keeping faith with a particular course of action has a 'witness value' for the actor. Alongside the first dichotomy between ideal-types of action, however, there is a second dichotomy that Weber considers as prevailing in pre-modern and non-western history. It is the dichotomy between action based on the compelling force of habit and action against it (that is, the contrast between 'traditional' and 'emotional action'). These ideal-types differ from the first two in that they bring behaviours to expression that over time are not explicitly conscious, because they are determined 'more or less unreflectively' by habit or emotion. This is what makes them so important for interpretative sociology and demands to be explained.

Emotional and traditional action differ from each other in terms of the relationship they entertain with the inertia of everyday life. Tradition, in fact, involves a non-reflected reproduction of habit, whereas on the impetus of punctual emotional states of mind, emotional action breaks with the regularities of everyday life. At the extreme of what can still be considered 'meaningful social action', Weber classifies traditional action as often taking the form of a dull, automatic reaction produced by the acquired habits that shape everyday life. Instead, emotional action distinguishes itself by the fact that it is an impulsive reaction due to the impact of unexpected or unfamiliar new events. In turn, this behaviour is eccentric with respect to the ideal-typical model of social action endowed with meaning. Yet, it conveys a considerable innovative force, capable of thoroughly reshaping social reality. The immediate dedication to the current feeling preceding all rationalization is essential to emotional action. Fear, anger, enthusiasm, love, jealousy or hate drive human beings to make profound and often irrevocable changes in their social life, often without allowing them to assess the consequences of their decisions. This output differentiates emotional action from rational action with regard to values, which implies the conscious elaboration of action guidelines that orientate the social actor in a planned manner over a longer period of time. Both, however, have in common that the meaning of action is found during the course of its development, and not beyond it, in the achievement of a particular goal.

## 5.3 The political power of non-rational choice

With these observations, Weber concludes his analysis of the types and dichotomies of individual action to turn his attention to the other two dimensions of the social world, which are not merely 'punctual', like action orientation, but 'relational' and 'stratificatory'. Weberian sociology has, in fact, a three-dimensional architecture, proposing a 'theory of social action', a theory of 'social structure' both in the horizontal (social relation) and vertical sense (social group), as well as a theory of social validity (*Geltung*). In the 'Basic Sociological Terms' (MWG I/23, 147–215) Weber reconstructs the typology of social relationships, starting from that of action orientation and showing how the latter constitutes the basis on which the complex structures of social reality are grounded. The matter is complex (Fitzi, 2004). Yet, here, the reconstruction will be limited to the role that the assessment of emotional action plays for Weber's theory building. Starting from the four-part typology of action, Weber introduces a distinction between two different processes that establish horizontal social relationships. The 'communitarian type', which Weber calls *Vergemeinschaftung*, is based on a subjective sense of belonging that those involved perceive in an emotional sense. This distinguishes it from the processes of association (*Vergesellschaftung*) that are based on the rational types of action orientation with respect to purpose or value. Thereby, Weber shows how relevant emotions are for cementing social ties, especially in situations of social crisis where the regular course of everyday life breaks down and rationally stated contracts do not hold anymore.

Through a number of logical steps that assess the relationship between social actors and social groups, involving the development of the concepts of representation (*Vertretung and Repräsentation*), imputation (*Zurechnung*) and social grouping (*Verbandsbildung*) Weber gradually moves from the ideal-typical reconstruction of horizontal to vertical social structures. The latter are characterized by 'asymmetrical social relationships', in which one part directs and the other executes, reciprocating the rule through an attitude of legitimation, or at least of acceptance for its authority. The assessment of asymmetric social relationship gives rise to the well-known distinction between power as domination (*Herrschaft*) and power as influence (*Macht*). The latter indicates the actor's ability to impose his will even against others' resistance and even if this does not structure a social relationship. Domination, instead, constitutes a structured relationship of command, or rather an asymmetrical two-way relationship between command and legitimation. Once the definition of *Herrschaft* has been established, however, the question for the sociology of emotions is how and within what limits emotional action can cement asymmetric relationships of domination.

Weber enquires into the topic by assessing the relational character of legitimation. In his view, this is the only approach that allows for the consolidation of a consistent typology of domination, including the type that is based on emotional action. This is one of the best-known chapters of Weber's theoretical edifice: the ideal-typical assessment of charismatic power. Here, emotional action is seen not only as the topical moment inducing the break with the unwritten laws of habit, but also as the privileged forging of new social ties, especially in pre-modern times. Following the intervention of a 'charismatic leader', a prophet, commander, demagogue or adventurer, a process of sudden and emotionally tense redefinition of coexistence is triggered, especially if his action is inspired by a substantial crisis of traditional social orders. The bearer of charisma comes, proclaims his mission and promises to guide his followers out of the predicament that hit them. Yet, the temper of emotion, enthusiasm and heroism dictated by the state of exception in which a charismatic personality comes to power, because it is considered capable of leading the social group towards a decisive event, are not destined to last. The emotional wave of charisma profoundly modifies social relations; however, it has a limited duration.

Like the typology of action, that of domination is also framed within a series of dichotomies. Here, the distinction between reason and emotion plays an essential role. The legitimacy of a 'ruling power' can be the expression of a system of rational rules and thus be objective, or else it can be rooted in the personal authority of a leader. The latter can be based either on the 'sacredness of tradition' (that is, of what is known, because it has 'always existed'), thus limiting the arbitrariness of power on the basis of rules of habit. Or the authority springs from the emotional dedication to the personality that breaks with traditional certainties to face the unknown in an attempt to overcome the state of exception, in which the social group has found itself. The belief in charisma thus comes into play as a 'gift of grace' of the person who is considered capable of guiding his followers towards salvation. Weber's definition of the third ideal-type of domination is based on the concept of religious charisma (Sohm, 1892). Here, the personality is regarded as having supernatural or superhuman, or at least specifically exceptional, powers and properties not accessible to others; or as being sent by the Lord and having exemplary value. Historically, the attribution of such exceptional qualities to a particular person has often been conditioned in a magical sense, as can easily be observed in both religious and political contexts. Economic crises, wars, pandemics, natural catastrophes and migratory flows shatter the daily certainties of habit, which stabilize the emotional substratum of social relationships, bringing out a malaise that demands to be addressed and resolved. In the most diverse forms, the 'charisma bearers' then appear on the scene, promising to eradicate the causes of the predicament.

Weber introduces the ideal-type of charismatic power last, contrasting its features with those of domination based on rationality or tradition. Charisma is characterized by being strongly personalistic, extra-ordinary and independent from the principles of economic profitability. This highlights its irrational and emotional character that does not tolerate the regulation of action in both the rational and habitual senses. Yet, in order to explain charismatic authority, it is essential to understand how militants, followers and adherents evaluate the charismatic gift of the leader, because the empirical persistence of charismatic power depends on a particular problem: the confirmation of the leader's gift of grace (*Gnadengabe*) in the eyes of his supporters. To reiterate the relationship of subordination it is thus crucial that the faith is confirmed again and again in the gift of grace. This originally occurs spontaneously, as a result of the psychological distress caused by the state of exception, in which the social group finds itself. The particular emotional atmosphere, both individual and collective, of such situations gives rise to confidence in the talents of a demagogue, to enthusiasm for the heroism of a commander, or to faith in the revelation of a new religion, advocated by a prophet, who sometimes supports its value with miraculous deeds.

The need to keep alive the legitimacy of a charismatic leadership through 'confirmation', however, must not lead to seeing it as a political relationship of an ephemeral character. In the ideal-typical case, the bearer of charisma asks not for consensus. On the contrary, he warns his supporters to understand the objective necessity of his mission, arising from the predicament, in which they find themselves and which can only be overcome under his guidance. Recognition of the charismatic endowment is therefore not dependent on the supporters' judgement but is imposed on them as a 'duty'. As long as they aspire to the salvific event inherent to the charismatic leader's mission, they must support him. The shift from despair to hope and to enthusiasm for the guidance of the charismatic leader thus informs the unconditional emotional dedication to his person. If, however, the confirmation of the gift of grace fails repeatedly, as the economic crisis worsens, the pandemic persists, the election or the war is lost, the bearer of charismatic power appears to be 'abandoned by his god'. The failure to achieve the salvific event eventually deprives him of charismatic authority. This can occur suddenly, in an irrational and violent way, leading, in an extreme case, to the ritual killing of the failing charismatic leader and the restoration of traditional power. Or it can take the form of a gradual dissipation of the emotional tension that underpins charismatic power, bringing the social group back into the mainstream of everyday power relationships.

This is what Weber calls the 'routinization of charismatic power' (MWG I/23, 533–591). By its very nature, charisma is the realm of exception, which in its ideal-typical form cannot be maintained over time. Its routinization is characterized by a gradual shift from the subjective principle of the person to that of the 'political reification'. The relationship of domination must profoundly modify its nature, by abandoning the emotional register of power legitimation and undergoing either a process of 'rationalization' or 'traditionalization'. The topical beginning of this process generally corresponds to the probable disappearance of the bearer of the charismatic gift, so that a question of succession emergences. This change is associated with the material interests of the 'charismatic apparatus' which supports the power system and seeks sources of income that are less random than those of the state of exception. As a rule, the charismatic power group is an emotional community without 'clerical staff', so that its 'administrative apparatus' has no specialist training. Its financial means is generally patronage or has a predatory character. The prophet is matched by apostles, the commander by followers, and the demagogue generally by men of trust, chosen based on their respective charismatic qualification. As the charismatic tension wanes, however, this apparatus must be reconverted in a day-to-day sense.

Finally, the charismatic leader is survived by his doctrine, or the eponymous tale of his deeds, which are used to ground the claim of validity for the functions and offices of the charismatic organizational apparatus that must be converted to everyday life. This transformation gives rise to the concept of 'office charisma', in which the charismatic qualities of a specific function do not depend on the person but derive from the institutional role entrusted to him or her. The 'de-emotionalization process' of the administrative apparatuses reaches its peak with the modern bureaucratic structure of power. Here, the rationalization of the political sphere results in the systematic exoneration of the institutions from every emotional randomness of the individual personalities that bear them. In a social structure that achieves the 'political disenchantment of the world', it thus appears that emotions are progressively marginalized. However, this is only partly true. There is, in fact, a strong emotional residue that persists in rationalized social structures. Its power is not only to be observed in the rise of 'Caesarism' as the modern form of political charisma in mass democracy (MWG I/15, 432–596; Weber, 1994). An emotional residue persisting within the frame of 'disenchantment' also determines the unexpected development of the religious conduct of life, which is typical for the modern 'rationalism of world domination', as Weber points out in the study on Ascetic Protestantism (MWG I/18).

## 5.4 Modernity as a child of non-rational choice

To differentiate the modern economic development model from pre-modern forms of capitalism, above all adventure capitalism, Weber coined the concept of 'modern capitalism', identifying it with the continuous profit aspiration of the rational capitalist enterprise. Its anthropological premise lies in the curbing, or at least the rational tempering, of the irrational impulse to enrichment aimed at consumption. Thus, modern capitalism is not an expression of the classical *auri sacra fames*, which is present in all historical epochs and geographical regions, but of its limitation. The peculiarity of modern Western capitalism consists not only in giving an irresistible impulse to the quantitative accumulation potential of capital, but it also baptises an unprecedented form of 'rationalism of world domination' that starts with the domestication of the human impulse towards the enjoyment of worldly pleasures. According to Weber, this attitude concerns both the social classes that capitalist societies are divided into. Entrepreneurs must aim to reinvest profits to assure the continuity of capitalist accumulation and workers must self-discipline themselves to the point where their performance can become part of a profit calculation. In the context of a causal-historical explanation, the question arises as if, on the one hand, this conduct of life is an historical-cultural product and, on the other, as if it existed before the birth of modern capitalism as a material production system.

According to Weber, the maxim of life conduct that imposes on the individual the duty to indefinitely increase his wealth, by the simultaneous disdain for its use for consumption, cannot be read as an expression of simple utilitarianism. On the contrary, it implies the modification of the causal chains of action and denies the 'anthropological constant' that induces individuals to spend money as a way to realize human needs, but also to enjoy the pleasures of life. From a sociological-historical point of view, it must thus be explained why the inclination for monetary accumulation, which in pre-modern times was perceived as immoral and was religiously sanctioned, became common practice from the Reformation onwards. Before that, the interest in profit was limited to the necessity of reproducing the means necessary to secure a living. 'Economic traditionalism' prevailed and was characterized by what today may be called the life conduct of 'Mediterranean humanity', which is based on the motto: 'working for living. Not living to work' (Latouche, 1999). In his study on ascetic Protestantism, Weber thus analyses the novel psychological impulses that the Calvinist religious faith awakened, which could induce a conduct of life that was so far removed from the 'anthropological constants' of economic traditionalism.

Calvinist religious dogmatics was based on two guiding ideas. On the one hand, the believer should actively intervene in the world, in order to subordinate its social orders to God's ethical prescriptions. The 'just religion' ought to modify the world, starting from the individual conduct of life. On the other hand, the 'worldly profession' was considered as the focus of this religious practice and this was elevated to the status of an instrument of religious asceticism. Accordingly, working hard and successfully was considered as the king's road to fulfilling the will of the Lord. The believer should be emancipated from the chaos of passions by subordinating them to the dictates of religious ethics, so that the conduct of life would be rationalized to the point where its emotional, sinful and irrational potential could be completely neutralized. Yet, according to Weber, this finding is not enough to explain why the transformation of the Calvinist religious dogmatics into a pervasive rationalization of life conduct became a mass phenomenon within the Protestant sects. For this reason, the study on the 'Protestant Ethic' undertakes a comprehensive historical-sociological reconstruction of the developments that characterized the pastoral practice of the Calvinist and Puritan clergy between the fifteenth and seventeenth centuries. The fundamental assumption of Calvin's religiosity was the doctrine of predestination that is the 'election' of the individual believer through God's grace. In his inscrutable omnipotence, the Lord destined only a part of humanity to eternal life. Hence, the worldly conduct of life could not influence the divine will thanks to magical intercession, as is the case with the sacraments of the Catholic Church. The inner-worldly activity served the exclusive purpose of glorifying the name of the Lord.

The grandiose coherence, yet also the pathetic inhumanity of the 'doctrine of predestination' placed particularly heavy burdens on the emotional balance of the faithful, spreading the feeling of the individual's unprecedented inner solitude. The Calvinist doctrine of salvation thus had a particular impact on the order of social life with two implications. In a positive sense, it gave a fundamental impulse to the processes that tended to rationalize economic and social relations. In a negative sense, Calvinist religious doctrine imposed a complete mortification of the most basic human needs, including the necessity to counteract the senselessness of suffering and the injustice of earthly life through a magical-religious interaction with God. Calvinism limited itself to responding to the question of divine justice in a fundamentally imperfect world – that is, 'theodicy' – with the doctrine of the inappellability of predestination. This imposed the accumulation of an unbearable psychic tension on the faithful that threw the individual into a state of complete existential uncertainty, denying the possibility of sharing with others the management of the emotional gap between earthly existence and the prospect of salvation. Thereby, a psychic discomfort emerged that had no immediate social outlet. According to Weber, it was this unease that provided the emotional fuel required to transform the abstract Calvinist religious doctrine into a concrete practical-rational behaviour aimed at regulating everyday life in an increasingly ascetic way. In order for this transformation to take hold and become generalized in the sense of an 'elective affinity' between ascetic Protestantism and the spirit of capitalist accumulation, however, an involuntary practical turn of Calvinist religiosity came to the fore. Weber insists on this point, since this not only represents the beginning of the decline of Calvinism as a religion, but it also informs the historical process that favoured the dissemination of inner-worldly asceticism starting from the Protestant sects.

Faced with the suffering that the doctrine of predestination caused to the faithful, the Calvinist clergy were gradually forced to spread certain guidelines for the conduct of life, to combat this distress. Thanks to a study of the historical development of the Calvinist and Puritan religious movement, Weber reconstructs the process whereby a progressive reinterpretation of the meaning for the ascetic, inner-worldly conduct of life came about. At a time when religion still played a fundamental role in the order of life, the search for certainty about the state of grace was a pressing need for the faithful. Asked how the doctrine of predestination could be endured, Calvin lapidarily replied that the Christian had to be content with faith, without knowing whether he belonged to the ranks of the elected. Confronted with the pressing demand for at least some signs of the 'state of grace' for the faithful, exempting them from the psychical oppression caused by the doctrine of predestination, two types of advice came to be dispensed in the daily exercise of spiritual care. On the one hand, the clergy insisted that it was without doubt a duty to consider oneself as chosen and to reject all doubt as an assault of the devil. This lack of self-confidence had to be interpreted as insufficient faith and thus as lacking the efficacy of God's grace. On the other hand, tireless professional work was strongly recommended as the main means to achieve self-confidence. Hoping to alleviate the enormous psychic oppression caused by the doctrine of predestination, the Calvinist-orientated humanity threw itself unsparingly into professional work whose material success could at least be read as a sign that it was not invisible to the Lord. Thereby, little by little, progressive enrichment was unintentionally promoted to an indirect criterion for the confirmation of the state of grace. The following transformation of the attitude towards capital accumulation, together with the acquisition of the ascetic inner-worldly conduct of life, thus instilled in Western humanity an 'elective affinity' with the spirit of capitalism that favoured its impetuous development. The emotions that had been thrown out of the door by the ascetic conduct of life, because of the doctrine of predestination, thus made their return by the window in the form of an existential anguish, imposing on ascetic Protestantism an historical turning point that profoundly marked the history of the modern occidental world.

In summary, it can thus be said that even if the process of the 'disenchantment of the world' programmatically eradicates emotions from everyday life, as 'ascetic Protestantism' did in the Calvinist and Puritan currents of the Reformation, they soon reappeared in the form of an anguish that has to be socially managed. This evidence emerges, if one traces back Weber's historic-causal reconstruction of the Reformation to the point where he reconstructs the endogenous crisis of 'inner-worldly asceticism', which led to the decline of the religious attitude of the conduct of life, favouring instead material success as a post-religious entrepreneurial strategy.

## 5.5 Conclusion

In order to take stock of Weber's contribution to a sociology of emotions, it may be noted that, for him, emotions are undoubtedly an integral part of social reality. Yet, their sociological meaning remains on a threshold, limiting their relevance to the effective impact they have on social action with reference to others. It is for this reason that simple, imitative or mass action remains excluded from Weber's understanding of social reality. The mere outburst of passions does not interest his research programme. If, however, emotions affect the unfolding of social action or social structuration, they become sociologically relevant. As a rule, the social realm for Weber is the playground of the two compelling forces of everyday life: habit and calculation. The modern development of society can be explained as the progressive predominance of an instrumental rationality of world domination to the detriment of the forces of tradition, with the consequent subversion of the related 'anthropological constants.' The everyday forms of social relationship, including both rational and traditional domination, are characterized by a substantial lack of heroism. Routine and not emotion guarantees their resilience. This is maybe the deepest meaning of Weber's concept of *Herrschaft*. A 'domination' based on an infinite series of small administrative procedures carried out by bureaucratically trained clerks who ideal-typically are accustomed to act far removed from every emotion: *sine ira nec studio*.

However, for Weber, this is not all that can be observed at the end of the 'process of disenchantment', because social reality hides an extraordinary reverse side that sociology must take into account. This is the realm of emotions, where sudden and irrational outbursts shatter the crust of everyday life, disrupting the framework of habit and rational calculation. The flame of passion when it takes hold of society is very intense, yet also short-lived. Therefore, emotions have a 'threshold value' for sociology. They are the fuel that grants non-reflected impulse-driven behaviour to suddenly reshape social relations. On the one hand, their impact on social reality is crucial. Yet, on the other, it is quite difficult to institutionalize the social transformation that emotions can trigger. To have concrete results, their innovative impetus must be brought back into the mainstream of everyday social life. Emotional action and charisma are the stars of the social scene. Yet, they can only be successful in the long run, if they withdraw from the stage in good time and leave a trace on the institutional fabric of everyday social life. If waves of emotional effervescence aim to extend their duration beyond the state of exception, they are neutralized by the habitual inertia of social structuration, regardless of traditional or rational type, and so leave no trace of their passage.

## References

Becker, G. S. (1976). *The Economic Approach to Human Behavior*. Chicago: University of Chicago Press.
Bell, Daniel (2010). *China's new Confucianism: Politics and Everyday Life in a Changing Society*. Princeton, NJ: Princeton University Press.
Coleman, J. S. (1990). *Foundations of Social Theory*. Cambridge, MA: Harvard University Press.
Fitzi, G. (2004). *Max Webers politisches Denken*. Konstanz: UVK.
Jaspers, K. (1989). *Karl Jaspers on Max Weber*. New York: Paragon House.
Kaesler, D. (2014). *Max Weber. Preuße, Denker, Muttersohn. Eine Biographie*. Munich: C.H. Beck.
Kaube, J. (2014). *Max Weber. Ein Leben zwischen den Epochen*. Berlin: Rowohlt.
Latouche S. (1999). *Le défi de Minerve: Rationalité occidentale et raison méditerranéenne*. Paris: La Découverte.
Le Bon, G. (1898), *Psychologie des foules*. 3, Paris: Alcan M.
Norkus, Z. (2001). *Max Weber und Rational Choice*. Marburg: Metropolis.
Radkau, J. (2005). *Max Weber: Die Leidenschaft des Denkens*. Munich: C. Hanser Verlag.
Schluchter W. (1991), *Religion und Lebensführung*. Bd. 2, *Studien zu Max Webers Religions- und Herrschaftssoziologie*, Suhrkamp, Frankfurt a. M.
Schluchter, W. (2005). *Handlung, Ordnung und Kultur. Studien zu einem Forschungsprogramm in Anschluss an Max Weber*. Tübingen: Mohr Siebeck.

Sohm, R. (1892). *Kirchenrecht*. Leipzig: Duncker & Humblot.
Tarde, G. (1890). *Les lois de l'imitation. Étude sociologique*. Paris: Alcan.
Weber, M. (1984–2020). *Max Weber Gesamtausgabe.* Tübingen: Mohr Siebeck. Quoted here as MWG followed by the volume number.
Weber, M. (1994). Parliament and Government in Germany under a New Political Order. In P. Lassman (ed.) & R. Speirs (trans.), Max Weber: *Political Writings* (Cambridge Texts in the History of Political Thought, 130–271). Cambridge: Cambridge University Press. doi:10.1017/CBO9780511841095.009.

Chapter 6

# Georg Simmel[1]

*Massimo Cerulo and Antonio Rafele*

## 6.1 Introduction

Georg Simmel (1858–1918) is considered one of the founders of sociology, the first sociologist to have written an entire text on love (1921) and various theoretical analyses on the manifestation of emotions, the latter understood as forms of sociality and reciprocal action, possible only within a relationship (1917–1919, 1909, 1908).

If in Comte, Durkheim and Weber, emotions are not explicitly thematised, without being considered as structuring elements of society and social interaction (Shilling, 2002), in Simmel's sociology the attention to emotional expressiveness and to the feelings of the subject living and acting in modernity is present in numerous writings (Fitzi, 2019), although a semantic distinction between the terms "emotion" and "feeling" is not produced. First of all, for Simmel, there can be no modern individual who does not "feel", who does not perceive emotions in the course of his social interaction. Like rain and sunshine, emotions and feelings "fall" on the subject, but the subject can choose how to use them in the course of their actions (Simmel, 1908). Consider the example of pity, an emotion that allows the subject to come into contact with the religious sphere – "pity is religiosity still in its fluid state" (Simmel, 1906) – and, consequently, with his individual interiority as a believing and, social being:

> The relationship of the respectful child to his parents; of the enthusiastic patriot to his homeland or of the cosmopolitan to humanity; the relationship of the worker to his class struggling to emerge or of the feudal lord proud of his nobility to his state; […] all these relationships with such an infinitely varied content can have a common tone that can be defined if we consider them in the form of their psychic aspect.
>
> (Simmel, 1906: 25)

Understanding social phenomena is therefore possible if an adequate account is taken of the role played by emotions in the interactions of individuals, the way they feel, relate to each other and create forms of sociality.

In his early works and then, in particular, in his major work, *Sociology* (1908), Simmel repeatedly points out how the advent of modernity, of so-called "metropolitan life", and of what he calls the "age of money" have erased "ancient" ways of manifesting emotions to make way for a modern intellectualism that stands as the dominant force in the management of most individual actions (Gerhards, 1986). One of the main characteristics of modern everyday life is, in fact, an "intensification of nervous life", a privileging, in everyday actions, of the use of the intellect (*Verstand*) – that more superficial faculty of the psyche, with its logical – combinatory character that allows individuals to manage multiple activities even simultaneously, adapting with ease and practicality to the frenetic rhythms of modernity – over reason (*Vernunft*) – that faculty of consciousness that gives the subject the possibility of reflecting on the world and giving it meaning, which therefore implies a confrontation with the emotions experienced.

In this tendency, Simmel hypothesises that the inhabitants of the metropolis become like "grains of dust" (*Staubkorn*), overwhelmed by the bombardment of stimuli, commitments and information present in modernity that could affect their ability to deepen interactions, to be moved, to "feel" (Idem). What could be defined as the "intellectualism" of consciousness, combined with the characteristics of the monetary economy, leads to the birth of the so-called "blasé man", whose essence consists in the attenuation of sensitivity to the differences between things: not because these are not perceived, but in the sense that their meaning and value are often equated due to the hurried rhythms imposed by modern daily life (see De Certeau, 1980). Being blasé is therefore a necessary defensive attitude through which the modern individual protects his capacity for reflection and emotionality from the voracious omnipresence of stimuli, information and routines that characterise his experience of everyday life (Nedelmann, 1999: 142).

## 6.2 The metropolis and the image of the self

In this section we rebuild, by reading some passages of Georg Simmel, the relationship between the metropolis and representation. In particular will be presented the following nodes: (a) the effects of the modern metropolis on individual sensibility and social organizations; (b) redefining the concept of lifestyle as an identity and social form; (c) the forms of individual and collective representation, of which televisionis the point of arrival, in light of changes introduced by the metropolis.

*The Metropolis and Mental Life* dates from 1903; it is directly related to Simmel's previous essay, *The Philosophy of Money* (1900), and in particular to its second part dedicated to money and its impact on lifestyle. Together with the subsequent essay, *The Philosophy of Fashion* (Simmel, 1905: 303–313), it constitutes the highest and most overt reflection Simmel dedicates to the metropolis and its consequences (Frisby, 1992,1994): fashion, allegory and morals, distraction and attention, freedom, solitude and lifestyle. The two essays articulate a sophisticated set of images that reveal details of the metropolitan experience from the inside (Cerulo, Rafele, 2020; Frisby, Featherstone, 1997).

The metropolitan type rests on the following psychological premise: "[T]he intensification of emotional life due to the swift and continuous shift of external and internal stimuli" (Simmel, 1903: 103). The number, frequency and intensity of the stimuli available and alluring in the metropolis is much greater than in the provincial towns. Such seemingly insignificant variants as quantity and speed can cause a qualitative leap in individual experience: the self is projected into a new techno-sensorial world, which challenges its previous mental balance. In order to adapt to the new rhythms of life, the self strengthens one particular organ:

> Instead of reacting emotionally, the metropolitan type reacts primarily in a rational manner, thus creating a mental predominance through the intensification of consciousness, which in turn is caused by it. Thus, the reaction of the metropolitan person to those events is moved to a sphere of mental activity which is least sensitive and which is furthest removed from the depths of the personality.
> (Simmel, 1903: 104)

This organ, which occupies the upper strata of the mind, can be defined as:

> the most adaptable of our inner forces. In order to adjust itself to the shifts and contradictions in events, it does not require the disturbances and inner upheavals which are the only means whereby more conservative personalities are able to adapt themselves to the same rhythm of events.
> (Simmel, 1903: 104)

The response to stimuli is moved to a malleable and dynamic psychic zone able to sense and neutralize as many stimuli as possible. As a means of absorbing and processing stimuli from the outside, emotionality is overcome, and becomes a mode of the past, consistent with provincial life, but totally inadequate for metropolitan life. If the provincial town is a *medium* that requires distinct practices and forms of organization, the metropolis is a *medium* that stimulates new strategies of aggregation. The technological difference between the provincial city and the metropolis reflects itself in the difference between a *moral*, and an *allegorical* intention, between a mode characterized by the preservation and repetition of habits, and one which instead tends to build and undo them rapidly, thus acknowledging that habits are ephemeral and illusory (Handel, 2003; Molseed, 1987). The metropolis weakens pre-existing boundaries between subject and object by conferring on the medium, rather than on the self, the power of originating historical and social processes (Nedelmann, 1990a, 1990b; Rammstedt, 1989). The advent of a new medium deviates and regenerates the course of time, by creating a new mental condition, and the potential for new modes and possibilities of living. The self is pure energy, the vital and inviolable structure that justifies the presence of things, because things exist only insofar as they are being used; but the self is also a mere reflection of the outside, the ever-developing product of the pressures coming from society (Rammstedt, 1991). The individual proceeds as if in suspended animation in the middle of thousands of "shocks" or stimuli. While being seduced by lights, posters, the gazes from passers-by, noise, colours and shop windows, the individual can let all these stimuli quickly glide away. In other words, the individual wanders through the streets of the metropolis *distractedly;* an organ is strengthened, one that is light, resilient and dynamic, half-way between consciousness and unconsciousness, capable of neutralizing any new stimulus or prompt from the outside. Distraction does not represent a degraded form of experience; it is an active and effective device: it allows an individual to keep pace with the rapid and fast-dispersing rhythms of the metropolis without inner upheaval, and it allows millions of people to live side-by-side, putting up with, and ignoring one another. From a different perspective, distraction creates a problem that is far from easy to solve: Is it possible to make this multitude of stimuli meaningful? Is it possible to obtain a clear and distinct image of the self, of one's characteristics and of one's potential? Distraction is a broad perception but it can only glide over things. As does everyday life, it flows rapid, light and uninterrupted. Consciousness can only surface by renting the veil of this *continuum,* by suddenly and momentarily interrupting the flow of experience, allowing the subject to leap to a higher mental level offering a sharper representation of the self. A continuous interplay or a to-ing and fro-ing between distraction and attention comes about, where the former serves to live with a life populated by stimuli that leave little space for thought, and the latter serves to register a quantitative and initially indistinct series of events, later to be transformed and elaborated into self-consciousness. The life of the self unfolds in a *pars construens,* which is swift, conscious and unconscious, and in a *pars destruens,* which is slow, lucid and entirely dependent upon the former. Indeed, it is only possible to deconstruct something once experienced, and then, only by working on it. To deconstruct the means to mortify, to treat living things as if they were dead objects, but also to enhance experience, to cast light on it: the individual follows life in a "reverse direction", focusing on details, on interference and gaps in the narrative, on those parts in which a clear and linear sequence leaves room for additions, for sudden interruptions and turns that modify and recreate the event experienced. The self makes a leap to a higher mental level and, in this kind of transfiguration, reaches a "high observation point" from which to look back and gain a distinct, though provisional, image of its own characteristics and potential, of its own strengths and weaknesses. In this moment of self-awareness, the self is lifted toward a liminal dimension, halfway between life and death, a dimension which grants a "better and deeper perspective", but which also numbs the senses. Consciousness appears to be essentially tactile, a reflection of experience, but also, automatically, a distancing from it: it is a prosthesis of experience, as well as a weapon against it.

Money, allegory and a multiplicity of stimuli produce an unprecedented psychic phenomenon:

> The essence of the blasé attitude is an indifference toward the distinctions between things. Not in the sense that they are not perceived, as is the case of mental dullness, but rather that the meaning and the value of the distinctions between things, and therewith of the things themselves, are experienced as meaningless.
> 
> (Simmel, 1903: 106)

On the one hand, money causes a levelling of the difference between values and objects, the public and the private, interiority and exteriority (Rammstedt, 2003); on the other hand, the speed at which different experiences follow each other makes them appear a mere prosthesis of the everyday. The excitement produced by the multiplicity of different situations encountered turns into its opposite: the feeling that all experience is ephemeral, vain and illusory. A circular and potentially infinite process aimed at its own self-reproduction originates within the self: illusion and disillusion, renewed illusion and renewed disillusion. Free from morals and a sense of duty, the individual lives life in the real or imaginary pursuit of *pleasure*. Pleasure is not derived from achieving a goal, or from preserving and safeguarding given values; rather it derives from a psychic condition of openness and alertness, nourished by illusions and disillusions related to things, people and experiences. The persuasion that illusions will materialize one day is the drive of individual life. However, it is not the realisation of illusions that matters; rather it is the tension that generates around them: the idea of *being able* to realize them (Campbell, 1987). From a different perspective, an individual's independence from the process of social change constitutes an integral part of freedom. Within narrow social groups, the creation of boundaries and a closure toward the outside, coincide with the imposition of strong ties on the individual. In order to hold a distinct role within the social group the individual is stuck with a precise function, and his freedom of action is accordingly reduced:

> In the measure that the group grows numerically, spatially, and in the meaningful content of life, its immediate inner unity and the definiteness of its original demarcation against others are weakened and rendered

mild by reciprocal interactions and interconnections. And at the same time the individual gains a freedom of movement far beyond the first jealous delimitation.

(Simmel, 1903: 107–108)

When social groups grow in size, and open up toward the outside, they also change from a qualitative viewpoint: their boundaries and unity tend to loosen, and the individual comes to enjoy a freedom of action never experienced before the advent of the metropolis. This freedom offers the possibility of asserting one's particular *style of life*, and of transforming one's imaginary world into a series of the minutiae of daily life: sex, clothes and consumption in general. Within a narrow and close social group, the individual feels a strong sense of belonging; however, this is countered by a limitation of freedom. On the contrary, within larger social groups, and therefore within the metropolis, freedom expresses itself also in the loss of a precise recognition of one's social identity. In the metropolis, everybody continues to have an identity and a role bound up with his name; a person's profile, however, is more fragile, because it becomes less noticeable and is inextricably linked to situations of anonymity.

Freedom and solitude are responsible for greater qualitative differences within social groups, yet they also imply the domination of modal strategies over final strategies, and of the private over the public sphere. Building one's own original, albeit marginal, profile, requires a deep interiorization of practices, tastes and choices. Once a tool for class differentiation, an individual's lifestyle is now perceived as a second skin, something which can make us visible to others as well as to ourselves. As a result, collective, vertical and codified identities weaken in favour of individual, private and provisional identities, intrinsically validated merely by their presence. Cohesion is not built through imitative processes, or generally shared values, but instead derives from unstable dynamics, resting on the interiorization of the other as a necessity for happiness and self-realisation. In this context, to live means to recognize one's habits, and to control and negotiate them with others on a constant basis. The individual no longer needs to be in conflict with the external world, but simply to partake of it by learning how to play the game along with, and better than, the others.

The isolation of the self and the consequent loss of any sense of the finality of time bring everyday life centre stage. The *everyday* becomes the matrix of all experiences, but also a system of modes and practices whereby the self reassesses the value, function and sense of ongoing events (Benjamin, 1936). Before becoming a habit, every single event presents itself to the individual as a potential narrative. In this phase it is experienced as a myth or a daydream, as a blind and instinctive force that demands to manifest itself. Daily use, repetition, and self-observation transform that potential into a familiar *habitus*, circumscribed and perfectly recognizable. A repeated experience becomes absorbed and integrated into behaviour, one more fragment of the history of one's psyche (Benjamin, 1940; Jedlowski, 1990). The sense and meaning of the various experiences come together in the self only *a posteriori*: things do not have an intrinsic or autonomous value. Their meaning only surfaces when the self makes an image of them, when it recognizes and relativizes them as a prosthesis of everyday happenings. The crucial question here is not, what does that specific event mean? Rather, what does that event mean for me, what is its impact on my daily life, and how does it stand in relation to the previous experiences I have interiorized? On this premise, the self experiences and interprets even great social structures, such as religion and politics, not as holistic systems, but as small fragments or details "stuck" between the folds of clothes and daily actions. The self appears to itself as a system always *in potential*, eligible for sudden reconfigurations, but constantly aiming toward illusory or concrete pleasure. The self is a dynamic singularity that cannot be pinned down; its action is justified by its relation and communication with other singularities. Interaction with people is unavoidable, yet is justified by mere interest (not in the sense of personal benefit). People spend time together for the sake of pleasure, aesthetically, in the original sense of the term, and to enjoy themselves, not for political or ideological reasons, or for a distinct purpose.

## 6.3 Emotions and daily life

How are emotions influenced by these tendencies? First, it must be made clear that, for Simmel, they constitute the subject together with the rational factor. Emotion and reason thus form an inseparable union that represents the core of the (modern) individual, who finds in himself criteria for judgement, evaluation and motivation to act. However, although they are an integral part of the subject (since they are born within it and characterise it, making each subject unique), in their manifestation they take on aspects that go beyond the singularity of the individual, thus becoming social phenomena: they, in turn, produce social interactions.

In this discussion, however, it is important to make it clear that emotions play an ambivalent role in modernity: they are both a means of communication and identification with others, and an instrument of self-understanding and thus of personal identification. They are elementary forms of sociality, bridges between the individual and society, because although the latter is certainly based on certain socio-structural assumptions, it could not take root without relying on feelings, beliefs, imaginary representations, desires and aspirations (Watier, 2002).

In this two-way relationship between the individual and society, there is emotional ambivalence. It is easy to find oneself "alone", (i.e., with very few people with whom one can claim to have an in-depth and continuous acquaintance) even though one is immersed in a plurality of daily interactions, especially in the professional sphere (see Cerulo, 2021). This loneliness is ambivalent because, on the one hand, it risks instilling in the subject a sort of "schizophrenic" behaviour (emotions of happiness and nervousness that alternate continuously) due to the uninterrupted emotional stimuli suffered by an increasingly frenetic and technological metropolitan life and aimed at professional competition. On the other hand, however, it allows him to seek out countless experiences and emotional interactions, regardless of family rules, neighbourhood, class, etc. The subject chooses to follow one path among a thousand possible others, and this tension, this wealth of possibilities, tinges modern existence with an irresistible fascination:

> The fascination that innumerable life experiences exert on us [is determined] in its intensity by the fact that through them we leave unexplored infinite possibilities of other enjoyments and opportunities to affirm ourselves. It is not only in the passing by of men, in their separation after a brief contact, in the complete estrangement from countless beings, to whom we could give, who could give us so much; in all this there is not only a sumptuous waste, a heedless grandeur of existence. This specific value of non-enjoyment also gives rise to a new, more intense and more concentrated fascination with what we actually possess. The fact that it is precisely this that is realised among the many possibilities of life gives it a tone of victory, the shadows of life's unexpressed and unenjoyed wealth form its triumphal procession.
> (Simmel, 1900: 210)

Immersed in this ambivalent existential and emotional dimension, the inhabitants of modernity, in order to keep up with the fast pace imposed by metropolitan experience, act or, better, re-act mainly through the use of the intellect, thus trying to protect what Simmel calls "sentimentality" from the acceleration of experience, the excess of stimuli and the continuous change imposed by the modern era (see Gassen and Landmann, 1993). We are therefore faced with a strategic manifestation of emotions selected based on the demands of the social context in which we find ourselves acting, the here and now of everyday life, and the objectives to be pursued. This is not, mind you, a denial of emotions, but a display of those most suitable for not being disturbed by the social situation in which one finds oneself. Thus, in normal daily interactions, fleeting, momentary, "impressionistic" expressions and emotional behaviour are increasingly taking shape.

The ambivalence of modernity, this being made up of trends and countertrends, forces subjects to live an essentially tragic relationship, caught in what Simmel calls the "dualism of individuality": being for oneself and being social (Simmel, 1908). On the one hand, the modern subject tends to withdraw into himself, in search of new spaces of individualisation and reflexivity; on the other hand, he cannot help feeling the social call that characterises him as belonging to a life in common with others. Existential ambivalence becomes, in Simmel, a principle of socialisation, a modern vehicle through which to grasp the facets of social reality.

This ambivalence also characterises the manifestation of emotions and represents a kind of social energy that guarantees the ego vital impetus: it is a dual instrument of knowledge in that it is directed towards oneself and, specularly, towards the other. Thus, although they emerge as conflicting forces and potential creators of tension in social interaction and, consequently, in the choice the subject must make about their manifestation, emotions are always elementary forms of sociality; in this sense, they cannot but be charged with further ambivalence: on the one hand, they help to create social interactions; on the other, they also arouse emotions.

In this direction, Simmel studies various forms of "emotional–sentimental" social interaction: sociability, discretion, modesty, shame, gratitude, loyalty, confidence, friendship, marriage, coquetry, and love. These emotions always play a dual and ambivalent role: on the one hand, they allow the subject to enter society, build social interactions, gain experience; on the other, they allow him to discover and identify himself and create a path of existential self-recognition through the emotions he perceives in his relationships with others. A few examples may further clarify the point.

One thinks of coquetry (*Koketterie*), which is a form of play that becomes a general form of interaction (Simmel, 1909). Studying the "flirtatious" behaviour of the subjects (starting with the coquetry typical of early twentieth-century upper-class women during the courtship process: their granting and denying themselves, embracing an invitation and immediately retreating to their positions), Simmel highlights how, through such a form of playful interaction, one can arrive at a thematization of social reality in a more convincing and profound way than in normal everyday interactions, marked by the respect of institutional and social rules that leave little room for imagination and facetiousness. In coquetry, subjects must trust their emotions, as a compass to orientate themselves within a playful, intimate relationship, ostensibly directed towards the other but, at bottom, an instrument of personal identification. Thus, the power to be free to assume a definitive position within the relationship translates, at the same time and ambivalently, into the freedom to use one's own power of fascination (and coquetry) towards the other.

Another example is gratitude, for which there seems to be little room in everyday social interactions. For Simmel, in fact, in modern interactions that are very often based on speed and utilitarian reciprocal exchange, a relationship is seldom devoid of instrumental interest, but rather is characterised by the desire to give for the pleasure of doing so, which corresponds to the emotion of gratitude. The latter could be defined as a counter-gift, not in the sense of opposition to the act of giving, but as an action that is born from the gift and lives in its memory:

> It can be said that deep down, gratitude does not consist so much in the fact that the gift is returned, but in the awareness that it cannot be returned. For we find ourselves in the presence of something that creates in the soul of the recipient a permanent disposition towards the other, something that brings to awareness the idea of the inner infinitude of a relationship, which cannot be completely exhausted or realised by means of any finite activity.
>
> (Simmel, 1917: 87)

Gratitude constitutes a positive response that Ego addresses to Alter in order to build a social bond that is free from instrumental or utilitarian perspectives. For Simmel, this form of sociality is configured as a unique reciprocal action and reveals the subject's totality: his being-for-itself that turns to the other in its entirety.

One of the most important emotions and forms of sociality for its function of creating cohesion within the interaction, gratitude is both a thank-you and an invitation, the gateway to one's own intimacy: "the most refined and strongest relationships are often linked to this emotion, independent of any single reception, which offers the other, as if by an obligation of gratitude, our whole personality and which also addresses the entirety of his" (Simmel, 1917: 74, 76).

A similar argument applies to friendship, defined by Simmel as a social emotion that allows interaction between individuals or groups. Friendship, being just an elementary form of sociality, creates a deep and spiritual union between two subjects, since it can play on the absence of the sexual factor, an element of vehemence and passion, and on a time span which is usually longer than that which characterises the feeling of love:

> The ideal of friendship leads to an absolute spiritual familiarity, which here often seems even more attainable than in love, because friendship lacks that unambiguous concentration on one element, which for love is sensuality. [...] For this reason friendship, which lacks this vehemence but also this unruliness of passion, can better unite the whole person with the whole person, can better overcome the closure of the soul, acting certainly not so impetuously, but to a greater extent and in a longer succession of time.
>
> (Simmel, 1917: 43)

Friendship, according to the German sociologist, is characterised by eight main elements. It is an emotion which:

1   is positive, because it binds individuals through feelings of friendliness and benevolence;
2   is secondary, because it does not manifest itself in the form of an immediate need, but is open to various types of social, cultural and situational influences;
3   unlike what can occur in love, is always based on mutual affection and therefore, while characterising the subjectivity of the individual, transcends his or her singularity;
4   can be caused by motivations and orientated towards ends external to friendship itself (it is therefore not self-referential);
5   is abstract, because it can be found in heterogeneous social spheres and in different categories of social actors;
6   is composite, because it can be accompanied by the manifestation of other emotions;
7   is dynamic because it can create new bonds or break previously established ones;
8   is socially productive, because it contributes to the social construction of reality.

(see Nedelmann, 1990a, b)

Friendship is theorised by Simmel as a sort of absolute emotion: the deepest and, at the same time, the most appropriate to the individual's presence in modern everyday life: it would not create discomfort, disturbances, uncertainties, but would allow an interaction with the other based on discretion and tact. In modernity, in fact, friendship becomes free from any ties of proximity, kinship or clan. Emancipating itself from the traditional, undifferentiated social circle in which it took shape in previous societies, the emotion in question finds new spaces and channels in which to manifest itself. The concept of freedom as a direct consequence of modernity returns. However if, on the one hand, the friendship bond is freed from its previous constraints, discovering spaces and times previously unthinkable, on the other hand, it discovers new difficulties in its development, running the risk of not being able to fully manifest its deep emotional charge. As social differentiation grows, so does distrust of others. It becomes difficult to express total intersubjective openness, so one trusts with distrust and out of necessity. Also, as Simmel points out, having abandoned traditional community life, each man has some secret to hide, which he takes care to keep concealed within those "ideal spheres" that characterise the discretion of each individual.

In modern times, material property is flanked by "psychological private property", unique to each subject and characteristic of his or her specific personality. This psychological private property must be safeguarded at all costs because it preserves the mystery of individuality that makes each subject not assimilable to another. If this property were to be violated, the individual would risk showing himself *in toto*, without any more secrets and, in so doing, the same effect of reciprocity (*Wechselwirkung*) between the subjects present in friendship would be lacking precisely because there would be no more secrets to discover.

If social interaction exists, then, for Simmel it is largely thanks to the form of sociality of discretion, which allows Ego to know Alter, but only partially and never fully, even in friendship. It is not by chance that in friendship (as in gratitude), the feelings of touch (*Taktgefühl*) and modesty (*Schamgefühl*), which for Simmel represent the subject's ability to mediate between curiosity about one's own emotions and respect for the other in the course of interaction, between the right to ask and the right to secrecy, acquire fundamental importance (Simmel 1908). In other words, friends must always be careful not to overstep that discreet boundary, which is synonymous with respect for the other, which preserves the relationship in a vital tension through a play of words and silences, sentences spoken or only hinted at, glances and illusions:

> [...] discretion does not consist at all only in the fact that the other person is a friend, but also in the fact that the other person is a friend. Discretion does not consist at all only in respecting the other's secrets, his intentional desire to hide this or that thing from us, but is already in keeping oneself at a distance from knowing everything about the other that he does not expressly manifest.
>
> (Simmel, 1917: 54)

The importance of the boundaries to be maintained during interaction emerges here. These are flexible boundaries that, while varying according to the form and intensity of the interaction itself, must always be maintained as they are vital to the continuation of the interaction.

## 6.4 On love

The last emotion we will review is that of love which, for Simmel, is configured as a direct and purposeless interaction, free from any utilitarian relationship and light years away from the instrumental reason characteristic of modern society. In modernity, this too is characterised by ambivalence: on the one hand, having freed itself from the family sphere, which was previously its main environment of manifestation, it finds a freedom of expression that gives the subject the possibility of living multiple experiences; on the other hand, due to the considerable increase in social differentiation, the love relationship becomes essentially tragic and individual: it only ignites in the face of individuality and shatters in the face of its insuperability (Simmel, 1921; Seebach, 2017).

As we have seen, Simmel's subject, forced to come to terms with his ineliminable solitude constitutive of the experience of modernity, is in search of some form of consistency that gives solidity to his ego. In this discourse, love is consistent in its continual search for individuality through the other, a tendency that makes the subject once again ambivalent in his actions: on the one hand, he tends to shy away from the responsibilities that dyadic experience brings with it; on the other, he feels the need to live in a continual search for the other and to experience different experiences with the latter. He is caught between unity and multiplicity; between the desire to "dare" the other and the fear of no longer finding himself.

Love is, therefore, configured as a totalising emotion, which produces a shattering experience for the individual in his or her entirety (also because, in interactions of love, one addresses the other as a whole, unlike other forms of interaction in which only a part of one's self is brought into play). Love always brings together two wholes: two subjects who reveal themselves to each other, for what they are and not only for that part of themselves that they want or need to show.

Simmel often returns to this discourse of unity, the pivotal point of his "philosophy of love". He sees love as a revolutionary force capable of creating havoc and disorder in existing reality, but at the same time of transforming the subjects themselves, reshaping their relationships, thus creating a new order and, in the end, a new social reality that can only be used by the subjects involved in the interaction. In fact, through the experience of love, the lovers create their own "love landscape". The external world takes on a different form in their eyes: in the company of the beloved everything changes and the world appears better than it really is. The experience of love thus becomes a sort of experiential bridge: through it one is driven to act, to be actively in the world and not to close it off from oneself. In fact, a deeper analysis shows how, according to Simmel, love creates its own love object. When Ego loves Alter, he, although turning to another subject, turns his love towards himself. Alter would then be the object through which it is ultimately possible to love oneself. It is a mirror-love made possible only by the presence of another subject within the constituted love-interaction (Simmel, 1921).

Once again, therefore, the individual is forced to live tragically, caught between the desire for extraneousness and the need to relate to the other. Oscillating within the modern process of social differentiation, it "is always member and body, part and whole, completed and in need of completion" (Simmel, 1917: 19). Ego needs Alter because it is only through its presence that it can experience love. It is thanks to the "contamination" with the other that it is possible to look at oneself from another perspective and go deep into the relationship with one's self. Yet, because of the characteristics of modernity, love is marked by conflict: between the different parts of the self, between the individual and society and, above all, between the subject and the other, bound by an interaction suspended between intimacy and solitude, between indiscretion and discretion, between the desire to become a We and the need to remain a separate I and You.

Modernity thus seems to appear as a gentle conspirator, careful to guarantee the polymorphism of reality. Like the wave of the sea that laps and then recedes, these modern forms of sociality described by Simmel display the characteristics of transience and fleetingness, in a relationship made up of secrets, fantasies and Ego-Alter games, in which the ambivalence of emotions and their manifestations plays a major role. Simmel's experience of modernity thus takes on the traits of an adventure, that is, of the present open to all that could be, of the here and now that oscillates between tendencies and counter-tendencies, ambiguities and contradictions, openness and closure to the outside world. We are dealing with an individual who goes ahead "by trial and error", aware of the different spheres of reality that make up his emotional experience.

Emotions are part of this modern "tragicness": as forms of sociality, they enable the subject to relate to others and to get in touch with himself. In doing so, they generate new emotions which, in turn, generate new social interactions. The effects are continuous and two-way, in the logic of trends and counter-trends that characterises Georg Simmel's fresco of modernity.

## Note

1 Antonio Rafele is the author of the section: "The metropolis and the image of the self"; Massimo Cerulo is the author of the following sections: "Introduction", "Emotions and daily life", "On love".

## References

Benjamin, W. (1936/2008) *The Work of Art in the Age of Mechanical Reproduction*. London: Penguin.

Benjamin, W. (1940/1999) *The Arcades Project*. Cambridge, MA: Harvard University Press.

Campbell, C. (1987) *The Romantic Ethic and the Spirit of Modern Consumerism*. Oxford: Basil Blackwell.

Cerulo, M. (2021) Emotions and Everyday Life: Some Cultural Issues from a Sociological Perspective. In W. Nericcio, A. Rafele and F.L. Aldama (eds), *Cultural Studies in the Digital Age*. San Diego: San Diego State University Press, 38–45.

Cerulo, M., Rafele, A. (2020) The Metropolis and Emotional Life. Experience, Rifts and Knowledge. In G. Giannakopoulou and G. Gilloch (eds) *The Detective of Modernity. Essays on the Work of David Frisby*. London and New York: Routledge.

De Certeau, M. (1980) *The Practice of Everyday Life*. Oakland, CA: University of California Press.

Fitzi, G. (2019). *The Challenge of Modernity. Simmel's Sociological Theory*. London and New York: Routledge.

Frisby, D. (1992) *Simmel and Since: Essays on Georg Simmel's Social Theory*. London and New York: Routledge.

Frisby, D. (ed.) (1994) *Georg Simmel: Critical Assessments, Vol. I*. London and New York: Routledge.

Frisby, D., Feathersone, M. (eds) (1997) *Simmel on Culture*. London: Sage.
Gassen, K. and Landmann, M. (eds) (1993) *Buch des Dankes an Georg Simmel. Briefe, Erinnerungen, Bibliographie*. Berlin: Duncker & Humblot.
Gerhards, J. (1986) Georg Simmel's contribution to a theory of emotions. *Social Science Information*, 25(4), 901–924.
Handel, W. (2003) Simmel und das moderne Geldwesen. In O. Rammstedt (ed.) *Georg Simmels Philosophie des Geldes. Aufsätze und Materialien*. Frankfurt: Suhrkamp, 245–264.
Jedlowski, P. (1990) Simmel on Memory. In M. Kaern, B. Phillips and R. Cohen (eds). *Georg Simmel and Contemporary Sociology*. Dordrecht: Kluwer, 131–154.
Molseed, M. (1987) The Problem of Temporality in the Work of Georg Simmel. *The Sociological Quarterly*, 28(3), 357–366.
Nedelmann, B. (1990a) On the Concept of "Erleben" in Georg Simmel's Sociology. In M. Kaern et al. (eds) *Georg Simmel and Contemporary Sociology*. Dordrecht: Kluwer, 225–241.
Nedelmann, B. (1990b) Georg Simmel as an Analyst of Autonomous Dynamics: The Merry-Go-Round of Fashion. In M. Kaern et al. (eds) *Georg Simmel and Contemporary Sociology*. Dordrecht: Kluwer, 243–257.
Nedelmann B. (1999) Fra due secoli: Georg Simmel ieri e oggi. In "Iride", XII, n. 26, January–April, 133–149.
Rammstedt, O. (ed.) (1989) *Georg Simmel Gesamtausgabe*. Frankfurt: Suhrkamp.
Rammstedt, O. (1991) On Simmel's Aesthetics: Argumentation, in the Journal Jugend, 1897–1906. *Theory, Culture & Society*, 8(3), 125–144.
Rammstedt, O. (ed.) (2003) *Georg Simmels Philosophie des Geldes. Aufsätze und Materialien*. Frankfurt: Suhrkamp.
Schilling, C. (2002) The Two Traditions in the Sociology of Emotions. *The Sociological Review*, 50(2), 10–32.
Seebach, S. (2017) *Love and Society. Special Social Forms and the Master of Emotion*. London and New York: Routledge.
Simmel, G. (1900/1978) *The Philosophy of Money*. London and New York: Routledge.
Simmel, G. (1903/2010) The Metropolis and Mental Life. In G. Bridge and S. Watson (eds), *The Blackwell City Reader*. Chichester: Wiley-Blackwell, 103–110.
Simmel, G. (1905/1971) *On Individuality and Social Forms*. Chicago: University of Chicago Press, 1971.
Simmel G. (1906) The Sociology of Secrecy and of Secret Societies. *American Journal of Sociology*, 11, 441–498.
Simmel, G. (1908/2009) *Sociology: Inquiries into the Construction of Social Forms*. Boston: Brill.
Simmel, G. (1909) Psychologie der Koketterie. *Der Tag. Moderne illustrierte Zeitung, Nr. 344*, 11 Mai, S. 1–3 und Nr. 347, 12 Mai, S. 1–3.
Simmel, G. (1917/1950) Fundamental Problems of Sociology: Individual and Society. In K. Wolff (ed.) *The Sociology of Georg Simmel*. New York: Free Press, 1–84.
Simmel, G. (1918/1968). *The Conflict in Modern Culture, and other Essays*. New York: Teachers College Press.
Simmel, G. (1921/1984). *On Women, Sexuality, and Love*. New Haven, CT: Yale University Press.

Chapter 7

# Vilfredo Pareto

*Vincenzo Romania*

## 7.1 Introduction

The work of Vilfredo Pareto (1848–1923) has long been neglected by sociological historiography,[1] with a few exceptions, amongst which stands out Talcott Parsons' The Structure of *Social Action* (1949 [1937]), a sociological classic that recognizes and pays particular tribute to the Italian sociologist: that of having contributed, together with Durkheim and Weber, to defining the field of sociological theory in antithesis to the utilitarian paradigm of social action.[2] Beyond those rare exceptions, his work has received only scant interest and there has been little work on his work on the canonical definition of the field of the sociology of emotions (see Cerulo, 2018). The main reasons that explain this oblivion are the prolixity and opacity of his writing; his insistence on the irrational character of human action, which differed markedly from the progressive climax of the classical period of sociology (Connell, 1997); and, finally, his political involvement in early Fascism, which had long been the subject of controversy (cf. Alexander, 1994). However, Pareto can be considered the only classical sociologist, together with Gabriel Tarde, to place emotions at the centre of his analysis of the social system.

## 7.2 Intellectual biography

Vilfredo Pareto was born in Paris in 1848 into an Italian family of noble origins and republican ideas which had been exiled to France for political reasons. After a few years, the family returned to Piedmont. Here, Pareto first followed classical studies and then graduated in 1869 in engineering, with a thesis on the fundamental principles of the equilibrium of solid bodies. In Turin, Pareto encountered Darwinism and the philosophy of John Stuart Mill, of which he became an interpreter and a critical reader, in opposition to Spencerian evolutionism.

After moving to Tuscany, Pareto worked as a physicist in the field of railway transport, but he also published economic and political writings, which

DOI: 10.4324/9781003088363-8

were very successful. His scientific background allowed him to approach pure economics and, in particular, the work of Leo Walras. This led him to succeed Walras in 1893 as the chair of Political Economy at the University of Lausanne. He taught at the Swiss university for the rest of his career, and from 1897, he also taught a course in sociology at the same university.

His career as an economist was brilliant and would produce a significant advancement in the understanding of the processes of subjective and collective utility (e.g. his famous concept of *Pareto optimality*, which indicates the best possible level of allocation of resources among the subjects within an economy). The results of this intellectual effort are contained in the *Manual of Political Economy*, written between 1890 and 1906 (Pareto, 2014 [1906]), where an intellectual tension between sociology and psychology is already visible. The Italian thinker considered it too reductive to explain human behaviour only from the heuristics of *homo oeconomicus*. Individual egoism could not be taken for granted and transformed into mathematical formulas. Rather, to understand economic behaviour, it was necessary to understand the relevance of psychological and ideological reasons and thus to distinguish, as he would theorize better in the following years, logical actions from non-logical actions.

From a political point of view, it is in this era that Pareto's distance from all socialist ideologies becomes clearer. While in Italy the intellectual scene was pervaded by the debate between scientific Marxism and idealism, Pareto clearly endorsed economic liberalism, which he considered the only political doctrine to be based on scientific assumptions. This, according to some psychoanalytical interpretations, such as that proposed by Borkenau (1936), originated from the radical conflict between the young Vilfredo Pareto and his father Raffaele, a political and intellectual figure who played a crucial role in the diffusion of Mazzini's ideas in Italy and Europe. This interpretation is hardly demonstrable, especially in the light of the new biographical evidence produced by Mornati (2018a; 2018b). What seems to us more relevant for the purposes of our discussion is to note how Pareto's political commitment corresponds to a consistent epistemological stance: liberalism, in its conception, fully implements the principles of positivism and defines the methodological individualism that would inspire all his subsequent intellectual production.

Therefore, the ideological scepticism of the liberal intellectual corresponded to the scientific scepticism of the positivist scientist (Bobbio, 1973). This is particularly evident in his critical study on *Les systèmes socialistes* first published in French in 1902 (Pareto, 1951). The thesis of the book is that in all societies, the government elites circulate and cyclically go through moments of ascendance (*anabasis*) and decay (*catabasis*). Socialism covers this process through the illusion of great Virtuist "passions" but aims, like all other ideologies, to conquer the positions of the elite. Emotions thus critically enter the interests of Pareto, whose intellectual figure increasingly resembles that of the great "debunker" of human passions, behind which are hidden completely instrumental ends.

Having progressively abandoned political economy and the study of political doctrines, in the last years of his life Vilfredo Pareto devoted himself entirely to the study of sociology. He worked for almost twenty years on his *Trattato di Sociologia Generale*, a text of over 2,000 pages published in Italian and French between 1916 and 1917, when the author was almost seventy years old. The text would appear in English in 1935 in the American translation, edited by Arthur Livingston, with the title *The Mind and Society*.[3] From this moment on and throughout the 1930s, Pareto's sociological fame grew and produced significant critical literature, both philosophical and sociological.[4] Together with Livingston himself, the pioneer of Pareto's sociology in America was Lewis Henderson, who in 1932, founded the Pareto Circle at Harvard. Among others, the Pareto Circle would be attended by great names in the social sciences of the twentieth century: George Homans, Pitrim Sorokin,[5] Joseph Schumpeter, Talcott Parsons, Elton Mayo, Crane Brinton, and Robert K. Merton.

During this period a real "Pareto cult"[6] was developing at Harvard. There are many reasons for this success: on the one hand, compared to the competing Chicago School, Pareto offered a systematic abstract model, compatible with that of the founder Pitrim Sorokin. Secondly, his sociology placed great emphasis on values and normative orientations, fundamental pillars in the construction of Parsons's theoretical architecture. Last but not least, his theory on the circulation of elites deconstructed the moral primacy of socialist doctrines and offered a strong interpretative framework against Marxism. Reflecting on Pareto's impact, Homans wrote that "as a Republican Bostonian who had not rejected his comparatively wealthy family, I felt during the thirties that I was under personal attack, above all from the Marxists. I was ready to believe Pareto because he provided me with a defense" (Homans, 1962: 4).

The fame of the Italian sociologist gradually waned after World War II, in parallel with the decadence of the functionalist paradigm. As already mentioned, the sociology of emotions would devote only a certain amount of attention to him in later years.

## 7.3 Logico-experimental and non-logico-experimental actions

Pareto's sociological production is quite extensive,[7] but the main theories are concentrated and outlined in the *Trattato* (1935 [1916]), on which we will focus in this chapter. The text is prolix and rich in digressions, but it follows a defined logical structure that can be schematically illustrated, as we shall outline below.

According to Pareto, all human action can be divided into two main categories: logico-experimental actions and non-logico-experimental actions. The first type is defined as follows because (1) it correctly links premises and results on the basis of deductive (*logical*) reasoning, and (2) it is based on observable and replicable (*experimental*) evidence. These are, in other words, actions based on scientific and objective – that is, shared – knowledge of what are the most appropriate ways to achieve a given goal. Those who perform them are not moved by instinct but by awareness. The rational actor, for Pareto, pursues his own interests by resorting to a solid scientific knowledge and a clear pragmatic and rational calculation of the consequences.[8] He is aware, based on his own experience and practical observation, of what are, for all practical purposes and for every possible observer, the most appropriate means to achieve a given goal. Such is the action of the *homo oeconomicus*, the rational actor theorized by positivism and the ideal citizen of liberal doctrines, three traditions in which Pareto clearly recognizes himself and which he synthesizes into this category.

However, according to Pareto, this model of social action is not enough to explain what human beings do in most contexts of their existence. In fact, all those actions determined by a transcendental subjectivity (e.g., of a religious, ideal, or value type) or by theories that transcend the logical-rational demonstration do not fall within the category of logico-experimental actions. Non-logico-experimental actions are all based on instincts, feelings of belonging, values, beliefs, emotionality, and the biology of the actor. They represent, according to the Italian sociologist, the most relevant component of human actions. Consistent with the thought of the French crowd psychologists, from Gabriel Tarde to Gustave Le Bon, Pareto shows how irrational, emotional elements emerge from social life and influence social behaviour in a decisive way. Pareto's conception is therefore *in nuce* contradictory: on the one hand, it underlines the importance of everything that transcends rationality, for social cohesion and collective utility, while, on the other hand, it denounces the atavistic weakness in human beings, explained by the prevalence, in their typical behaviour, of non-logical action.

Like Durkheim, Pareto does not offer any psychological explanation of why individuals act illogically but rather focuses on collective feelings (he often uses the term *sentiment*), namely those emotions that are socially constructed and objectively shared by all. Like the French thinker, Pareto uses the theme of emotions to fundamentally differentiate sociology from psychology: "Non-logical actions originate chiefly in definite psychic states, sentiments, subconscious feelings, and the like. It is the province of psychology to investigate such psychic states" (Pareto, 1935, I: 88). This great dichotomy between logic and feeling closely resembles the model of social action studied by Max Weber, but it would seem that the two authors never influenced each other (Bobbio, 1964 and 1973).

## 7.4 Non-logical actions and rationalizations

Having defined the distinction between logical and non-logical actions, Pareto adds a further piece to his theoretical model. Non-logical actions, while representing the predominant part of human behaviour, he says, never appear as such in social representations: "Human beings – indeed – have a very conspicuous tendency to paint a varnish of logic over their conduct" (Pareto, 1935, I: 79). The Italian sociologist believes, in other words, that individuals are continuously engaged in justifying and rationalizing their instincts and emotions (Rutigliano, 1994). The subject has a certain relationship to the theory of *rationalization*, developed by Sigmund Freud and his follower Ernest Jones (1908). In Jones's theory, in particular, rationalization represents a process implemented by an individual to hide emotions or inconvenient aspects of reality. Indeed, in Freud's overall work, rationalization is a process performed by the ego that has to do with the resolution of inner conflicts placed in the unconscious and semi-conscious dimension. Pareto does not deal with subjective psychological elements, but mainly with how language and philosophical, doctrinal, and ideological representations provide individuals with elements of the rationalization of subjective emotional experiences. He deals, in other words, with the collective resources of the rationalization of subjective emotional experiences. As Raymond Aron suggests:

> the underlying reason for the distinctiveness of the Paretian method is that, compared with the psychoanalytic method, it is not psychological since it deliberately ignores the sentiments or states of mind of which the residues are merely the expression. Pareto renounces exploring the subconscious and unconscious; he concentrates on an intermediary level between the depths of consciousness and acts or words directly apprehensible from the outside.
>
> (Aron, 1971: 171)

In summary, according to Pareto, (a) social action is driven mainly by non-logical drives; (b) however, only logical actions are considered publicly plausible; (c) given this contradiction, people engage in a continuous process of rationalization of illogical behaviour; and (d) this process produces beliefs, common-sense orientations, ideologies, doctrines, religious precepts, and normative orientations that make the illogical acceptable. According to Pareto, "the human being has such a weakness for adding logical-developments to non-logical behaviour that anything can serve as an excuse for him to turn to that favourite occupation" (Pareto, 1935, I: 104).

There exists, in other words, a fundamental conflict between man's inner passions and the public behaviours that suppress their manifestation. From this conflict arise all the great narratives that guide human behaviour. The irrational is, in fact, unspeakable in a world that makes rationality its supreme meta-value. With this, Pareto is once again comparable to Weber in facing the fundamental conflict of all modernity: the iron cage of rationality. And this is further comparable to Freud in reading the process of civilization as a process of the rational suppression of instincts (Freud, 2002). As Norberto Bobbio explains,

> Pareto had been struck by the varied and captious way in which these passions had been hidden, simulated, masked by pseudo-rational constructions. The classical quarrel between passion and reason did not appear to him as a quarrel between the lower and upper part of the human soul, but between natural instinct and its counterfeiting, between spontaneity and construction.
>
> (Bobbio, 1964: XX)

From this conclusion, Pareto moves to define the mission of sociology, which is twofold. First, its task is to reveal the artificially rational character of non-logical actions, to show how, beneath the surface of the rationality of ideologies and beliefs, deeply irrational forces remain that move human behaviour: "Hence our need to do a thing of supreme importance for our purpose here – to tear off the masks non-logical conduct is made to wear and lay bare the things they hide from view". Secondly, the sociologist is called upon to distinguish truth from the social usefulness of non-logical actions, that is, their function for the integration and balance of the social system: "The experimental truth of a they and its social utility are different things. A theory that is experimentally true may be now advantageous, now detrimental, to society; and the same applies to a theory that is experimentally false" (Pareto, 1935, I: 171). Or, again:

> In the course of our study, therefore, we shall have to try to separate those two parts; and then not stop with the reflection that a certain argument is inconclusive, idiotic, absurd, but ask ourselves whether it may not be expressing sentiments beneficial to society, and expressing them in a manner calculated to persuade many people who would not be at all influenced by the soundest logico-experimental argument.
>
> (*ivi*, I: 264)

Unlike the positivism of the origins, Pareto separates scientific truth – which is concretized in logical reasoning – from the pragmatic utility of social actions and their social representation. He is convinced, in fact, that even non-logical actions possess some social utility and that, at the same time, logical action could also produce negative effects for the community. In this sense, he is a critical positivist who recognizes the crucial importance of the pragmatic validation of knowledge and clearly detaches himself from the approaches of Comte and Spencer, who are repeatedly his critical targets.

## 7.5 Residues

The most substantial and demanding part of the *Trattato*, however, concerns the analysis of the verbalizations that humans use to make non-logical actions appear rational. Pareto is, in fact, convinced that the best way to study non-logical actions is to explore the arguments that support them.[9] Unlike what Durkheim does in *Elementary Forms of Religious Life* (1965 [1912]), Pareto's data are not ethnographic but consist of social representations, developed within particular societies, cultures, religions, and political groups to justify models of social action that have neither a logical basis nor an empirical-experimental validation.

In every theory that supports non-logical actions, according to the Italian sociologist, two types of elements can be distinguished: the arguments, which are the superficial and variable part that he calls *derivations*; and the fixed elements of human behaviour, fundamental for every representation, which he calls *residues*.

Residues, in other words, are what remains when all logical-rational elements and all superficial arguments are eliminated from a theory. They are the direct reference to an element of human behaviour that does not need further interpretation. They are the most important and yet most indefinite part of social representations. They are the arguments that refer directly and constantly to the ultimate drivers of non-logical actions. Pareto sometimes defines them as sentiments or "manifestations of sentiments" and other times as *instincts*,[10] using the terms as synonyms.[11]

The fundamental residues are classified as follows:

1. *Instinct for combinations*. This can be defined as the instinct of human beings to creatively combine objects, elements, and phenomena. Otherwise, it is an associative instinct or, more specifically, the tendency of the human mind to produce differential associations between elements of the material and immaterial worlds. It is the element which, according to Pareto, stimulates innovation and social change.
2. *Group-persistence (instinct of persistence of the aggregates)*. This has a nature somewhat opposite from the first. It is, in fact, the tendency to preserve the integrity and uniformity of relationships, identifications, and existing groups. It manifests itself in the attachment to a community, to a place, to a social group. It produces stability and stagnation.
3. *Need to manifest sentiments through external acts (activity, self-expression)*. This kind of residue concerns what Pareto calls "powerful sentiments", which are associated with striking symbolic acts. These are, as usual, collective sentiments, based on the model of the Durkheimian rituals. The most significant prototype is religious exaltation: "One may feel a calm and thoughtful need for 'doing something'. But that sentiment may rise in intensity to the point of exaltation, exhilaration, delirium. [...]

Religious chants, contortions, dances, mutilations performed in states of delirium, belong to [this] variety. However, mutilations and more generally, voluntary sufferings often involve another kind of residues – the ascetic type" (Pareto, 1935, II: 648).

4   *Residues connected with sociality.* This is the tendency of a social group to adopt homologous and uniform behaviour and the individual to sacrifice himself for the needs of the community. This instinct is proactive and pro-social. Its manifestations are neophobia, self-pity extended to fellow others, cruelty to strangers to defend one's community, sharing one's goods, renouncing selfish good for collective ends, seeking social recognition, and sacrificing one's life for one's community. It is connected to recognition. In fact, Pareto affirms: "The sentiments of sociality manifested by various sorts of residues are nearly always accompanied by a desire for the approbation of others, or for avoiding their censure" (ivi, II: 690).

5   *Integrity of the individual and his appurtenances.* This is, on the contrary, a defensive and egoistic residue concerning the defence of one's identity and possessions. It is, in other words, the preservation of the private sphere, which is not affected by the social sphere.

6   *Sex residue.* This is the residue in which Pareto demonstrates more explicitly the importance of considering the biological element in the understanding of human behaviour.

In summary, according to Pareto, there are six fundamental "drives" of non-logical action – and many of these involve human action. Two of these (1 and 2) express the dialectic between social stability and social change; two others (4 and 5), the dialectic between identification and distinction. The third refers to the public expression of common feelings of belonging, while the last represents a clear link between social dynamics and biological determinism. In brief, Pareto proposes a model of social action conciliating primordial instincts and passions with modern and industrial mechanisms of social differentiation. There are three fundamental elements of the residues: (a) human nature, (b) the individual as a rational, self-determining entity, and (c) the society with which it enters into a dialectical relationship. The rational component of interests remains outside the residues because it is included in the logical-experimental actions. The author thus outlines a system of social action that claims to be applicable to any human group.[12] The differences between cultural, political, and religious groups are reduced to epiphenomena. All human behaviour is driven by fundamental forces that transcend the manifest differences that are proper to the whole of humanity.

For Pareto the residues cover a large part of human behaviour and therefore overlap with the concept of "human nature", which is inherently emotional. Clearly, in each of the six categories of residues proposed by Pareto, an emotional element is included. This is evident in different exerts of the

*Trattato*, as in the one that follows: "Human beings are persuaded in the main by sentiments (residues), and we may therefore foresee, as for that matter experience shows, that derivations derive the force they have, not, or at least not exclusively, from logico-experimental considerations, but from sentiments" (ivi, vol. IV: 885).

The thesis is that there is "a group of constant and generalized sentiments" determining human life. Indeed, according to Pareto, the same residues have a capacity for emotional contagion or of "redundancy" that recalls very closely the contemporary Durkhemian theory of social effervescence:

> The acts in which sentiments express themselves reinforce such sentiments and may even arouse them in individuals who were without them. It is a well-known physical attitude, and individual putting himself in that attitude may come to feel the corresponding emotions.
>
> (ivi, II: 647)

In conclusion, Pareto develops a general social system, inserting emotions within the dynamics of structuration and the institutionalization of social action. Therefore, the classification of residues offers an original – and perhaps not totally unconscious – combination among the great paradigms of European classical sociology: Comtian positivism, Simmel's formal sociology, the Weberian theory of social action, the Durkheimian theory of social solidarity, and finally, a certain Darwinian evolutionism, deprived of the historical-finalistic component.

## 7.6 Derivations and social equilibrium

If the model pretends to offer an overall explanation of human behaviour, the differences between the various human groups can be noticed, according to Pareto, especially at the superficial level of the arguments or symbolizations: the so-called *derivations*.[13] While the residues vary very little over time, the derivations are highly variable historical, cultural, and social products. They constitute the most visible element of rationalization, which is the ideological justification of non-logical or illogical behaviour: "The derivations comprise logical reasonings, unsound reasonings, and manifestations of sentiments used for purposes of derivation: they are manifestations of the human being's hunger for thinking" (ivi, III: 889).

Since they are verbalizations, Pareto coherently distinguishes them in linguistic-argumentary categories:

1. *Assertions*, namely the mere enunciation of real or imaginary facts, sentiments, or mixtures of facts and sentiments.
2. *Authority*, that is, the legitimation of a given action based on the authority of men, traditions, divinities, or personified entities.

3   *Accords with sentiments or principles*, or the legitimation of a given action based on sentiments, interests, or normative principle, or on the belief in metaphysical and supernatural entities.
4   *Verbal proofs*, concerning the rhetorical capacity to prove an argument through incidental sentiments, metaphors, allegories, or analogies.

Therefore, Pareto lists among the derivations those rhetorical tools that give strength to a discourse on the preferability or plausibility of a given course of non-logical action, from the illocutive and perlocutive point of view.[14] Two of them (1 and 4) refer to the direct, illocutive rhetorical force of speech; the second derivation concerns the *a priori* legitimation of a derivation – what in rhetoric is called *argomentum ab auctoritate*; the third, instead, explicitly concerns the speaker's ability to involve his audience's emotions.

With respect to derivations, emotions still play a crucial role, but of a different kind than for residues. They stimulate the construction of consensus based on the mechanisms of persuasion. Using the terms of sociolinguistics, it can be said that Pareto focuses on the *emotional function* of speech. The so-called "agreement with sentiments and principles", in particular, indicates all those arguments that recall values, principles, and shared beliefs that stimulate emotional involvement in the public.

This has two purposes consistent with the two tasks of sociology: to show how some arguments in favour of non-logical actions are useful, despite their irrationality, and to unmask all ideological constructions. Pareto, in fact, directs his most potent criticism towards political doctrines (from socialism to nationalism) that resort to rhetorical strategies (metaphors, personifications of the people or the nation) to give strength to illogical feelings.

From the interaction between residues, derivations, interests, and elements external to society derives social equilibrium. Unlike other classical sociologists, Pareto does not believe that society is the product of social structures or organic syntheses. Rather, borrowing the metaphor of dynamic equilibrium from rational mechanics, he believes that social systems are produced by the interaction and combination of several elements. Indeed, the form of human society

> is determined – aside from external environment – by sentiments, interests, logico-experimental reasonings used for satisfying sentiments and interests, and, in a secondary way, by derivations, which express and sometimes intensify sentiments and interests and serve in certain cases as instruments of propaganda.
>
> (ivi, IV: 1478)

His insistence on social representation and the unveiling of their artifact character led Brigitte Berger to say, "Society is essentially interpreted by Pareto through an analysis of 'knowledge,' that is, of the manifold and commonly deceptive ways in which society interprets itself" (Berger, 1967: 267). Pareto's is, in fact, a tireless struggle to unmask the ideological character of legitimate interpretations of social facts. In this sense, one can consider him an Enlightenment thinker who shifts Machiavelli's cynical realism to the sociology of knowledge. But he is also a thinker who, like Kant, criticizes the very biological base of the human being, those that prevent a full liberation of the rational potential of the species.

Each element interacts with the others, and the emerging structure is the product of this dynamic process of exchange, which gives rise to cycles, and, in particular, to the rise and fall of political elites and sociocultural models. Pareto's approach is therefore fully attributable to the paradigm of methodological individualism. Although it differs from the positivistic-evolutionist model, it retains its systematic and universalistic claim to define the nature of man and society.

## 7.7 Discussion

The sociology of Pareto developed in an historical period dominated by a dominant paradigm: rational utilitarianism, supported by both philosophy and the economic sciences, and finally, by sociological positivism. According to this approach, human behaviour, oriented to the maximization of subjective happiness, would naturally tend towards rationality and the suppression of emotionality.

Pareto does not detach himself from it morally or politically, but, rather epistemologically. Unlike sociological positivism and classical liberal economics, the Italian sociologist, in fact, goes beyond the limits of the rational actor and shows how sentiments, values, instincts, and a sense of belonging are crucial elements in directing human behaviour. However, the Italian sociologist does not exalt the irrational. Rather, he advocates historical pessimism, which looks with scepticism at the social transformations that pass through his time and considers humans from a negative point of view, as beings who cannot rise above their own instincts.

As Talcott Parsons explains, Pareto rejected the hypothesis of the most naive and dogmatic positivism according to which it was considered possible to build a society on exclusively logical-rational bases. This is because in human behaviour there always remains a dimension that cannot be expressed through statements, that cannot be reduced to formulas, whose character is – precisely – emotional, normative, and moral:

> Pareto approached the study of action free from positivistic dogmas. Moreover, his recognition of the concrete inadequacy of economic theory implied, in a direct way which Marshall did not provide, the unacceptability of the utilitarian position for general social theory. And having defined logical action in a way closely corresponding to the conceptions

of economic theory he proceeded to a systematic investigation of some of the principal nonlogical elements of action. For Pareto, this eventuated in a complex classification of residues and derivations which, along with the "interests" and the principal facts of social heterogeneity he incorporated into his generalized social system.

(Parsons, 1949: 299)

In his reaction to the limits of utilitarian theory, according to Parsons, Pareto shows how social action is directed to transcendental ends or to symbolic ends/means relationships. The concept of *sentiments* that he introduces is broader and less specific than that typically used by the modern sociology of emotions. It corresponds, in the author's words, to "any spiritual state other than social logical reasoning, and vice versa". It synthesizes ethical, instinctual, and social drives in one ideal-typical category. Emotions, in fact, are not exhausted by instinct.

On the contrary, Pareto states that every social emotion – that is, collectively defined – is the result of a process of social construction. This social construction, however, mainly concerns the forms of the *emotional display* rather than the basic emotions, which, conversely, are thought of as constants. An example of this is given in *Les Systems Socialistes*, when he analyses the forms of religious sentiment:

> it is essential not to confuse the religious sentiment existing in men with the forms it takes. The oscillations thus exist for the former than for the others, but in general they are much less intense for the sentiments than for the forms. One must therefore beware, when one sees a certain religious form declining, of the conclusion that the feeling is also in decline; it may not be much changed in intensity and manifest itself in other forms.
> 
> (Pareto, 1951: 17)

It is again Parsons who brilliantly explains the complexity of this theory, which mixes biological determinism and social constructionism:

> The sentiment itself is a human creation. It may itself be relatively vague and indefinite, only achieving definiteness by a process of development, if at all. Furthermore, there may be conflicts of sentiment which are only to a relative degree clearly formulated and which may be concealed by indefinite residues. Analysis will reveal innumerable ways in which, remaining on the normative level itself, complexities of the kind Pareto so acutely analyzes may arise.
> 
> (Parsons, 1949: 217)

Consistent with other sociological theories of his time, the Italian sociologist believes that there is a common human nature and still believes, even if implicitly, that emotions, sentiments, feelings, and passions do not vary over time. Only their representation, the forms of their expression, and their philosophical or doctrinal rationalization vary. In this sense, even if not further developed, in separating the origins and expression of emotional states its sociology contains *in nuce* a very articulated and therefore modern theory of emotions in which biological, cultural, and normative data interact with and co-structure each other.

The limits of this embryonic sociology of emotions are instead the following: the imprecision of terminology; the clear contrast between logic and emotion; the emphasis on the universal character of emotions; and the consequent inattention to the dimensions of subjectivity, the cultural definition of emotions, and their situational regulation.

In the more than 2,600 paragraphs of his work, Pareto speaks of emotions in mutable and imprecise terms. He never uses the term "emotion", but in the definitions of residues and derivations he refers, above all, to the indefinite concept of "sentiment". In other passages of his work, he still refers to "passion, propensity, inclination, disposition, need, appetite, instinct, psychic state", terms which, as Antonio Mutti explains, "often return and are used interchangeably" (Mutti, 1994: 152). This imprecision is partly intentional. Reason is conceived as inherently precise and feeling as inherently indefinite. However, Pareto does not develop a phenomenological conception of what is and how one experiences and manifests emotion, but rather offers an analysis that we could call second-hand. He investigates, in fact, the verbal and behavioural manifestations of emotions, and their externalization in the behaviour of the individual and that of the community. Minimal references to the subjective experience of emotions are offered when he mentions its neurophysiological effects (Pareto, 1935, II: 647).

This is, moreover, perfectly consistent with the heuristic and epistemological model in which his work is located. Unlike the historicists, Pareto does not consider *comprehension* a valid method; rather, he tries, with an intellectual operation that is not always successful, to offer a positivist but critical point of view on human feelings. His is still an approach that aims, like Durkheim's, to constitute an alternative sociological field to the psychological. Therefore, emotions are rather studied from an intermediate point of view between individual action and the structural component that influences the cycles of society.

The link that Pareto establishes between non-logical actions and feelings thus places a clear incompatibility between reason and emotions. Consequently, emotions are defined mainly negatively, as the force from which non-logical actions originate due to human weakness, as well as biases that prevents us from looking objectively at natural and social phenomena. Again, reason is conceived as analytical and feelings as synthetic; reason seeks demonstration, while feelings (or sentiments) seek justification; reason is defined, while feelings are undefined and contradictory; reason is calm, while feelings can be extremist (Mutti, 1994: 156–58).

However, in his work, there is also room for a positive conception of emotions themselves. In fact, Pareto recognizes a positive potential (particularly visible in the conceptualization of the instinct of combinations) in stimulating scientific discovery. Furthermore, they have a crucial utility for social cohesion, since they define the ultimate ends to which a given community orients its collective action and, consequently, its values.

In conclusion, this classic author's interest in the theme of emotions is structural and based on a background pessimism about human nature and the historical dynamics of the West. Pareto is, in fact, convinced that the human being is irremediably emotional and that any deviation from this original datum, in an evolutionary sense, can only happen very slowly. However, he is among the first classical sociologists to clearly define a link between social action and emotions, and he is therefore an author of great relevance in our study of the relationship between the classics of sociology and emotions.

## Notes

1 Among the international critical works, the more significant are Henderson 1935; Parsons 1949 [1937]; Bousquet 1960; Perrin 1966; and Aron 1971. After the 1960s, a new international interest in Pareto's work has been recorded only in recent decades (see Femia and Marshall, 2009). By contrast, in Italy secondary sociological literature on Pareto is consistent. Among the most important texts are Bobbio 1964; Pizzorno 1973; Mutti 1992; and Rutigliano 1994.
2 Before publishing his famous book, Talcott Parsons dealt specifically with Pareto in three works: the entry "Vilfredo Pareto" in the *Encyclopedia of Social Sciences* [Pareto, 1933]; a review of *Mind and Society* published in the *American Sociological Review* in 1935; and the essay "Pareto's Central Analytical Scheme" (Parsons, 1936).
3 This choice closely recalls the title of the almost contemporary *Mind, Self and Society* (1934), a posthumous edition of George Herbert Mead's lectures, edited by Charles Morris. Nevertheless, the two authors developed substantially divergent theoretical perspectives.
4 As far as journals are concerned, two articles appeared in the decade of 1930–1940 in the *American Journal of Sociology*. The first was a critical article by M. A. Bongiorno on the *Trattato* (Bongiorno, 1930), and then in 1940, an essay by Timasheff on the concept of *Law in Pareto's Sociology* (Timasheff, 1940). In 1936, the *Journal of Social Philosophy* dedicated a special issue to the Italian sociologist, and Morris Ginsberg published an introductory essay in *The Sociological Review*. As far as monographs are concerned, the most important works are by Homans and Curtis (1934) and the already mentioned Henderson (1935).
5 Sorokin (1928) had already dealt with Parsons in *Contemporary Sociological Theories*.

6   At Harvard in the 1930s there was certainly, led by Henderson, what the then Communist or fellow-travelling or even just mild American style liberals in the University used to call 'the Pareto cult'.... The Pareto cult was never one that influenced a majority of the faculty, but it had fairly wide repercussions.
(Crane Brinton, *Letter*, 17 February 1967, cited in Heyl, 1968: 317)

7 For a review, see Pareto (1966).
8 "[W]e apply the term *logical actions* to actions that logically conjoin means to ends not only from the standpoint of the subject performing them, but from the standpoint of other persons who have a more extensive knowledge – in other words, to actions that are logical both subjectively and objectively in the sense just explained. Other actions we shall call *non logical* (by no means the same as 'illogical')" (Pareto, 1935, vol I: 77, §150). Significantly, the author clearly defines what he means by logical actions, without, however, offering any practical example, while he does not define – if not in the negative – non-logical actions, to whose practical exemplification he devotes a large part of his work. In other words, the *Trattato* is based on the deductive definition of logical action and the extensive inductive exemplification of non-logical actions.
9 The material he works on is mainly composed of philosophical texts, essays on classical and medievalist historiography, epistemological texts, religious doctrines, and political manifestos.
10 An example is the following: "Residues correspond to certain instincts in human beings, and for that reason they are usually wanting in definiteness, in exact delimitation" (Pareto, 1935, vol II: 509, §870).
11 In the proposed scheme, therefore, residues and derivations do not constitute real references but are rather analytical-formal instruments that refer, synthetically, to a large amount of empirical data. It is, once again, an epistemological model that recalls the Weberian ideal type.
12 This makes it possible to compare Pareto's proposal with that of other contemporary authors, for example William Isaac Thomas who at the same time. proposed a theory of fundamental *desires* common to all human beings (see Romania, 2015).
13 We will pay less attention to them because they are less central to our theme.
14 Therefore, we can say that, albeit with the intellectual tools of his time, Pareto anticipated some elements of the so-called *linguistic turn* of social sciences.

## References

Alexander, J. (1994) Vilfredo Pareto: The Karl Marx of Fascism. *Journal of Historical Review*, 14(5), 10–18.

Aron, R. (1971) *Main Currents in Sociological Thought: Durkheim, Pareto, Weber*. Vol. 2. New York: Penguin.

Berger, B. (1967) Vilfredo Pareto and the Sociology of Knowledge. *Social Research*, 34(2), 265–281.

Bobbio, N. (1964) *Introduzione*. In V. Pareto (1964), *Trattato di Sociologia Generale*. Turin: UTET, XIII–XXXIV.

Bobbio, N. (1973) *Pareto e il sistema sociale*. Milan: Sansoni.

Bongiorno, M. A. (1930) A Study of Pareto's *Treatise of General Sociology*, *American Journal of Sociology*. November 1930, 349–370.
Borkenau, F. (1936) *Pareto*. London: Wiley.
Bousquet, J. H. (1960) *Pareto: le savant et l'homme*. Lausanne: Payot.
Cerulo, M. (2018) *Sociologia delle emozioni*. Bologna: il Mulino.
Connell, R. W. (1997) Why is classical theory classical? *American Journal of Sociology*, 102(6), 1511–1557.
Durkheim, É. (1965), *Elementary Forms of Religious Life*. New York: Free Press (orig. vers. 1912).
Femia, J. V. & A. Marshall (eds). (2009) *Vilfredo Pareto Beyond Discisplinary Boundaries*. London: Routledge.
Freud, S. (2002) *Civilization and Its Malcontents*. London: Penguin.
Ginsberg, M. (1936) The Sociology of Pareto. *The Sociological Review*, 28(3), 221–245.
Henderson, L. J. (1935) *Pareto's General Sociology: A Physiologist's Interpretation*. Cambridge, MA: Harvard University Press.
Heyl, B.S. (1968) The Harvard "Pareto Circle". *Journal of the History of the Behavioral Sciences*, 4, 316–334.
Homans, G. C. (1962) *Sentiments and Activities: Essays in Social Science*. New York: Free Press.
Homans, G. C. & Charles P. Curtis, Jr. (1934) *An Introduction to Pareto: His Sociology*. New York: Alfred A. Knopf.
Mornati, F. (2018a) *Vilfredo Pareto An Intellectual Biography. Volume I: From Science to Liberty (1848-1891)*. London: Palgrave Macmillan.
Mornati, F. (2018b) *Vilfredo Pareto An Intellectual Biography. Volume II: The Illusions and Disillusions of Liberty (1891–1898)*. London: Palgrave Macmillan.
Mutti, A. (1992) Il contributo di Pareto alla sociologia delle emozioni. *Rassegna Italiana di Sociologia*, 4, 465–487.
Mutti, A. (1994) *Il contributo di Pareto alla sociologia delle emozioni*. In E. Rutigliano *La ragione e i sentimenti: Vilfredo Pareto e la sociologia*. Milano: Franco Angeli. (1994), 149–170.
Pareto, V. (1935) *The Mind and Society: A Treatise on General Sociology*, ed. by Arthur Livingston, 4 vols. New York: Harcourt, Brace (orig. version 1916).
Pareto, V. (1951) *I sistemi socialisti*. Turin: UTET (orig. vers. 1902).
Pareto, V. (1966) *Sociological Writings*, selected and introduced by S. E. Finer. New York: Praeger.
Pareto, V. (2014) *Manual of political economy: a critical and variorum edition*. Oxford: Oxford University Press (orig. vers. 1906).
Parsons, T. (1933) *Vilfredo Pareto* in *Encyclopedia of Social Sciences*, 11th edn E. Seligman. London: Macmillan. Rpt. 105–108 in C. Camic (ed.), *Talcott Parsons: The Early Essays*. Chicago: University of Chicago Press (1991).
Parsons, T. (1935) Review of *The Mind and Society* and *Pareto's General Sociology*. *American Economic Review*, 25(4): 502–508.
Parsons, T. (1936) Pareto's Central Analytical Scheme. *Journal of Social Philosophy*, I, 244–262.
Parsons, T. (1949) *The Structure of Social Action*. Glencoe IL: The Free Press, Second Edition (First Edition: McGraw-Hill, 1937).
Perrin, G. (1966). *Sociologie de Pareto*. Paris: PUF.

Pizzorno, A. (1973) Pareto e la crisi delle scienze. *Rivista di Filosofia* 64(3), 203–218.
Romania, V. (2015) William Isaac Thomas: profilo intellettuale di un classico della storia del pensiero sociologico. *Sociologia: Rivista quadrimestrale di Scienze Storiche e Sociali*, (1-2015), 27–42.
Rutigliano, E. (1994). *La ragione e i sentimenti: Vilfredo Pareto e la sociologia.* Milano: Franco Angeli.
Sorokin, P. (1928). *Contemporary Sociological Theories.* New York: Harper.
Timasheff, N. S. (1940) Law in Pareto's Sociology. *American Journal of Sociology*, 46(2), 139–149.

# Chapter 8
# Charles Horton Cooley

*Mariano Longo*

> All our life has a history, that nothing happens disconnectedly, that everything we are or do is part of a current coming down from the remote past. Every word we say, every movement we make, every idea we have, and every feeling, is, in one way or another, an outcome of what our predecessors have said or done or thought or felt in past ages.
>
> (Cooley, (1902)1922: 34)

## 8.1 Introduction

The sociology of emotions is generally conceived as a recent development. Indeed, the emergence of a sociological sub-discipline devoted to the topic of emotions dates back to the early 1970s, when the relation between emotions and society was clearly thematized, and sociology started dealing with such topics as emotional display, emotional rules, emotions and social action (Stets, Turner, 2004). Yet, considering emotions as a completely recent sociological topic is misleading. Although classical sociology did not produce a sociology of emotions, emotions have been dealt with by social thinkers in the nineteenth and at the beginning of the twentieth century. Nonetheless, as sociology consolidated as an independent academic field, sociologists tended to expunge emotions from their analysis. Sociology had, by now, defined its specific scope and emotions were conceived as an appropriate object for biology or psychology rather than sociology. In the passage from classical to post-classical social theory, sociology produced highly cognitive approaches, which divested the social actor of its emotional component and regarded it solely as a rational and cogitative being. The model of actor which post-classical sociology produced – what Alfred Schutz, (1962) called the sociological puppet – was unemotional. Emotions were thus held as irrelevant, or at least marginal, in sociological analysis.

As a matter of fact, emotions are a relevant component of classical sociology, which is particularly evident in such authors as, Weber, Durkheim, and Simmel (Longo, 2019). As the discipline was still striving for the definition of its field, classical authors were more free than later authors would be as

DOI: 10.4324/9781003088363-9

to the self-limitation of topics and themes. The relevance given to emotions and sentiment is even more evident in the development of American sociological thought, as it was being elaborated between the nineteenth and twentieth centuries. By synthesizing the thoughts of one of the earliest American sociologists, namely Lester Frank Ward, Robert Bierstedt underlines that, according to Ward, emotion, not reason, is the chief component of human action, hence the element triggering and determining human activity: "Ward – writes Bierstedt – gave the distinction of the *primum mobile* to feelings, not ideas. Men are moved by the power of sentiment, not intellect" (Bierstedt, 1981: 52). Yet emotions and sentiment are not understood by Ward as a positive social force, as they are potentially anti-social. As compared to the gloomy representation proposed by Ward, sociologists such as Cooley, Park, Burgess and Znaniecki analyse the relations between emotions, sentiments and society from a more optimistic point of view. Although they give great relevance to the emotional component of the social actor, they all conceive of emotions as a socialized component of the individual, and in so far as they are socialized, they represent a relevant factor of social stability and integration of the individual in society.

What I propose in this chapter is an analysis of Charley Cooley's approach to emotions. Cooley proposes a strong interconnection between the individual and the social and his sociology of emotions must be understood as a part of his overall theoretical achievements.

## 8.2 Self and society

Although strongly influential within the so-called Chicago School, Cooley never taught in Chicago and his original, somewhat unsystematic thought, is difficult to locate within a specific sociological tradition. His style is impressionistic, often driven by ethical rather than argumentative intent (Mead, 1930, Lewis and Smith, 1980: 163), which makes his works unusual to the modern reader. In a timely and somewhat ungenerous obituary review of Cooley's thought, George Herbert Mead (1930) stressed the relevance of Cooley's conception of the self. The self, although located in a physical body, is made up chiefly of cultural (hence social) elements (Willey, 2011: 170). Mead stresses the innovation of Cooley's approach as compared to the old Western tradition which substantialized the Ego (a sort of substratum independent of sociality and communication). The self has no substance: it is the output of a relational process. As Mead puts it, according to Cooley, the self "arises through the imagination of the idea that others entertain of the individual" (Mead, 1930: 696) hence, through a process of internalization of what one thinks others think about oneself. As a counterpart, society is conceived of as a "relation among personal ideas" (Cooley, (1902) 1922: 19), or the organization of the ideas social actors have about each other. The self is social, as it emerges as a reflex of social relationships and social communication, and, at the same time, the solid facts of society are mental, as both the idea one constructs of oneself (the self) and the personal ideas one conceives of other individuals and the relations they may have (society) are mental. Cooley aims to show the strong interconnection between the individual and society, the self and societal organizations, as emerge in his famous and icastic sentence "Self and society are twin-born, we know one as immediately as we know the other, and the notion of a separate and independent ego is an illusion" (Cooley, 1909: 5). What the above quoted lines point to, is that self and society are two sides of the same reality, which entails that "society is mental", because "the human mind is social" (Cooley, (1902) 1922: 81).

In his obituary essay, Mead tends to underestimate the strong social and communicative component of the constitution of the self and set the standard of a critique to Cooley, which tends to consider him as prone to a mentalist (hence idealist) representation of the self and society (see, e.g., Farberman, 1970). As a matter of fact, Cooley never denies the objectivity of the social actor: people are real, according to Cooley, and endowed with an instinctive self-feeling, which has to be domesticated within social intercourses. Yet, sociality is possible only in so far as we interact with other people by referring to the ideas we have about them: "the personal ideas are the immediate personal reality, the thing in which men exist for one another, and work directly upon one another's lives" (Cooley, (1902) 1992: 124). Cooley stresses that society is mental as a counterpart of the idea that the mind is social, and by both assertions Cooley means that both the self and society are rooted in communicative processes. Cooley is not denying the physical component of the individual and society: he is only stressing the relevance of ideas and communication as fundamental elements both for the constitution of the self and for the organization of society (Schubert, 2006). Communication (hence a social fact) is the *trait d'union* between the self (emerging from constant conversations with oneself and the other) and society (intended as the mental representation of personal ideas and their relations). There is no duality, since communication set the very possibility of both the human self and human relations (Lewis and Smith, 1980: 163). Communication is, in fact, "the mechanism through which human relations exist and develop – all the symbols of the mind, together with the means of conveying them through space and preserving them in time" (Cooley, 1909: 61). The mind is shaped by communication and, in its turn, it shapes the external world, but only in so far as it adopts signs and symbols which are already socially defined and shared. As Emma Engdahl correctly puts it: "both self and society are understood as artifacts of intersubjective processes. This indicates that the influence that we have on society is what makes us present in it, and that the influence that society has on us is what makes it present in us" (Engdahl, 2005: 43).

## 8.3 Sociability and sympathy

According to Cooley, the construction of the self is emotional in so far as it has to be connected to our instinctual perception of ourselves. This perception, which Cooley calls self-feeling, is only indistinct at birth and may be described, in William James's terms, as a form of excitement connected to possession (Hinkle, 1963: 708). In *Human Nature and Social Order* Cooley makes explicit reference to James, and his idea that "a man's self is the sum of all he CAN call his" (James, quoted in Cooley, (1902)1922: 170). Self-feeling is hence constructed around all an individual perceives as his own (including his body, his relations and his moral values). This feeling is indistinct at birth and is gradually shaped, as the individual has communicative interaction with their fellow people, thus converting it into a social, rather than an instinctual, feature of the social actor. Indeed, the sense of appropriation combines with what Cooley calls sociability, such that self-feeling is gradually domesticated through a sympathetic connection to other people. Sociability is a general sentiment drawing us towards our social surroundings. As such, Cooley identifies sociability as the raw material on which other, more differentiated, social sentiments build up (Cooley, (1902)1922: 86). More specifically, sociability is "the capacity and need for social feeling, rather too vague and plastic to be given any specific name like love. It is not so much any particular personal emotion or sentiment as the undifferentiated material of many" (Cooley, (1902)1922: 86). The feeling of one's self is thus a precondition for life with other people, its function being "stimulating and unifying the special activities of individuals" (Cooley, (1902)1922: 171), which makes interaction possible. Although the self is configured as a feeling, Cooley stresses its radical social character and icasticaly comments " 'I' is a militant social tendency" ( Cooley, (1902)1922: 181) by which he stresses both that the self is moulded by society and that it is functional to social relations.

It is thanks to the social experience in primary groups that the individual develops a social identity, thus transforming indefinite dispositions and feelings into sentiments and ideas. Thus, the genetic components of the self are socially made relevant through socialization and communication. This process is possible due to sympathy, which one could define as our capacity to tune up with other people. Sympathy is hence our faculty, which is both emotional and cognitive, to envisage the thinking, feelings and emotions of other people. Sympathy, intended as the capacity to share both our cognitive and emotional sphere with others, is "the basis for the altruistic or organic or holistic development of personality, groups, and ideas" (Hinkle, 1963: 709. Wiley (2011: 171) stresses that the idea of sympathy is better understood if compared to Mead's concept of role-taking. According to Mead, role-taking is a cognitive process, by which a cogitative self enters into relationships with other people through communication and by recurring to abstract ideas. The process is particularly relevant in the construction of the self in primary socialization, during which a not-yet-socialized I becomes aware of himself as a socialized Me (Wiley, 2011: 171). Sympathy, understood as the capacity to share both thoughts and emotions with our fellow-people is, according to Willey (Wiley, 2011: 171), Cooley's emotional and cognitive version of role-taking. Cooley is quite clear when underlining that sympathy is a form of understanding, not to be confused with compassion, as it is in the common use in English. Sympathy "denotes the sharing of any mental state that can be communicated, and has not the special implication of pity or other 'tender emotion' that it very commonly carries in ordinary speech" (Cooley, (1902)1922: 136). For Cooley, sympathy is defined as "the sharing of any mental state that can be communicated" (Cooley, (1902)1922: 136). Sympathy may be conceived as a conversation with another person, which implies "to have more or less understanding or communion with him, to get on common ground and partake of ideas and sentiments" (Cooley, (1902)1922: 136). As compared to Mead's strong cognitivism, Cooley's sympathy may therefore be intended as a form of emotional understanding, our capacity to interpret not only thoughts but also states of mind (Nungesser, 2013: 71–72). This form of emotional understanding is relevant for the development of personality and is, as Cooley writes, "guided and stimulated in its selective growth by feeling" (Cooley, (1902)1922: 156).

Both sociability and sympathy are relevant components in the development of the social self and its emotions. As the individual growths within the context of his social relations, the originally amorphous self-feeling undergoes a process of differentiation and refinement, yet it keeps having, as its essential feature, a strong connection with a sense of appropriation (Cooley, (1902)1922: 171). An undistinguished self-feeling is converted into a plurality of sentiments of oneself, each depending on the social relation we entertain (Hinkle, 1963: 708). Personal thoughts become more diversified and new social feelings emerge, so as to adapt "to the (growing) complexity of life itself" (Cooley, (1902)1922: 34). The meaning of I and mine – hence of the self-feeling – is learnt in the same way as we learn other feelings such as "hope, regret, chagrin and thousands of others", that is by "having the feeling, by imputing to others with some kind of expression and hearing the word along with it". As the feeling evolves, it becomes a social sentiment, "defined and developed by intercourse" (Cooley, (1902)1922:192). Cognition and emotions are faculties which the individual learns to manage in social intercourse. Both are raw and crude at the beginning of life, and are refined as we develop personal ideas, e.g., ideas of the others with whom we enter into relations. And the process of refinement is circular, in the sense that the more personal symbols we develop, the more we refine our feelings and cognition, and the greater becomes our capacity to interpret symbols, hence allowing us to achieve a cognitive and emotional relationship with the world and other people:

> An infant's states of feeling – Cooley writes - may be supposed to be nearly as crude as his ideas of the appearance of things; and the process that gives form, variety, and coherence to the latter does the same for the former. It is precisely the act of intercourse, the stimulation of the mind by a personal symbol, which gives a formative impulse to the vague mass of hereditary feeling-tendency, and this impulse, in turn, results in a larger power of interpreting the symbol. It is not to be supposed, for instance, that such feelings as generosity, respect, mortification, emulation, the sense of honor, and the like, are an original endowment of the mind.
>
> (Cooley, (1902)1922: 114)

The process may be better understood by referring to what Cooley effectively defines as the "looking-glass self", hence the self as mirrored in our fellow people (Cooley, (1902)1922: 183–184). Socialization implies that the perception of oneself is no longer instinctual, as it is now defined by the way we think other people perceive us. What we perceives as ours is, in fact, dependent on the attitude others have towards us: "The self at any particular moment– Cooley writes – (…) is simply the system of objects and ideas which, because of the attitude of others toward us, we cherish as distinctively our own" (Cooley, Angell and Carr, 1933: 119). And, as the self is social, it implies a process of differentiation of the individual from the plurality of his fellow people: "It always possesses a social setting; that is, it is an assertion of the ways in which we are distinctive from our fellows" (Cooley, Angell and Carr, 1933: 119). Self-feeling is hence always connected to our perception of the thought of others, which affects "specialized endeavor of higher as well as lower kinds" (Cooley, Angell and Carr, 1933: 119). It cannot be limited to the instinctive sense of appropriation, but also to higher motives, connected to our social values (such as the sense of duty). It is, as such, utterly social, as clearly emerges from the following quotation: "There is no sense of "I," as in pride or shame, without its correlative sense of you, or he, or they" ((Cooley, Angell and Carr, 1933: 120).

It is the reference to the perception other people have of the individual which allows us to domesticate the sense of appropriation characterizing our instinctual self-feeling. The perception of one's self is no longer a kind of egotistic appropriation of the world, since it is shaped by the mirroring quality of social relations. Cooley breaks up the mirroring effect into three components: "the imagination of our appearance to the other person; the imagination of his judgment of that appearance, and some sort of self-feeling, such as pride or mortification" (Cooley, (1902) 1922: 184). In the first stage, we mirror ourselves in the attitude others have towards us. The second phase is essentially social and is linked to the judgement we think other people have of us. Cooley writes: "The thing that moves us to pride or shame is not the mere mechanical reflection of ourselves, but an imputed sentiment, the imagined effect of this reflection upon another's mind" (Cooley, (1902) 1922: 184). As the self develops, it is no longer defined by one's assertion of being here now (as when a child claims possession of the world) but by the capacity to tune up with our social surroundings in terms of the appropriateness of our behaviours, pride or mortification being relevant emotional indicators (Engdahl, 2005: 47).

## 8.4 Primary group, feelings and sentiment

Primary groups are characterized by face-to-face, intimate relations. The main sense in which they are primary is that "they are fundamental in forming the social nature and ideals of the individual" (Cooley, 1909: 23). As a consequence, the individual and the group are to be intended as a common whole "so that one's very self, for many purposes at least, is the common life and purpose of the group" (Cooley, 1909: 23). Primary groups are, therefore, the places of social interaction in which the we-feeling (our perception of being part of a collective) develops. In primary groups "(o)ne lives in the feeling of the whole and finds the chief aims of his will in that feeling" (Cooley, 1909: 23). This is the reason why social actors refer to the primary group where they belong by adopting the first-person plural "we". Primary groups (family, neighbourhood, community) are hence the informal social structures in which both the self and the social nature of man develops. Cooley writes:

> This nature consists chiefly of certain primary social sentiments and attitudes, such as consciousness of one's self in relation to others, love of approbation, resentment of censure, emulation, and a sense of social right and wrong formed by the standards of a group.
> (Cooley, (1902)1922: 32)

What is specific of human nature is, hence, our disposition towards the others, whereas the content of our behaviours, emotions and thoughts depends on the features of the intimate groups, such that "(i)f these are essentially changed, human nature will change with them" (Cooley, 1909: 32–33).

The process of constitution of the self, which takes place in primary groups, shows the deep interconnection between the individual and the social: primary groups produce, in fact, solidarity, empathy, a sentiment of kindness which helps consolidate social relations among its members. A benevolent and altruistic disposition towards the others, so typical of primary groups "contributes to an ideal of moral unity of which kindness is a main part. Under its influence the I-feeling becomes a we-feeling, which seeks no good that is not also the good of the group" (Cooley, 1909: 189–190). The reference to the groups of intimates permits us to specify in what sense Cooley considers the self as social: it is social, not only in so far as it is the output of a process of domestication of the I-feeling, but also because it emerges in a social context characterized by the we-feeling, the perception of ourselves as belonging to a group whose members share a purpose, sentiments and morality.

Primary groups are humanizing agents in so far as they convert innate drives ("lust, greed, revenge, the thirst for power, and the like" (Cooley, Angell and Carr, 1933: 59)) into sentiments, in a relational process which conditions raw emotions "through sympathetic insight into sentiments such as love, ambition, and resentment" (Cooley, Angell and Carr, 1933: 59). Sentiments are "instinctive emotions organised around ideas", thus culturally conditioned instinctual drives. They are moulded and humanized within our relation with other people, yet the process is more effective within primary groups, where the identification with the social context

> occurs spontaneously, over and over again, is not limited by conscious purpose, is accompanied by full and free play of pre-verbal as well as verbal communication with all that that implies for the emotional conditioning of personality, and finally, that it is a universal type of experience affecting the entire human race.
> (Cooley, Angell and Carr, 1933: 59)

Passions (another way to name instinctive emotions) are not intended by Cooley as properly human. They are, as it were, linked to the animal component of human beings and as such, we need "the spirit of family or neighborhood association (in order to) control and subordinate them" (Cooley, (1902) 1922: 36). It is through the mediation of family and community that they may be converted into sentiments, once they are "brought under the discipline of sympathy" (Cooley, (1902) 1922: 36). Lust is converted into love, revenge into resentment, greed into ambition, such that they turn from disintegrative into integrative social factors. Cooley analyses greed as a specific example, stressing how experiencing greed may have a positive effect on the social structure but only if it is socially conditioned and controlled:

> The desire of possession is in itself a good thing, a phase of self-realization and a cause of social improvement. It is immoral or greedy only when it is without adequate control from sympathy, when the self-realized is a narrow self. In that case it is a vice of isolation or weak social consciousness, and indicates a state of mind intermediate between the brutal and the fully human or moral, when desire is directed toward social objects – wealth or power – but is not social in its attitude toward others who desire the same objects.
> (Cooley, (1902) 1922: 36)

It is socialization, as well as the close connection with intimate people, which makes greed social, hence a sentiment which no longer has a disruptive power. The instinct of appropriation and the desire to possess is tempered due to our being part of a primary group of intimate relations. Cooley writes: "Intimate association has the power to allay greed. One will hardly be greedy as against his family or close friends, though very decent people will be so as against almost anyone else" (Cooley, 1909: 36). The simple fact of sociality and association tends to mitigate greed as an instinctive emotion, hence the softening effect of sociality upon the instinctive component of human nature and the moralizing power of social intercourses and sociality as such (Cooley, 1909: 36).

Social sentiments emerge as a refinement of raw emotions in the self-same process of refinement of cognition, hence "in conjunction with communication and could not exist without it" (Cooley, (1902)1922: 155). They are, therefore, social from the outset, as they are connected to symbols, produced in the communicative intercourse with others:

> It is these finer modes of feeling, these intricate branchings or differentiations of the primitive trunk of emotion, to which the name sentiments is usually applied. Personal sentiments are correlative with personal symbols, the interpretation of the latter meaning nothing more than that the former are associated with them; while the sentiments, in turn, cannot be felt except by the aid of the symbols.
> (Cooley, (1902)1922: 36)

In the following quotation, drawn from *Social Organization* (Cooley, 1909) the interconnection among feeling, sociability and the sympathetic connection with other people is emphasized:

> By sentiment I mean socialized feeling, feeling which has been raised by thought and intercourse out of its merely instinctive state and become properly human. It implies imagination, and the medium in which it chiefly lives is sympathetic contact with the minds of others. Thus love is a sentiment, while lust is not; resentment is, but not rage; the fear of disgrace or ridicule, but not animal terror, and so on. Sentiment is the chief motive power of life.
> (Cooley, 1909: 177)

Not only does sociality domesticate instinctive emotions, it also produces differentiation, hence a variety of nuances a raw feeling may assume according to the functional needs of social intercourses. As Cooley writes "social emotion is also elaborately compounded and worked up by the mind into an indefinite number of complex passions and sentiments, corresponding to the relations and functions of an intricate life" (Cooley, (1902)1922: 88).

## 8.5 Nature and culture

The instinctual component of human nature is not dismissed by Cooley. On the contrary, he thinks of human life as characterized by a strong connection between nature and culture: they are to be distinguished, but find a juncture in human beings, which are both natural and cultural (hence social). By assuming an organicistic perspective (Hinkle, 1963; Nungesser, 2013), Cooley thinks of life (both animal and human) as a common whole, and this is more evident when one takes a diachronic perspective:

> The stream of this life-history – Cooley writes – (...) appears to flow in two rather distinct channels. Or perhaps we might better say that there is a stream and a road running along the bank — two lines of transmission. The stream is heredity or animal transmission; the road is communication or social transmission. One flows through the germ-plasm; the other comes by way of language, intercourse, and education.
> (Cooley, (1902) 1922: 4–5)

"Germ-plasm" is a term Cooley uses to qualify heredity. A strong supporter of Charles Darwin, Cooley gives relevance to the genetic component of human behaviour. In the introduction added to the second edition of his *Human Nature and Social Order*, Cooley poses the question of emotions within a discussion on the relevance of both the hereditary and the social environment. Self and society are the complex outputs of the intertwining between the heredity and the cultural (Cooley, (1902) 1922: 4–5) such that it is hard to distinguish what contributes to what. Human behaviour is not predetermined by instinct but is, on the contrary, made possible by what Cooley defines as "instinctive emotions" as opposed to instincts among lower animals, instinctive emotions do not produce "fixed modes of behavior" (Cooley, (1902) 1922: 29). They are, as it were, genetic prerequisites for plastic actions: "(t)hese instinctive emotions predetermine, not specific actions, but, in a measure, the energy that flows into actions having a certain function with reference to our environment". Some instinctive dispositions are clearly related to our animal nature (e.g. anger and fear). Yet, simple emotions are not sufficient to explain human behaviour. As Cooley writes: "all such dispositions (...) are rapidly developed, transformed, and interwoven by social experience, giving rise to a multitude of complex passions and sentiments which (...) change very considerably with changes in the social life that moulds them" (Cooley, (1902) 1922: 27).

Take as an example anger: "Human anger (...) motivates conflict with opposing persons or other agents, being similar in function to the anger, clearly instinctive, of all the fighting animals" (Cooley, (1902) 1922: 24). Yet one could not predetermine human behaviour from anger as an instinctive emotion, since the way anger is managed depends on the specific situational context or cultural patterns (Cooley, (1902) 1922: 26). Raw instinctive emotions are hence flexible, being moulded by society (language, intercourse and education), which gives them specific content. Since Darwin believed that "the effects of habit are inherited, he did not discriminate as clearly as we could wish between what is hereditary and what is learned from others" (Cooley, (1902) 1922). Indeed, although there is a thread of continuity between instinct and culture, instinctive emotions are, as it were, culturally and socially redefined, according to specific culturally determined situations. Let me specify the connection between instinctive and social emotions by quoting Cooley directly:

> Though man does not show long trains of overt behavior based on inborn patterns he does seem to experience inner states, called emotions, which are unlearned. These emotions are a result of certain innate visceral reactions stimulated through the nervous system. What happens, then, is that these visceral reactions become "conditioned" to a great variety of external situations, and whenever one of these situations arises, the appropriate internal, innate pattern functions, giving us an emotion like fear, anger, or love.
> 
> (Cooley, Angell and Carr, 1933: 32)

Cooley establishes a complex relation between the instinctive base of raw emotions and their socialized component. An instinctive emotion, although being a relevant component of human behaviour, is socially meaningful only in so far as it is culturally defined. It is to be configured as "an impulse whose definite expression depends upon education and social situation" and, as an impulse "(i)t does not act except through a complex, socially determined organism of thought and sentiment" (Cooley, (1902)1922: 27). Thus anger may, for instance, be differentiated according to levels of socialization and cultural domestication. Cooley detects three levels in which this raw feeling may vary, from the instinctual, impulsive outburst of rage to the ethical manifestation of indignation:
It is thus possible rudely to classify angers under three heads, according to the degree of mental organization they involve; namely, as

1. Primary, immediate, or animal.
2. Social, sympathetic, or imaginative of a direct sort. This is resentment and is caused by an idea imputed to some other person's mind attacking our naive, narrowly personal self.
3. Ethical or highly rational. This is called indignation and is caused by behavior which outrages some standard which we cherish as part of our broader self (Cooley, Angell and Carr, 1933: 131).

As a general process, Cooley states that thoughts and sentiments are socially determined and, since they may be defined in a variety of culturally different ways, they produce a highly complex differentiation of instinctive emotions, which:

> are rapidly developed, transformed, and interwoven by social experience, giving rise to a multitude of complex passions and sentiments which no one has satisfactorily elucidated. Indeed, as these change very considerably with changes in the social life that moulds them, it is impossible that they should be definitely and finally described. Each age and country has its own more or less peculiar modes of feeling, as it has of thinking.
> (Cooley, (1902)1922: 26)

Cooley asserts that fixed instincts (hence instincts as determined by heredity, typical of animals), work regardless of any cultural control: "life presses a button and the hereditary mechanism does the rest" (Cooley, (1902)1922: 29). Human instincts are, on the contrary, characterized by plasticity, which is the chief feature of human nature: we are human because we are endowed with plastic instincts. In his introduction to sociology, Cooley (who parallels in this regard Gehlen's philosophical anthropology (Nugesser, 2013)) exemplifies his idea of the plastic, teachable character of human nature:

> By human nature – he writes - we mean those characteristics which are human in being superior to those of the lower animals, and also in the sense that they belong to mankind at large, and not to any particular race or time. These can perhaps be analyzed into (i) a highly complex yet flexible type of behavior, and (2) certain characteristic attitudes and sentiments which are always developed by close association with other people.
> (Cooley, Angell and Carr, 1933: 54)

Yet, the universality of these characteristics is to be connected to the type, not to their content, which is always determined by the social context, hence by specific relations with other people. In particular, sentiments such as "self-consciousness, enjoyment of approbation, pain at censure, a sense of right and wrong, rivalry, and hero-worship" are bound to "vary in content from one culture to another but the general types will be found in all" (Cooley, Angell and Carr, 1933: 53). Thus, human nature may not be identified with any specific behaviour or disposition, "such as pecuniary selfishness or generosity, belligerency or peacefulness, efficiency or inefficiency, conservatism or radicalism, and the like" (Cooley (1902)1922: 33). Accordingly, behaviours and dispositions are determined by specific social and institutional contexts.

As raw instincts are teachable, they need a guide, which is to be detected in reason. Reason guides and coordinates instinctive emotions, so that they adapt to the variety of cultural and social situations. In a somewhat emphatic analogy, Cooley equates reason to an officer and instinctual emotions to his recruits. Reason, in fact "takes the crude energy of the instinctive dispositions, as an officer takes his raw recruits, instructing and training them until they can work together for any end he may propose, and in any manner that the situation demands". Thus reason, which is itself a natural disposition, "is a principle of higher organization, controlling and transforming instinctive energy". For example, lust as a teachable instinct is domesticated by reason, which allows one to conform to socially established rules: a man is, for example, converted into a wooer, who wins the favour of his beloved according to a set of conventions regulating courting as a social activity (Cooley, (1902)1922: 30). As Hinkle effectively puts it "Cooley held that innate emotional dispositions receive definitive expression through education and social situation, and effective coordination through reason" (Hinkle, 1963: 705).

It is due to the teachable nature of the human mind that not only the microphenomena of emotional control are possible, but also history as a macro, diachronic process. History, indeed, "is a process possible only to a species endowed with teachable instinctive dispositions, organized, partly by reason, into a plastic and growing social whole" (Cooley, (1902)1922: 30–31). Here a double plasticity is at work: the plasticity of human beings and human nature, which can adapt to different cultural contexts and the plasticity of culture, which may change and evolve, thus producing history as a diachronic process. The adaptability of human nature to different contexts is better understood by referring to diachronic processes of cultural and social change. Historical changes are all compatible with the teachable nature of human instincts, so that there is no reason to suppose a change of human nature in the course of human history, but an adaptation of our genetic make-up to the new circumstance (Cooley, (1902)1922: 31–32).

It would therefore be misleading to impute social changes and historical developments to instinctual tendencies (including instinctual emotions). Cooley takes as an example war, which as a social phenomenon is strongly connected to a variety of dispositions, all part of our genetic make-up. Yet the way war is perceived, conceived of and assessed is down to specific cultures and modes of education. Saying that "war is due to an instinct of pugnacity" is a misrepresentation of reality, since, although "(w)ar is rooted in many instinctive tendencies", these tendencies "have been transformed by education, tradition, and organization, so that to study its sources is to study the whole process of society" (Cooley, (1902)1922: 27). Historical phenomena must not be reduced to the instinctual substratum of human nature, which, on the contrary, is deeply conditioned by cultural and social factors. Cooley hence calls for "detailed historical and sociological analysis" (Cooley, (1902)1922: 28).

A pessimistic version of human nature conceives of it as immutable, which makes any attempt to improve society and social relations ineffective. Cooley may, on the contrary, stress the moralizing and educative function of social institutions. Institutions may take advantage of the changeable character of human nature and act upon such plasticity to improve conducts and behaviours. Teachability is, as it were, the premise for social reforms and, as such, it may be identified as "an inexhaustible source of changing conduct and institutions. We can make it work in almost any way, if we understand it, as a clever mechanic can mould to his will the universal laws of mass and motion" (Cooley, (1902)1922: 33). The teachable constitution of human nature sets the very possibility for progress and reform, thus establishing a stable link between the natural characteristics of the species and ethical and political programs aiming at social change.

## 8.6 The micro–macro link

What is remarkable in Cooley's approach is that the self-same human characteristics (e.g., sociability and sympathy) which are adopted to explain the micro-phenomenon of the constitution of the self, are employed to account for macro phenomena such as civilization and democracy. Both may be intended as the gradual extension of characteristics and values of the primary groups to society as a whole. Life in primary groups gives new members of society access to ideas as love, freedom, justice, and solidarity. Well acquainted with pragmatism (Lewis and Smith, 1980), Cooley states that such notions are not to be intended as the abstract product of philosophical investigation, but the result of the lively experience of people within "simple and widespread forms of society, like the family or the play-group". In this elementary form of association, "mankind realizes itself, gratifying its primary needs, in a fairly satisfactory manner, and from the experience forms standards of what it is to expect from more elaborate association" (Cooley, Angell and Carr, 1933: 60). Cooley stresses the relevance of primary groups by underlining that they may be conceived of as "an enduring criterion" by which different institutional and social contexts are evaluated and judged, thus establishing a functional connection between the everyday organization of social life and the meso and macro level of institutions and social systems (Cooley, Angell and Carr, 1933: 60).

The civilizing function of society is strictly connected to emotions and sentiments. Modern society seems to Cooley as more capable than other forms of social organization to modify the emotional structure of social intercourses. Two processes are at work here. The first (which we have already hinted at) is the differentiation of emotional types and contents. The variety of stimuli and forms of social relations caused by the increased complexity of society produces new types and shades of emotions, so that the individual may better adapt to differentiated social and institutional contexts. A more complex society, this is the idea, is one which determines a more articulated emotional structure (Cooley, 1909: 177). The second process is "a trend toward humanism meaning by this a wider reach and application of the sentiments that naturally prevail in the familiar intercourse of primary groups" (Cooley, 1909: 178). These sentiments tend to spread outside the group of intimates, such that they substitute more aggressive or formal emotions, which in earlier epochs were associated with those relations not belonging to the narrow circles of intimates (Cooley, 1909: 178).

Differentiation has two consequences: the attenuation and the refinement of sentiments. An "animated moderations in feeling" is the final output. Whereas, in simpler societies, sentiments could be extreme (an "alternation of apathy and explosion"), modern social actors are exposed to extending social complexity, which demands a specific economy in the manifestation of emotions. Sentiment becomes more diversified and, at the same time, milder, "so that the man most at home in our civilization, though more nimble in sentiment than the man of an earlier order, is perhaps somewhat inferior in depth" (Cooley, 1909: 178). The civilizing process is more evident, Cooley writes, among the lower classes, where an equalitarian democratization of emotions is at work, which entails a generalized domestication of affects, such that "(t)he sharp contrast in manners and feelings between the "gentleman," as formerly understood, and the peasant, artisan and trading classes has partly disappeared" (Cooley, 1909: 179).

The historical process of civilization is not linear. Cooley clearly states that there have been historical periods (the Italian Renaissance for example) when the refinement of sentiments was more intense and comprehensive than in modern societies. Nonetheless, this has to be imputed to "the maturity of special types of culture, rather than of general progress" (Cooley, 1909: 179). The overall trend, however, is one of increasing domestication of emotions, connected to modernity and democratization. According to Cooley, a variety of interconnected factors has contributed to the stability of the process of humanization. The improvement of material conditions has made us less accustomed to coarseness and violence; new means of social communication have determined an increased possibility for social intercourses, whose final consequence is a refinement and diversification of sentiments; a more stable social order has determined less propensity to violence; the spread of democratic values has made differences among classes and "the degrading spectacle of personal or class oppression" less tolerable (Cooley, 1909: 179). As compared with occasional and unstable cases of refinement of sentiments (Cooley makes reference here to classic Greece), the process is now irreversible, "in no more danger of dying out than the steam engine" (Cooley, 1909: 180).

A determining factor is the development of new communication media, which enlarges the possibility for social intercourse outside the direct experience of face-to-face interaction. "Everything that tends to bring mankind together in larger wholes of sympathy and understanding – Cooley writes – tends to enlarge the reach of kindly feeling" (Cooley, 1909: 191). This enlargement process is chiefly due to the development of new forms of communication, that allows the enlargement of the social mind. In essence, the process is one by which communitarian bonds (those that bind the members of families or primary groups) expand to society as such, thus enlarging the we-feeling, once typical only of primary groups. Cooley takes as an example newspapers, and their capacity to produce a common ground of shared opinions and principle and, hence, to extend the we-feeling beyond the situation of co-presence: "Indeed – Cooley writes – the decried habit of reading the newspapers contributes much to a general we-feeling, since the newspaper is a reservoir of common-place thought of which everyone partakes – and which he knows he may impute to everyone else – pervading the world with a conscious community of sentiment which tends toward kindliness" (Cooley, 1909: 192) Humanism as an attitude towards others has in fact this enlarging function, since it "strives with renewed energy to make the we-feeling prevail also in the larger phases of life" (Cooley, 1909: 192).

Democracy is hence to be intended as the extension of the values of primary groups to the larger society. Historically, Cooley identifies in the Teutonic tribes and villages the place where public discussion, public agreement and public opinion started being effectively adopted to reach shared decision (Cooley, 1909: 108). Democracy has adopted the model of participative decision-making of former times and may hence be considered as "the general and public phase of this larger consciousness, this public mind and public opinion" (Bierstedt, 1981: 110). By adopting a naïve and ethnocentric attitude, Cooley considers the United States as the epicentre of the civilizing and democratizing process. The American democracy is configured as a political system fostering the conversion of formal relations among strangers into direct, open, straightforward intercourses typical of primary groups. The sense of community expands, so as to include the nation intended as a single unit, in a way which anticipates Parsons' idea of the societal community (Parsons, 1965). Here is the somewhat idealistic representation of human relation in the American national community:

> In idea, and largely in fact, we are a commonwealth, of which each one is a member by his will and intelligence, as well as by necessity, and with which, accordingly, the human sentiment of loyalty among those who are members one of another is naturally in force.
> 
> (Cooley, 1909: 182)

And in such a social context, where clear-cut rules of behaviour are set, justice and truth may prevail. Indeed, democracy, not only as a political system but as an overall mode of organization of human life, "aims to organize justice, and in so far as it succeeds it creates a medium in which truth tends to survive and falsehood to perish" (Cooley, 1909: 184). Sympathy is no longer a sentiment we share with the people in our narrower social circles, but with all those belonging to our society and, in an all-encompassing vision, with the overall human species. And, as sympathy widens outside the boundaries of primary groups, the sentiment of justice extends, to include all sorts of people, even "alien nations and races, civilized or savage, and to help them to their just place in the common life of mankind" (Cooley, 1909: 181). Moreover, the American democracy is able to favour "social courage and hopefulness, a disposition to push forward with confidence regarding the future both of the individual and of society at large" (Cooley, 1909: 187). In a domesticated society, even a negative sentiment such as discontent assumes a positive function. It produces a different prefiguration of the future, which is now conceived as open for the realization of new ideals. Discontent "works out programmes and hopefully agitates for their realization. There is a kind of piety and trust in God to be seen in the confidence with which small bodies of men anticipate the success of principles they believe to be right" (Cooley, 1909: 188).

## 8.7 Concluding remarks

The individual and society are strictly interconnected in Cooley's thought. Any neat separation of these two aspects would be artificial. And this holds for emotions, which are never conceived of as the output of the individual mind or genetic make-up, but as a product of social intercourse and culture, both able to convert raw sentiments into a refined social product. Instinctive emotions must be tamed, as they represent the intrusion of the sensual, the bodily, the primordial within social life. When discussing morality, Cooley stresses that reason is the only human faculty able to choose between right and wrong, conformity and deviancy, integrative or disruptive behaviours. The emotional is not incompatible with the rational, but only if it has been socially tamed and is now driven by reason. Emotions must be either domesticated (such that they may produce integration and cooperation), or suppressed (in case they attempt to dismantle the integrity of the we-feeling) (Cooley, (1902)1922: 362; Bierstedt, 1981: 102). When the domestication of emotions works, it is both able to produce well integrated individual minds and set a process of enlargement of the social mind to an ever-wider context, beyond the narrow social milieu of primary groups.

In Cooley's highly idealistic conception, the diffusion of kindness, a sentiment typical of primary groups, is an indicator of civilization. We are naturally attracted towards other people, as we need the co-presence of others to develop as individual minds. Civilization accounts for the widening of mutual interconnection, which are not only functional (as in Durkheim, 1893), but also emotional. Cooley quotes Kropotkin in this regard, to stress the relevance of mutuality. The theoretician of mutual aid considered cooperation a general natural trend (Benvenga, Longo, 2020). Thus, against the common notion that only competition may foster evolution, Cooley stresses that "this fusing kindness underlies all higher phases of evolution, and is essential to the cooperative life in which thought and power are developed" (Cooley, 1909: 189). Yet, if mutual aid is, as Kropotkin stated, a general, diffuse natural trend fostering cooperation among lower animals, it is society and civilization which brings this tendency to its fullest development. "Among the conditions that most evidently have this effect (e.g. to enlarge the reach of kindly feeling, n.d.r.) are facility of communication and the acceptance of common principles. These permit the contact and fusion of minds and tend to mould the group into a moral whole" (Cooley, 1909: 191). Egoism and conflict are not expunged, as both are to be conceived as relevant aspects of social change (Cooley, 1909: 193–194, 199). Yet they are tolerated only in so far as they are not disruptive forces, thus contributing to the general progress of mankind.

Domestication, differentiation and mitigation are key words to understand the socialization of instinctual emotions. By making reference to these processes, Cooley is able to develop a civilizing theory *avant la lettre*, which at places resemble Elias' great achievement (Elias, 1939; 1969). Violent anger in primitive life is "crude, impulsive, wasteful" and is "felt against the opponent as a whole and expressed by a general assault". The civilized man, on the contrary "strikes at tendencies rather than persons, and avoids so far as possible hostile emotion, which he finds painful and exhausting. As an opponent he is at once kinder and more formidable than the savage" (Cooley, 1909: 200).

Cooley gives society a civilizing function, which reminds us of Durkheim's conception of the social (Durkheim, 1914). But, whereas in Durkheim, society and the individual are neatly separated, as is evident in the notion of the *homo duplex*, Cooley opts for a different model, where the taming of selfishness depends on sympathy both as a sentiment and a cognitive comprehension of our fellow man and the judgement they have of ourselves. Let me quote a brief passage:

> The perfectly balanced and vigorous mind can hardly be selfish, because it cannot be oblivious to any important social situation, either in immediate intercourse or in more permanent relations; it must always tend to be sympathetic, fair, and just, because it possesses that breadth and unity of view of which these qualities are the natural expression. To lack them is to be not altogether social and human.
>
> (Cooley, (1902)1922: 217)

There is no sharp distinction *à la* Durkheim between the natural and the social, the individual and society. Whereas Durkheim considers morality as an external social fact imposed upon the social actor, Cooley's self is, from the outset, social, which accounts for its being moral. The self-feeling, once converted into a sentiment, is, paradoxical as it may sound, an instrument of social control. Love, honour, mortification etc. are always relational sentiments and, as such, can direct one's actions in accordance with social norms and rules. In such a way, the sentiment of oneself is converted into a controlling force. Moreover, the social self and its constitution denies possessive individualism. This idea, still prominent in the discipline of economics, conceives as a specific character of the human species to be individualism and selfishness. Cooley's perspective is different, as the self is a product of society, as well as of our natural disposition towards others, so that the interconnection between the individual and the social works at its best when the social actor is not driven by self-interest, but by a widespread identification with social values (Willey, 2011).

The complexity of Cooley's approach to emotions is undeniable. It is an all-encompassing perspective, able to integrate the individual, its social surroundings, diachronic processes and society. Dispersed throughout his essays, one may find illuminating insights and ideas. Yet all are diluted by moralistic arguments which partly accounts for the misfortune of Cooley as a classic of sociological thought. Cooley's optimistic attitude is, as it were, the consequence of the narrow perspective from which he looks at society: the American provincial community is the model against which he defines features and characters of society as a whole. Bierstedt emphasizes Cooley's ethnocentrism, when describing him as follows:

> Cooley writes from a position of moral and intellectual security. He knows what is right and what is true and what is good. He has a quite security in the superiority of the Anglo-Saxon race and the Christian religion. He is sure that intemperance must be suppressed and heathen converted.
>
> (Bierstedt, 1981: 105)

Yet, regardless of his ethnocentric optimism, regardless of his moralistic attitude and impressionistic mode of argumentation, Cooley's sociology of emotions is full of insights and promising intuitions. In so far as they are socialized, emotions are to be intended as social facts and must be analysed within a sociological perspective. Cooley is able to anticipate the everyday management of emotions (Hochshild, 1975; 1979), which are always relationally displayed and culturally controlled. He hints at the relevance of utterly social emotions, such as shame, which would be subdued to intellectual scrutiny by later symbolic interactionists (Scheff, 2000). He can envisage the civilizing function of society, through a process of domestication of instinctive emotions, thus anticipating Norbert Elias. He proposes a naïve micro-macro connection, when asserting the strong correlation among emotions, communication and the extension of the we-feeling to society as a whole, intended as a national community. It is no surprise, therefore, that his approach is being subjected to a process of rediscovery and re-evaluation, which will probably have, as its final output, the redefinition of the place of Charles Horton Cooley within the sociology of emotions (Nungesser, 2013).

## References

Benvenga, L., Longo, M. (2020) Kropotkin. Mutualismo e Anarchia. *The Lab's Quartely*, XXII (3), 131–151.

Bierstedt, R. (1981) *American Sociological Theory. A Critical Theory*. New York: Academic Press.

Cooley C. H.; Angell R.C., Carr, L.J. (1933) *Introductory Sociology*. New York: Charles Scribner's Sons.

Cooley, C. H. (1902)(1922). *Human Nature and The Social Order*. New York: Charles Scriber's Sons.

Cooley, C. H. (1909) *Social Organization. A Study of the Larger Mind*. New York: Charles Scriber's Sons.

Durkheim, É. (1893) *The Division of Labour in Society*. Translated from French by Halls, D.W. 1984. London: MacMillan.

Durkheim, É. (1914) *The Dualism of Human Nature and Its Social Conditions*. Translated from French by Blend, C. In R.N. Bellah (1973) *On Morality and Society*. Chicago: University of Chicago Press, 149–165.

Elias, N. (1939) *The Civilizing Process: Sociogenetic and Psychogenetic Investigations*. Translated from German by Jephcott, E. Oxford: Blackwell.

Elias, N. (1969) *The Court Society*. Translated from German by Jephcott, E. 1983. New York: Pantheon Books.

Engdahl, E. (2005) *A Theory of the Emotional Self. From the Standpoint of a Neo-Meadian*. Örebro University, University Library.

Farberman, H. A. (1970) Mannheim, Cooley, and Mead: Toward a Social Theory of Mentality. *The Sociological Quarterly*, 11(1), 3–13.

Hinkle, R.C. (1963) Antecedents of the Action Orientation in American Sociology before 1935. *American Sociological Review*. 28(5), 705–715.

Hochschild A. R. (1979) Emotion Work, Feeling Rules and Social Structure. *The American Journal of Sociology*, 85(3), 551–575.

Hochschild, A. R. (1975) The Sociology of Feeling and Emotion: Selected Possibilities. *Sociological Inquiry*, 45(2–3), 280–307.

Lewis, D. J., Smith, R-L. (1980) *American Sociology and Pragmatism. Mead, Chicago School and Symbolic Interactionism*. Chicago: Chicago University Press.

Longo, M. (2019) *Emotions through Literature. Fictional Narratives, Society and the Emotional Self*. Abingdon: Routledge.

Mead, G. H. (1930) Cooley's Contribution to American Sociological Tough. *The American Journal of Sociology*. XXXV (5): 693–706.

Nungesser, F. (2013) *Charles Horton Cooley: Human Nature and the Social Order*. In K. Sengeand, R. Schützeichel (eds). *Hauptwerke der Emotionssoziologie*. Wiesbaden: Springer, 68–79.

Parsons, T. (1965) Full Citizenship for the Negro American? A Sociological Problem. *Daedalus*, 94(4), 1009–1054.

Schutz, A. (1962) *Common-sense and Scientific Interpretation of Human Action*. In A. Schutz, *Collected Papers I. The Problem of Social Reality*. The Hague: Martinus Nijhoff, 3–47.

Scubert, H.-J. (2006) The Foundation of Pragmatic Sociology. Charles Horton Cooley and George Herbert Mead. *Journal of Classical Sociology*, 6(1), 51–74.

Sheff, T. J. (2000) Shame and the Social Bond: A Sociological Theory. *Sociological Theory,* 18(1), 84–99.

Stets, J.E., Turner, J.H. (Eds) (2004) *Handbook of the Sociology of Emotions.* Cham: Springer International Publishing.

Wiley, N. (2011) A Mead-Cooley Merger. *The American Sociologist.* 42(2/3), 168–186.

# Chapter 9

# George Herbert Mead

*Lorenzo Bruni*

## 9.1 Introduction

George Herbert Mead (1863–1931) can be considered, for all intents and purposes, as a classic of sociological thought. This affirmation is not universally shared. Indeed, Mead is often defined primarily as a psychologist or a philosopher, and his standing as a sociologist has not always been accepted. Mead's elevation to the canon as one of the leading lights of sociology has come about in two fundamental stages. Herbert Blumer and Jürgen Habermas are the two thinkers whose interpretive work has made the greatest contribution to Mead's status as a sociological institution (see Côté, 2016; Huebner, 2014; Carreira da Silva, 2006).

Blumer was the first to promote Mead's canonization within the discipline of sociology (Blumer, 1981; 1969). The reception of Mead's work on the part of the founder of symbolic interactionism is credited with laying the groundwork for the legitimization of Mead's thought in the disciplinary field of sociology, providing the impulse for a substantial program of empirical research (see Carreira da Silva, 2006). Mead's elevation to the status of an institutional figure in sociology was definitively certified by Jürgen Habermas and by the central role that he attributes to Mead in *The Theory of Communicative Action* (1987). Habermas, as is well known, makes ample reference to Meadian theory with the aim of formulating a sociological hypothesis on the social solidarity between strangers in the transition from a prevailing model of goal-orientated strategic action to a model of communicative action. The German sociologist credits Mead with being the sole artificer of a symbolically mediated theory of social interaction.

Mead's reflections on emotions are distinguished from other classic sociological formulations by one peculiarity. Like other sociologists, Mead believes that emotions are exquisitely social. But the characteristic feature of his conception is his proposal of a singular definition of the social dimension of emotions. For Mead, emotions are the raw material for the cognitive development of intersubjective human relations. Emotions constitute a sort of

DOI: 10.4324/9781003088363-10

connective fabric, social in origin, between a dimension of feeling and a more cognitive dimension determined by human behaviour.

Mead's works do not include a systematic treatment of emotions. This may account for the frequent underestimation of the role of emotions in the overall economy of his thought. Indeed, Mead is "often interpreted as overly rational and lacking a theory of emotions" (Deegan, 2017: 12). Nevertheless, Mead's reflections on emotions are of great importance, above all because of the originality of the position he develops and because of its intimate relationship with the general framework of his social theory. Mead's conception of emotions can be deduced both from his general social theory and from several essays explicitly devoted to the subject.

Section 9.2 presents a brief overview of Mead's scientific and intellectual profile. Section 9.3 reconstructs the fundamental elements of his social theory, with specific attention to the contextual genesis of self-consciousness and its social significance. Section 9.4 examines the reception of Mead's social theory in the work of two sociologists of emotions: Susan Shott and Thomas Scheff. Sections 9.5 and 9.6 focus specifically on Mead's conceptualization of emotions. Our attention turns to a detailed analysis of two essays: *The Social Character of Instinct,* and *Emotion and Instinct*, where the theme of emotions is treated in a circumscribed manner. While the third section examines how Mead's social theory has been used to study emotions in two approaches in the field of symbolic interactionism, the fourth and fifth sections analyse Mead's conception of emotions in the narrow sense, concentrating on those texts in which the author explicitly addresses the theme of emotions.

## 9.2 A brief intellectual profile of G.H. Mead

George Herbert Mead is one of the major contributors to the development and dissemination of pragmatism, especially in the years following the First World War, even though many of his works date to an earlier historical period (see Huebner, 2014; Joas, 1997; Cook, 1993). Pragmatism can be defined as a movement of Western philosophy, developed between the end of the nineteenth and the beginning of the twentieth century, whose main area of inquiry is the dimension of *experience*, understood as an open-ended and active process, pertaining equally to the thinking and feeling dimensions of human activity.

Mead's intellectual development is situated within the broad perspective of research and investigation of the concept of *experience*, which must be studied starting from human activity of a perceptive nature all the way through to more reflective activities, which take on a fully social significance (see Joas, 1997; Calcaterra, 2003). From a philosophical and epistemological point of view, Mead can thus be considered a pragmatist. From a scientific point of view, he is a social psychologist. For a long time, the terms "social" and "psychology" were not deemed to be compatible because traditional psychology tended to identify the discipline with the study of the individual taken singularly, or with the study of mental functioning, understood as the organic activity of the brain. Mead, instead, proposes a program of research whose focus is the nexus between society and shared meanings, on the one hand, and the formation of the mind and the development of personality, on the other.

Mead's scientific position can also be defined as behaviourist. He believes that it is necessary to observe human behavior as it appears in order to study it and understand it scientifically. His interest, however, is in a social variant of behaviourism. In fact, Mead's approach is conventionally defined as *social behaviourism*. Human behaviour cannot but be understood as starting from an undeniable fact: the existence of society (see Morris, 2015: 20). Individual human acts must always be observed and understood within the broader category of social acts. Behaviourism, for Mead, indicates a particular approach to the study of experience understood in terms of *social conduct*, which must be explored scientifically while, at the same time, taking into account the importance of internal states, especially of consciousness, but in light of their social genesis.

Without going deeply into Mead's biography, which is not our concern here, it is worth recalling that in 1894 he accepted a position as Assistant Professor in the Department of Philosophy and Psychology at the University of Chicago, thanks to the intervention of his colleague and friend John Dewey, becoming the Chair of the department in that same year (see Joas, 1997: 22). In the history of sociological thought, this is a rather significant event, since that is where Mead came into contact with the Chicago School of sociology, a school of thought closely tied to the social issues then emerging in the pulsating heart of the fast-growing metropolis of Chicago (Joas, 1997: 23).

It is important to note the fragmentary and unsystematic nature of Mead's scientific production. In his intellectual career, he never organized his own thoughts in systematic and complete works. Many of his published scientific articles are reworked texts of conference papers or lectures given during his university courses. Mead's published volumes are all the products of posthumous collections of previously unpublished texts not subjected, therefore, to revision by their author (cf. Huebner, 2015: 391). Some of the better-known volumes are: *The Philosophy of the Present* (1932), in which Mead outlines the fundamental themes of his philosophy; *Movements of Thought in the Nineteenth Century* (1936), an historical-philosophical essay; and *The Philosophy of the Act* (1938), which collects reflections developed by Mead in the last fifteen years of his life and concerning a pragmatic philosophy of time.

The author of texts on psychology, philosophy, ethics, and pedagogy, Mead is known to the sociological audience above all for the contents of his social theory, brought together and condensed in *Mind, Self, and Society*, a collection of his notes prepared for lectures in his social psychology classes held from

1927 to 1930. The text is made up of twelve sets of classroom materials, which include students' notes and stenographer transcripts, together with eight fragments of manuscripts written by Mead himself (Huebner, 2015). The editorial work of collecting and publishing this plurality of sources was undertaken by Charles Morris in 1934.

## 9.3 Mead's social theory

We now turn to a reconstruction of the main elements of Mead's social theory. From a sociological perspective, Mead's thought represents a strong discontinuity with respect to structural–functionalist approaches. In orientations of this kind, individuals are considered only as a means through which initial factors operate to produce certain actions (cf. Blumer, 1981; 1969). The original aspect of Mead's sociological reflections consists in interposing between initial factors and actioning a process of self-interaction. Unlike structural-functionalist sociological conceptions, individuals, for Mead, are not limited to responding to external and objective factors. Individuals come to terms with themselves in the situations where they act, by entering into relationships with themselves and giving rise to an internal dialogue, which plays out by making our own the responses that others have to us. Individual action is not the mere product of a determining external reality. Subjects participate in the formation of the situations in which they find themselves, by representing those situations, by interpreting them, by contributing to their construction.

Individuals are endowed with a *Self*, with the capacity to think their own thoughts. That capacity, in Mead's view, is social, because it comes about and is triggered only in case of interaction with other *Selves*. For this reason, Meadian theory is unlike other sociological conceptions, which tend to see society as an entity that imposes itself on individuals, prescribing structures, norms, roles, and values. This does not mean that Mead's theory rejects, in an overly ingenuous fashion, the existence of a social structure, but that the importance of that structure does not lie in a presumed priority attributed to action nor in the hypothetical existence of parts of the social system that operate autonomously (cf. Blumer, 1969). Rather, the concrete and effective importance of the social structure is defined by the extent to which it enters into the process of interpretation and definition from which common action emerges. Mead views society as a set of continually interacting persons, who encounter a plurality of situations imposed on them by the conditions of life (Blumer, 1969). Within social situations, each person, endowed with his or her own *Self*, interprets the actions of others, contributing to the social construction of *common actions*, which are, in fact, the products of a cooperative process of interpretation.

From the point of view of the theory of consciousness, an integral part of his social theory, Mead elaborates a proposal that makes it possible to account for the formation of thought and the reproduction of human action by way of an approach that is consummately sociological. The mind cannot be defined solely as the seat of the psyche. The mind is not, as it is conceived by neuroscientific reductionism, the organic seat of biochemical reactions. Or, rather, it is not only that. The mind is self-consciousness, and self-consciousness is always constituted within the social relationships of partners to interactions. Mead, then, presents a social theory of consciousness, which – in harmony with other modern intersubjective concepts of self-consciousness – moves beyond the conception of psychic activity as the exclusive domain of the individual. Among these intersubjective conceptions, Mead's theory distinguishes itself for its marked reference to the concrete and symbolic social dynamics that generate consciousness, but, like other interactive approaches, Mead holds that individual consciousness can exist only in a social context. In phylogenetic terms, consciousness emerges within the social process.

The human capacity for reflection is not an innate characteristic, but rather develops from social behaviour, by assuming the attitudes of others towards ourselves. While the emergence of self-consciousness – the typically human capacity of the individual to make himself an object to himself – resides primarily in the assumption of the attitudes of others towards ourselves, the willingness to put ourselves in the other's shoes is, in turn, intertwined with Mead's observations on the genesis of meaningful gestures. The distinction between simple gesture and meaningful gesture, though present in other works by Mead (1910; 1912) is the subject of a long analysis in *Mind, Self, and Society*. A meaningful gesture, "calls out in the individual making it the same attitude toward it (or toward its meaning) that it calls out in the other individuals participating with him in the given social act, and thus makes him conscious of their attitude toward it (as a component of his behaviour) and enables him to adjust his subsequent behavior to theirs in the light of that attitude" (Mead 2015: 46).

Mead's conception of meaning is externalist and social: awareness of what a gesture means can be achieved only with reference to the response that the same gesture elicits in others. The response elicited by the gesture becomes, in turn, a new symbol for the individual who first performed the gesture, who will very probably be led to recalibrate his own behaviour on the basis of the effects caused by it. In Mead's own words:

> The conscious or significant conversation of gestures is a much more adequate and effective mechanism of mutual adjustment within the social act – involving, as it does, the taking, by each of the individuals carrying it on, of the attitudes of the others toward himself – than is the unconscious or non-significant conversation of gestures.
> 
> (Mead, 2015: 46)

Mead opens part three of *Mind, Self, and Society* by addressing the preconditions for the formation of the *Self*. Mead's social theory of the *Self* asserts that there is no consciousness anterior to social interaction. Self-consciousness would not be such, "unless the individual brought himself into the same experiential field as that of the other individual selves in relation to whom he acts in any given social situation" (Mead, 2015: 138). The *Self* emerges, we repeat, within social behavior. In essence, Mead's social-theoretical thesis is the following:

> The unity and structure of the complete self reflects the unity and structure of the social process as a whole; and each of the elementary selves of which it is composed reflects the unity and structure of one of the various aspects of that process in which the individual is implicated. In other words, the various elementary selves which constitute, or are organized into, a complete self, answering to the various aspects of the structure of the social process as a whole.
>
> (Mead, 2015: 144)

A little further along in the same essay, Mead introduces another fundamental concept of his theory: the *generalized other*, defined as the attitude of the community or social group that confers on the individual his unity as a *Self*. In order to develop his own integrated self, an individual must – beyond taking on the attitudes that other individuals manifest towards him – make his own the attitudes of others toward the various moments of social activity as a whole. The constitution of a complete *Self* involves the progressive internalization by the individual of an ever-increasing number of activities performed within society, which coincide, in fact, with the idea of the *generalized other*.

The dynamic aspects of the bond between the individual and social spheres, between formation of the personality and processes of socialization, are addressed in Mead's social theory by way of recourse to two concepts: *me* and *I*. The *Self* is constituted by the *me* and the *I*. The discussion of the differentiation of these two components animates, not without some interpretive difficulties, most of the pages of *Mind, Self, and Society*. The *me* represents a cognitive objectification related to the generalized assumption of the social expectations reflected in the attitudes of others towards ourselves. The *me* is what allows the individual to address himself in the same way that he addresses social objects. The *I*, on the other hand, is the subject of acts, but, as such, can never appear – in the sense of delineating itself as a determined objectification – while the action is in progress. Otherwise, the *I* would resolve itself into an object rather than a subject. The *I* is a necessary correlative of the *me*, since the determinate organization that the community gives to our attitudes requires a response.

The *"me"* does call for a certain sort of an *"I"* in so far as we meet the obligations that are given in conduct itself, but the *"I"* is always something different from what the situation itself calls for. So, there is always that distinction, if you like, between *"I"* and *"me"*. The *"I"* both calls out the *"me"* and responds to it. Taken together they constitute a personality as it appears in social experience" (Mead, 2015: 178).

The *Self* is thus essentially definable in terms of a social process, which unfolds through an open relationship between these two phases. If there was no relationship between these two phases, there would not be, on the one hand, any effective coordination of social life nor, on the other, any conscious responsibility on the part of the subject.

Experience, as we have seen, a central concept of pragmatism, thus comes to be interpreted by Mead in a sociologically original way. It is definable as a social process through which what is unforeseeable and unprecedented in the generalized expectations of society comes about by virtue of an open relationship between the two components of the *Self*.

## 9.4 Mead and the sociology of emotions

Mead's thought has not only been canonized within the sociological discipline understood in the broadest sense, but it has also found an important place within the narrower field of the sociology of emotions. We will now examine the positions of two sociologists who have played important roles in the effort to place Meadian theory within the parameters of the sociology of emotions.

First, Mead's thought is a fundamental element in the work of Susan Shott, unquestionably one of the biggest contributors to the institutionalization of the sociology of emotions, thanks above all to the publication of her essay *Emotion and Social Life* (1979). Shott relies on Mead's theory to develop a conception of the emotions in harmony with the central methodological tenets of symbolic interactionism. According to Shott, emotions are constituted by the combination of two co-extensive dimensions: physiological–sensorial and cognitive. Social structures are the necessary dimension that allow the individual to connote emotions as cognitive phenomena. Put differently, emotions become the object of sociological study to the extent that their physiological arousal is consolidated in a cognitive definition. This passage occurs primarily through the mediation of the social role played by current and effective social norms (Shott, 1979: 1323). The aspects of Meadian theory that contribute to Shott's sociological interpretation of emotions seem to be concentrated above all on this interpretation: emotions play a fundamental role in social control. This function can be performed by emotions to the extent in which the subject, in the course of interaction, takes on the role of *partner*. The reference to the Meadian concept of the *generalized other* is obvious end explicit. Shott defines *role-taking emotions* as those emotions whose expression and manifestation depend on the individual's capacity to make his own the attitudes of others towards himself. Emotions are functional in ensuring a form of self-control that contributes to the individual's social integration. *Role-taking emotions* may also include positive emotions such as, for example, pride.

Shott's analysis is in substantial agreement with the concept of *feeling rules* elaborated by Arlie Hochschild (1979). According to Hochschild, feeling rules prescribe or discourage the expression of certain emotions. For her part, Shott holds that "whether emotional explanations are considered appropriate to a given situation, and which emotion, if any, is warranted, are suggested by social norms" (Shott, 1979: 1319). In Shott's view, emotive experience is socially constructed. There exists a social framework, which conditions and modifies the actor's experience, interpretation, and expression of emotion. Mead's influence on Shott is most apparent, however, in the notion that an equally important role in this process of symbolic construction is played by "the construction of emotion by the actor". An interactionist approach to the study of emotion, that is, can concentrate "on the actor's definitions and interpretations and on the emergent, constructed character of much human behavior, both of which are central to the actor's experience of an emotion" (Shott, 1979: 1320).

Mead's influence on Shott is best expressed in four propositions, which are the fundamental points of Shott's theory of emotions:

1. Analysis of the interpretive processes of the social actor is essential to an adequate understanding of human conduct. The reference here is clearly to the margins of creativity at the disposal of the individual with respect to the normative frameworks that define the social situation in which he acts.
2. Human behaviour is a social outcome that is continuously reconstituted in the course of its unfolding. As we have seen in the preceding section, individual action must be interpreted in terms of a dynamic and open-ended process through the fabric of social relations. Human behaviour is not something pre-defined whose outcome can be foreseen in a certain and determinate way before the action has completed its course.
3. Individual action is influenced just as much by impulses and internal states as it is by external stimuli and social factors.
4. Social structures and normative regulation are frameworks that orientate human action rather than determine it.

The content of these last two propositions is in evident continuity with the previous two.

In addition to its contribution to these four general propositions, Mead's influence on Shott's sociology of the emotions can also be seen in her discussion of the nexus between social control and *role-taking emotions*:

> If there is any area in which the sociological relevance of sentiments is most evident, it may be that of social control; and symbolic interactionist theory is quite useful here, as well. One sort of feelings, which I shall call role-taking emotions, is really the foundation for the large part of social control that is self-control. Unlike other feelings, which do not require role taking for their evocation, role-taking emotions cannot occur without putting oneself in another's position and taking that person's perspective.
>
> (ibid.: 1323)

In order to experience a *role-taking emotion,* an individual must first take on the attitude of the other towards himself. That is, the subject must, as proposed by Meadian theory, have taken on the role of a generalized other, even if only by imagining it. Taking on the attitude of the other towards ourselves gives rise to two types of *role-taking emotions*: reflexive emotions, which are directed towards oneself and include guilt, shame, embarrassment, pride, and vanity; and empathetic emotions, which are felt in the moment we put ourselves in another's place and thus come close to feeling what the other feels. The expression of reflexive emotions is modulated by our perception of how we appear to others or the generalized other. Shott's basic thesis is that both reflexive and empathetic *role-taking emotions* define moral and normative orientations for human behaviour and, thus, foster social control. Think, for example, of how guilt, shame, and embarrassment act to further the goal of checking and punishing deviant behaviour. Indeed, these emotions are evoked in the moment that "one commits or contemplates some 'immoral' action, then takes the role of the generalized other and accepts its perceived judgment of oneself as morally inadequate" (Shott, 1979: 1325).

Although perhaps less evident that what we have seen in relation to Shott, Mead's influence is also traceable in the reflections of Thomas Scheff. Scheff is certainly one of the most influential American sociologists still active and, like Shott, he is an exponent of the interactionist approach to the study of emotions. During his long academic career, Scheff has devoted his attention not only to emotions but also to mental illness, restorative justice, and collective violence.

In this case, Mead's influence can be seen above all in Sheff's reflections on shame. The theme of shame involves nearly the totality of Scheff's scientific production (2004; 2003; 2000; 1996; 1995) but the most significant of his contributions which illustrate his fundamental theses are probably *Shame and the Social Bond* (2000) and *Shame in Self and Society* (2003). As with Shott, here too, Mead's influence reverberates primarily in the idea of understanding shame as a cognitive objectification of others' attitudes toward oneself. Scheff's sociological theory of shame turns around two large hypotheses. The first is that shame comprises an extended family of emotions. The second is that shame represents a feeling of threat to the strength of the *social bond* (Scheff, 2004; 2003; 2000). In Scheff, shame becomes an extended family of emotions that includes within it embarrassment, shyness, feelings of inadequacy or failure, and humiliation in the broad sense. The common denominator of all these different emanations of the same root emotion consists in the recognition that shame is to be considered a manifestation of a threat to the social bond. Indeed, as a potential threat to the social bond, shame cannot be conceptually disjoined from the emotional or semi-emotional fields akin to it. Scheff thus proposes a broad sociological interpretation of shame.

What inevitably signals the emergence of shame is not self-reflection in and of itself but self-reflection as a social process tied to others' reactions to us. In Scheff's notion of shame, and here the reference to Mead is evident, we see ourselves through the eyes of others. At the same time, the various meanings that we ourselves attribute to others' reactions to us will affect the manifestations of this basic emotion. As Scheff writes, we are ashamed to show ourselves as evasive in the eyes of an extremely competent person, or to show ourselves fearful in the eyes of a brave person, and so on. Shame and pride participate in a process of imagination and anticipation of others' judgments of ourselves (Scheff, 2000).

The affinities between Shott and Scheff are evident, above all in the social construction of emotions, which is mediated by the process of *role-taking* and the possibility, recognized in the role-taker, to creatively appropriate himself of what has been socially given, conserving margins of interpretation and the autonomous attribution of meaning. Furthermore, both Shott and Scheff display an underlying concern for the conditions that ensure the endurance of the social bond. The points of contact between the two authors are obviously tied to a shared and more or less explicitly acknowledged Meadian influence.

## 9.5 The social character of instinct

The general aspects of Mead's social theory recalled in section one allow us to understand clearly how it is possible to interpret emotional subjectivity as a social outcome, and how it can be deduced from a general conception of the *Self* understood as a dimension co-extensive with the social process itself (Côté, 2016; Engdahl, 2005; McCharty, 1992). The person who feels and expresses emotions constitutes himself in the social process within which human experience unfolds. Our emotions are acquired, therefore, through a process of identification with others, in complete harmony with the other general elements of Mead's social theory. The identification with others, however, must be viewed as a process of decentration, or as a continuous willingness to readjust one's own action in reference to others. In this sense, the definition of the social character of emotional subjectivity that can be deduced from Median social theory leads us back to some of the concepts we have already discussed. To take just one as an example, we could say that the socially emotive level proper to the dynamic of the assumption of others' attitudes towards ourselves can be understood to coincide with the *I* component of the self. The *I*, in this sense, can be interpreted, in emotional terms, as a disposition to an open-ended resynchronization with others' reactions to ourselves by, for example, a bodily or expressive readjustment. While such an adjustment does not amount to a cognitive dimension – proper instead to the *Me* component – it presents a social connotation not reducible to a merely organic or biological – instinctive component.

As mentioned above, Mead's work does not include a proper systematic theory of emotions. For this reason, Mead's conception of emotions must be deduced both from the central conceptual elements of his social theory, and from some essays devoted specifically to the theme of emotions. We will examine two of those essays, in particular, *The Social Character of Instinct* and *Emotion and Instinct*, analysing several of their key passages. We will proceed by citing ample passages from the essays, which will be accompanied by some brief comments. The essays in question are not dated, though presumably they were written between 1892 and 1910 (Carreira da Silva, 2007), and remained unpublished until 2001, when they were included in *Essays in Social Psychology*, edited by Mary Jo Deegan.

> The primitive instincts of the human animal are practically all social. It is at best a difficult task to isolate and define human instincts, but whatever group one gathers together is bound to refer to conduct that is determined by the movements of other individuals whose conduct is like our own. In fact, the earlier history of the race and the history of childhood shows us that primitive consciousness even of the physical world is social, and only becomes a physical consciousness with the growing powers of reflection.
> (Mead, 2017a: 3)

Mead begins the essay entitled *The Social Character of Instinct* with a statement of his thesis that human instincts are all to be considered – in terms of practical activity, linked, that is, to the concrete actions of human beings – as social in nature. This is a rather radical and original thesis. Instincts, generally thought to be the expression *par excellence* of the organic component of human action, are interpreted here completely as social phenomena. Human instincts are elicited by the behaviour of the individuals with whom we share a social conduct, or rather a way of acting coordinated by common meanings, as explained in section one. The other main theme stated in the opening of Mead's essay, obviously tied to the first, also has a social genesis, and is not rooted in a merely biological or organic dimension.

Within this field of social consciousness arise gradually objects — social objects, the selves, the me, and the others. I wish to discuss for a few moments the process by which these objects arise. That these instinctive social processes are intimately connected with the emotions, that many of the so-called expressions of the emotions are vestiges or early stages of instinctive reactions, has been recognized in all psychological treatment of the emotions and the instincts, but, so far as I know, the function which these expressions of the emotions may have in the process of mediating social conduct and then in forming the objects within social consciousness has not been adequately studied.

(Mead, 2017a: 4)

Mead's intention in this essay is to demonstrate the central function of emotions in the social process. The passage cited above helps us to see quite clearly that, in Mead, there is no important difference between instinct and emotion. Indeed, at times these are proper synonyms even from the semantic point of view. Emotions are an integral part of social conduct and, as such, are the expression of a fundamental disposition to act by continually readjusting one's own behaviour in accordance with others' reactions. This instinctive–emotional interactive disposition plays a decisive role in the emergence of social consciousness, or rather in the constitution of social objects, among which is the *Self*, the general theory of whose genesis we discussed at length in section one.

We have already defined social conduct as that in which the acts are adjusted to the movements of others. Perfection of adjustment implies response to the earliest indications of the overt act. Just as the fencer reads in the eye of his opponent the coming thrust and is ready with the parry before the thrust is made, so we are continually reading from the attitude, the facial expressions, the gestures, and the tones of the voice the coming actions of those with reference to whom we must act. Such beginnings of acts, and organic preparations for action, which have been called expressions of emotion, are just the cues which have been selected and preserved as the means of mediating social conduct. Before conscious communication by symbols arises in gestures, signs, and articulate sounds, there exists in these earliest stages of acts and their physiological fringes the means of co-ordinating social conduct, the means of unconscious communication. And conscious communication has made use of these very expressions of the emotion to build up its signs. They were already signs. They had been already naturally selected and preserved as signs in unreflective social conduct before they were specialized as symbols.

(Mead, 2017a: 5)

Manifestations of emotions accompany bodily changes or the enactment of not completely conscious gestures, and they trace complex of reciprocal actions and reactions that are an integral part of social conduct, even though – as in the case of Mead's two fencers – they are still not completely reflexive. This means that the expression of emotions comes in some way to be sensed by the person who feels them, albeit without necessarily reaching full awareness of the emotion that he is feeling. Indeed, the reading of the other's emotional reactions should not be understood as a complex cognitive interpretation, similar to the production of a reflexively elaborated meaning. At the same time as we sense the other's emotional reaction, we give rise to an emotional reaction even before reflexively elaborating the content of our feeling. For this reason, Mead suggests that consciousness is already emotively constituted in social terms even before being developed by way of an intersubjective communication made up of sounds and symbols articulated in cognitively more determined forms, on the way to achieving linguistically complete interaction. The emotive basis of consciousness precedes its linguistic basis because it is the outcome of an open-ended process of continuous readjustment to the reactions of others to our emotive manifestations. The emotively social nature of our conduct can then extend itself in forms that present a fully cognitive content, such as spoken language.

The idea of social conduct as a progressive open-ended process suggests that linguistically reflexive communication – the conscious use of language – plants its roots in the emotive dimension and is then articulated in increasingly determinate forms. The emotions are a fundamental component of a pre-linguistic phase of intersubjective communication. They are the expression of an only partially reflexive social conduct that, in a subsequent phase of its unfolding, extended above all to linguistic communication, acquires a more reflexively determined symbolic character. This process is confirmed in rather explicit terms in the following passage.

> In the first place, the emotional consciousness belongs at the beginning of the reflective process. It comes before the possibility of thought or of reflective action (...) It is the earliest stuff out of which objects can be built in the history of presentative consciousness, and this earliest instinctive consciousness is primarily social.
>
> (Mead, 2017a: 6)

Emotive consciousness precedes cognitive consciousness. The emotions are the raw material of consciousness, which is instinctive and social at the same time. It could be said, then, that emotive consciousness already has an intentional connotation. We use the term intentional here only to emphasize that consciousness is directed toward something; it addresses itself to social objects. Consciousness is *consciousness of something*. It has its own content which is content is fundamentally social, even if it is not yet fully defined in cognitive terms. The primary content of consciousness is a content of feeling, Mead writes, adding, however, that this primary content is not sensorial. What we feel upon seeing the attitudes of others is not merely the body, or the face, of the other, but rather the imminent acts that they are about to commit. There is not, therefore, in the conception of consciousness deducible from Mead's reflections on emotions in *The Social Character of Instinct*, a contraposition between the social sphere and the instinctive sphere, on the one hand, and between feeling and cognition, on the other. At the same time, there is no evidence of a contraposition between the emotion and cognition.

## 9.6 Emotion and instinct

The essay entitled *Emotion and Instinct* is a shorter and less-developed composition. Mead examines the relationship between emotions and interest, recognizing the essentially emotive character of interest. In this case, too, it would seem that emotions and interest constitute two phases of the social act.

> There is, however, another side to this investigation that promises more valuable and interesting results, and that is the relation between the emotions and interest. We recognize the essentially emotional character of interest, but the affinity and the developmental relationship between them is not so plain. One distinction between them is evident almost at the first view. This is their positions within the act. Interest underlies the going after and struggle for the end, while the emotion characterizes the immediate grasping and enjoyment of the object sought.
> (Mead, 2017b: 27)

The two dimensions, interest and emotions, are phases of the social act involved in the unfolding of the relationship between the individual and the individual's desired object. Mead recognizes the emotional nature of interest, but also appreciates a fundamental difference that distinguishes emotions from interest. The emotion "characterizes the immediate grasping and enjoyment of the object sought", and interest instead "underlies the going after and struggle for the end" (Mead, 2017a, 2017b: 27).

> In each of these cases, and this applies to all actions in so far as they are predominantly passionate, the consciousness is occupied with the emotion and the activity approaches reflex action, and in all of these cases the emotion answers to the immediate presence of and appropriation of the object sought — an appropriation that takes place by means of instinctive processes that are not present in consciousness as means to an end, but as parts of the end and resultant itself.
> (Mead, 2017a, 2017b: 27–28)

Both emotions and interest are phases of a social act through which the individual relates to the desired object, but the emotion, in so far as it is passionate, has to do with the tension toward the gradual overcoming of the obstacles placed between the individual and the desired object. This essay, too, highlights the progressively dynamic character of the social dimension of emotions, which, starting from an instinctive basis of immediate appropriation of desired objects, can become a means for achieving increasingly complex objectives, or, even better, as Mead writes, it can constitute "that in which intelligence is chiefly expressed" (Mead, 2017a, 2017b: 29). The essay reiterates the same idea that underlies *The Social Character of Instinct*, namely, emotions are at the same time socially instinctive and cognitively intelligent. Emotions are both instinctive and cognitive.

The conceptually characteristic element of the essay is that emotions are definable as social on a less determinate level than interests. The social dimension of interest is more defined, emotions involve an immediate appropriation of the object to which they are oriented, while interest marks a *more intelligent* distance from the same object. In this sense, interests become means for achieving more articulated and more complex goals.

> The passions of one period are the reservoirs of the interests of those that follow it. It also follows that the interest is much more definitely social in its organization than is the emotion. For the appropriation has a most direct individual evaluation, but the intelligent act, must, in so far as it is objective, partake of the social organism of which the form is a metaphor.
>
> (Mead, 2017a, 2017b: 29)

If, that is, emotion absorbs consciousness in its entirety, the action directed toward an object may be compromised, if not totally blocked. If, instead, the emotional tension manages to channel itself into forms of acting orientated toward the pursuit of an interest, the act can successfully be carried to completion. Impassioned emotion, that is, leaves room for its reflexive articulation, which accompanies the completion of the act previously or potentially interrupted by excessive emotive tension.

To conclude this section, we wish to propose an example to better explain the fundamental dynamic involved in the relationship among social act, emotion, and interest. Let's return to the emotion of shame, mentioned above in the discussion of Shott and Scheff. Take the more circumscribed example of the shame felt by a person evicted from his home, having lost his job and hence no longer able to pay his rent. If the shame he feels should absorb his consciousness in its entirety, the manifestation of that emotion could transform itself into a form of humiliation that precludes any kind of action directed towards overcoming this problematic situation. If, instead, the shame does not totally absorb his consciousness, but actually finds an outcome by channelling itself into new forms of social action, it may solicit the concrete pursuit of an interest, such as, for example, looking for adequate alternative housing.

## 9.7 Conclusion

The conception of emotions that can be deduced from Mead's writings outlines an approach that can be defined as non-dualist and anti-reductionist. Meadian anti-dualism, as we have seen, is rooted both in the general principles of his social theory, which outline the relationship between the individual and society, and in the definition of a socially mediated relationship between bodily feelings and the cognitive dimension of human conduct. These dimensions, far from being dualistically separated, are, in fact, linked by their belonging to a socially interactive sphere, of which the emotions are the original and fundamental element. As we have outlined in this chapter, for Mead, emotions undergo an open-ended and progressive unfolding. They are the product of a continual decentration, of an unceasing disposition to assuming the attitudes of the other participant in the interaction. Emotions emerge socially and unfold open-endedly in the pragmatic development of human activity, as an anticipation of reciprocal reactions.

In conclusion, we can synthesize in what follows Mead's main contribution to the study of emotions as we have discussed it in this chapter: linguistically mediated and cognitively reflective human communication is always rooted in the social nature of primitive instincts, whose affective content is represented by emotions. The interactive material of emotions constitutes a non-reflexive social act that precedes the specialization of this same material in more socially determined symbols and cognitions. Emotions are not, therefore, completely private – they do not belong to the sphere of the inner experience of the individual – nor are they completely externalized, or definable as social solely in terms of cultural constructions connected to social beliefs, norms, and roles. The social nature of emotions is essentially the outcome of an extended complex of intersubjective relationships, which are the foundation of human social acts within the world.

## References

Blumer, H. (1969) *Symbolic Interactionism: Perspective and Method.* Berkeley, CA: University of California Press.
Blumer, H. (1981) *George Herbert Mead.* In B. Rhea (ed.), *The Future of the Sociological Classics.* London: George Allen and Unwin, 136–169.
Calcaterra, R. (2003) *Pragmatismo: i valori dell'esperienza.* Roma: Carocci.
Carreira da Silva, F. (2006) G.H. Mead in the History of Sociological Ideas. *Journal of the History of the Behavioral Sciences,* 42(1), 19–39.
Carreira da Silva, F. (2007) *G.H. Mead. A Critical Introduction.* Cambridge: Polity Press.

Cook, G. A. (1993) *George Herbert Mead: The Making of a Social Pragmatist*. Urbana-Chicago: University of Illinois Press.

Côté, J.-F. (2016) *George Herbert Mead's Concept of Society: A Critical Reconstruction*. London and New York: Routledge.

Deegan, M.-J. (2017) *Introduction*. In G. H. Mead, *Essays in Social Psychology*. Edited by M.-J. Deegan. Abingdon and New York: Routledge, 11–44.

Engdahl, E. (2005) *A Theory of the Emotional Self*. Örebro: Örebro University Press.

Habermas, J. (1987) *Theory of Communicative Action, Volume Two: Lifeworld and System: A Critique of Functionalist Reason*. Boston: Beacon Press.

Hochschild, A. (1979) Emotion Work, Feeling Rules and Social Structure. *American Journal of Sociology*, 85(3), 551–575.

Huebner, D. R. (2014) *Becoming Mead: The Social Process of Academic Knowledge*. Chicago: Chicago University Press.

Huebner, D. R. (2015) *Appendix*. In G. H Mead, *Mind, Self, and Society. The Definitive Edition*. Edited by C.W. Morris, Annotated Edition by D.R. Huebner and H. Joas. Chicago: Chicago University Press, 391–487.

Joas, H. (1997) *G. H. Mead. A Contemporary Re-examination of His Thought*. Cambridge: MIT Press.

McCarthy, E.D. (1992) *Emotions are Social Things: An Essay in the Sociology of Emotions*. In D.D. Franks and E.D. McCarthy (eds), *The Sociology of Emotions: Original Essays and Research Papers*. Greenwich: JAI Press, 51–72.

Mead, G.H. (1910) What Social Objects Mmust Psychology Presuppose? *Journal of Philosophy, Psychology and Scientific Methods*, 7, 174–180.

Mead, G.H. (1912) The Mechanism of Social Consciousness. *Journal of Philosophy, Psychology and Scientific Methods*, 9, 401–406.

Mead, G.H. (1932) *The Philosophy of the Present*. Edited by A.E. Murphy. Chicago-La Salle: Open Court Publishing.

Mead, G.H. (1936) *Movements of Thought in the Nineteenth Century*. Edited by M.H. Moore. Chicago: University of Chicago Press.

Mead, G.H. (1938) *The Philosophy of the Act*. Edited by C.W. Morris, J.M. Brewster, A.M. Dunham, and D.L. Miller. Chicago: University of Chicago Press.

Mead, G.H. (2015) *Mind, Self, and Society. The Definitive Edition*. Edited by C.W. Morris, Annotated Edition by D.R. Huebner and H. Joas. Chicago: Chicago University Press

Mead, G.H. (2017a) *The Social Character of Instinct*. In G.H. Mead, *Essays in Social Psychology*. Edited by M.-J. Deegan. London-New York: Routledge.

Mead, G.H. (2017b) *Emotion and Instinct*. In G.H. Mead, *Essays in Social Psychology*. Edited by M.-J. Deegan. London-New York: Routledge.

Morris, C.W. (2015) *Introduction*. In G.H Mead, *Mind, Self, and Society. The Definitive Edition*. Edited by C.W. Morris, Annotated Edition by D.R. Huebner and H. Joas. Chicago: Chicago University Press, 17–43.

Scheff, T. (1995) Shame and Related Emotions: Overview. *American Behavioral Scientist*, 38 (8), 1053–1059.

Scheff, T. (1996) Self-esteem and shame: Unlocking the puzzle. In R. Kwan, *Individuality and Social Control: Essays in Honour of Tiamotsu Shibutani*. Greenwich, CT: JAI Press.

Scheff, T. (2000) Shame and the Social Bond. *Sociological Theory*, 18, 84–99.
Scheff, T. (2003) Shame in Self and Society. *Symbolic Interaction*, 2, 239–262.
Scheff, T. (2004) Elias, Freud and Goffman: Shame as the master emotion. In S. Loyal and S. Quilley (eds), *The Sociology of Norbert Elias*. Cambridge: Cambridge University Press.
Shott, S. (1979) Emotion and Social Life: A Symbolic Interactionist Analysis. *American Journal of Sociology*, 84(6), 1337–1334.

# Chapter 10

# Norbert Elias

*Gabriela Vergara*

## 10.1 Introduction

The social processes that characterize the twenty-first century offer an excellent opportunity to produce theories and methodologies that are capable of addressing this complexity, intensity and speed. But this task cannot be carried out in a satisfactory way without taking into account other theories and researches that were previously constructed, even in other contexts.

We live in a time that is marked by the unavoidable presence of digital societies that configure particular sensibilities in relation to time/space, transform the world of labour and consumption (through marketing and e-commerce), but also work reproductively in homes and educational institutions. We are also witnessing a sustained deployment of social movements that fight against racial and gender violence, ranging from those who seek recognition of the multiple ways of living sexuality, to the constant demands of gender equality. However, migratory processes, the increasing number of people who rely on social policies, the increasing number of people in general (and children in particular) who live in conditions of malnutrition and die due to poverty, are stressed in the intersection with the marketization of the affective and turn bodies/emotions into a central node for the whole of social sciences and, specifically, for sociology, from which to approach different processes, practices and experiences (Scribano, 2018).

It is, in this scenario, where the Norbert Elias's work can be brought into this century[1] to re-think and update a set of categories, relationships between concepts, and ways of seeing sociology itself. At least three assumptions support this assertion:

1 First, because his sociohistorical studies made it possible to connect processes of vast scope with others of a reduced scale. This makes it possible to transcend the macro/micro dichotomy and, at the same time, constitutes a contribution to qualitative methodologies, as they enable the investigation of significant experiences, not because of their quantitative

manifestation, but because of what their dimensions "say" about the processes of social structuring.
2   Secondly, because their analyses within their own configurations and networks of interdependencies, renew the ways of thinking about corporeity, emotions and the in-corporated social. In this way, it is possible to transcend the inner/outer dichotomy, that between individual/society, thereby enabling a way to understand that all subjectivity is inter-subjectively constituted.
3   Third, because in the provocative dialogue with other disciplines (such as history or biology), his works invite us to problematize, in epistemological and ontological terms, the split between nature and society, which, precisely, becomes a theoretical, ethical and politics problem when we think about the effects of capitalism in its configuration and maintenance (the COVID-19 pandemic relieves us of making further explanations in this regard).

These assumptions compel us to revisit this theoretical work, to which it is possible to make a brief connection with Elias' biography, even more so if we think about it from the standpoint of a sociology of bodies/emotions.

Norbert Elias's life, crossed by world wars and most especially Nazism, led him to feel marginalized in England, without a place or a voice. A trajectory plagued with intermittences and troubles characterizes this sociologist (Béjar, 1994), who presents a particular theoretical perspective which makes it difficult to situate him within a particular social current. His closeness to certain German thinkers allowed him to build his own special view of social processes. This was possible by his carefully neutrality, resulting from an exercise of distancing with which he sought to separate ideologies of science. For this reason, while Parsons elaborated a theory of North American society and the Frankfurt theorists, exiled in the United States, criticized the paradoxes of the Enlightenment, Elias delved into history to find answers that would allow him to understand – and somehow endure – the horrible present in which he had to live. And his perspective of history also implied strengthening his analysis of social processes, then discussing great figures of history with historians, as proposed in "The court society".

Perhaps for this reason, Elias's biography can be read from the categories that he himself elaborated for the analysis of the social in terms of "established/marginalized". And in this sense, he can no longer be considered an "outsider" in his own sociological field because the themes of his work became important to other thinkersers (Smith, 1984). Its relevance is maintained, both by the dilemmas it causes to constructivist and realist epistemologies, and by the new sociological areas in which its thought can be applied, such as the case of race, as well as his different views on the relationship between biology and sociology (Newton, 2006).

In his "return to the scene" at the end of the 60s, he presented himself as an intellectual who sought to transcend the modes of thought of the sociological positions of the time. This was evident in his intense work during the decades that followed, which were reflected in a set of writings that connect sociology with history and psychiatry, and deepens the view in terms of a sociology of knowledge, in relation to emotions, with the state and with groups (Smith, 2009).

Theoretical proposal of Elias then, sought to build an object of study for sociology, starting from the figurations or configurations, highlighting the place of the processes. For this reason, it was located as an alternative to the Parsonian view of the social condensed in the notion of "system". In this context, bodies, emotions, affections, and networks of interdependencies form a theoretical web that is difficult to split, but that, for analytical and expository purposes, we have decided to organize as explained below.

In the first place, we will describe the social construction of the body, based on the concepts of *process and figurations*, which allow us to understand how, simultaneously, social transformations are becoming a body in the subjects, who reproduce through socialization, naturalized patterns of behaviour generating conditions for the unintended unfolding of the great civilizing process.

Second, we show the main transformations in the subjective world of individuals, based on shame and displeasure, emotions defined in terms of social fears that allow behaviour to be adjusted to the parameters of what is acceptable and expected for the social group.

Third, connecting the two previous analytical axes, we will return to the place of emotions in social regulation, which operates explicitly in subjects, as well as implicitly in the conditioning that marks these configurations.

The plot that is formed between these three dimensions accounts for the intrinsic relationship between social processes, interdependencies, practices and emotions and, in this way, allows us to problematize from a critical viewpoint, how bodies/emotions can be a central node for domination. This is one of the places where we consider it relevant to reread part of Elias's work, with the aim of dwelling on some of his analyses and concepts, in order to find theoretical contributions for a sociology of bodies/emotions (Scribano, 2012).

As we noted elsewhere (Scribano and Vergara, 2009), "re-visiting" Elias's thought allow us to understand the functioning of social support mechanisms and the devices for regulating the sensations that become bodies/emotions in the processes of social production/reproduction.

## 10.2 The social construction of the body

For Elias, the body has been a crucial place to observe social transformations in the long term. In analysing European society across three centuries, he noted deep changes in customs, habits, routines, manners, and daily gestures.

The body was transformed along with the emotions and affections, but this was also possible, because emotions become actions.

The civilizing process, at the level of individuals, involved important changes in the behaviour and sensibilities of people, which were mainly focused on the passage from external social constraints to internal constraints. The physical/corporal needs were increasingly hidden from the social gaze due to the generalized presence of emotional forms of self-control.

From the Erasmus of Rotterdam's book (*De civilitate morum puerilium*), Elias elucidate that these are general norms that are not intended for a particular social class, but by observing them he began to understand how throughout the centuries a whole set of patterns from eating to blowing one's nose gradually expanded:

> More clearly than by inspecting particular accounts of contemporary manners, by surveying the whole movement one sees how it advanced (...) And, like the handkerchief. The napkin had also appeared already, both still -a symbol of transition- as optional rather than necessary implements: if you have a handkerchief, the precepts say, use it rather than your fingers. If a napkin is provided, lay it over your left shoulder. One hundred and fifty years later both napkin and handkerchief had, like the fork, become more or less indispensable utensils in the courtly class.
> 
> (Elías, 2000: 91)

Bodily fluids and food find decent social and slowly established forms (first in distinguished social circles, then moving towards bourgeois classes) by which the body itself learns to use objects as mediations. However, hands and noses, the senses of touch and smell, have become socially modified in the long term. People must learn to use new mediations with the world, and with these mediations, increased self-constraints of biological needs. To eat and breathe, to take objects and smell them, are basic functions of a body. But in human societies these practices turn into new ways to live with others.

And, if on an historical level, Elias manages to account for the socialization of the body, of the incorporation of society into daily practices within the framework of the civilizing process, on a conceptual level he manages to show, early in the twentieth century, that the dichotomies of individual/society on the one hand and freedom/determination on the other, are diluted under a relational gaze:

> (...) a scientific debate that claims something more than mere affirmations about 'freedom' and 'determination', must start with what can be observed effectively, that is, multiple men who are more or less dependent on each other and, at the same time, more or less autonomous, that is, who govern themselves in their mutual relationships. As long as a man

> lives and is healthy, he possesses, even if he is a prisoner or a slave, a certain autonomy, a field of action within which he can and must make decisions. On the contrary, even autonomy, even the field of action of the most powerful king has fixed limits; it is involved in a network of dependencies whose structure can be precisely defined.
>
> (Elias, 1996: 48; own translation)

Social interactions not only dilute the image of the individual-in-society, but also warn about the ways in which conditions and possible openings coexist, something that we will return to at the end of this chapter. Social regulation and constraints are a basic feature of social life, and the bodies are the "locus" of this control. Socially constructed bodies have social life because they are configured in a network of interdependencies. But it is neither absolute nor complete. There is always a space to create other practices with other subjects, in what Scribano (2009) defined as "interstitial practices".

Now, the subjects who carry a body with life and health, occupy social positions from which their actions and practices are configured. The body is socially constructed on a physical basis and, in general, acquires specific ways of learning to act in the groups of which it is a part. For this reason, in the research of court society,

> the analyses are aimed at elaborating the interdependencies of the individuals that form a court society and, in some specific cases, especially in that of Louis XIV himself, at showing the way in which an individual man uses the field of decisions that his position grants him, within a specific configuration, in the strategy to direct his personal conduct.
>
> (Elias, 1996: 49; own translation)

The quote gives an account of the social and structural dimension of the bodies that act according to the place they occupy in the social space or, rather, in a configuration; their decisions and behaviours depend on that web of interdependencies in which they are immersed.

From this conceptual level, the social made body reappears as part of those interactions, when we see it from empirical researches. Within a particular figuration, the corporal dimension expresses the social conditioning, and through it, it is possible to preserve, in certain situations, places of legitimacy or power. For example, in court society, the gaze and observation – which also served as self-observation – contributed to the manipulation of others. In other words, the senses of the body, also socialized, are inscribed in the interdependencies of a particular configuration, where each movement and gesture acquired new meanings within the power relations of the courtly world. In this way, clear distinctions were also made with respect to other social groups, both noble and bourgeois.

Elias gives an account of this relationship between bodies and social groups:

> Their existence as rentiers made possible and forced, for example, elegance in bearing and good taste in the sense of their mature social tradition, as conditions to be included and promoted in their society.
>
> (Elias, 1996: 155)

The duality of the verbs used in the quotation – "make possible" and "force" – updates the interest in not being trapped in sterile dichotomies. But it also accounts for how interdependencies operate in and through bodies. Specifically, of the acceptable ways to dispose, present, and manifest before others. The quote also allows us to consider that there are different kinds of bodies in society, according to social position and condition, not only as a way to be distinguished, but also as a clear example of how society becomes a body, in an imperceptible way, in everyday life.

On the contrary, in the nineteenth century, the bourgeoisie were conditioned by their profession:

> which required a more or less regulated job and a great routine in affections. Thus the conduct of men and their relationship with each other were formed in the first place from profession. Here was the center of the constraints that the social interdependencies of men exerted on individuals.
>
> (Elias, 1996: 155; own translation)

The profession organizes times and practices but also affections, an aspect that we will develop in the next section. In other words, according to the position occupied, you will have a regulated body, you will have specific disposition to perform, to feel and to perceive the world. Taste, dressing, routines, and the senses are all different dimensions connected to the body that are transformed by social configurations and social process.

Following the above, we can indicate that bodies have three possible places of construction from life (and this supposes an ontogenesis, which for Elias did not have great changes): the powerful long-term processes that allow us to notice transformations in gestures, dispositions, and habits. Therefore, it is in the specificity of a particular configuration that, according to the position occupied and the interdependencies that exist there, bodies are also moulded according to these conditions, but also offer a possible path to freedom.

Finally, we must explain that what makes this social learning possible is the very body structure of human beings, who, like the rest of the species, are born and die, but who differ since,

> without having acquired a body of social knowledge they cannot survive or even become human. In fact, they are biologically constituted in such

a way that it is both possible and necessary for them to orient themselves through learned knowledge.

(Elias, 1998: 304; own translation)

Bodies can be social because they are biologically determined for a social learning process that operates on the body itself and on emotions. This axiom is very important because it allows us to make the very idea of the social construction of the body more complex, since it does not occur in a vacuum, from nothing, but from a real, concrete, biological structure, created and not created by human beings. Overcoming the dichotomies between the sciences and opening a new conduit to think the social in a biologically human way, Elias hypothesizes from the emotions as a privileged, if not the only, place to find the specificity of the human.

## 10.3 Emotions in interactions

Social interactions are not only articulated from the whole set of knowledge, dispositions, movements and gestures apprehended and incorporated socially, but also imply the presence of emotions that sustain, organize and give meaning to such practices. In this sense, Elias identified that one of the first qualities of the bonds that the subjects establish among themselves within the configurations are affective. Beyond sexual relations, there is another class of long-lasting, stable emotional stimuli:

> some of which find a solid bond and anchor and others, on the contrary, remain free and unsatisfied, in search of bonding and anchoring in other people. The concept of affective valences oriented towards other people offers a fruitful starting point in the attempt to substitute the image of man as homo clausus with that of the 'open man'.
> 
> (Elias 1995a: 163; own translation)

Affective valences allow us to demonstrate that social relationships are not characterized by sexual encounters but instead by emotional ties that are characterized by a greater permanence. This is exemplified by the loss of a loved one, which does not imply an absence of someone outside the self, but on the contrary,

> it means that he loses a part of himself. One of the valences of the figuration of his satisfied and unsatisfied valences had fixed her on the other person. And this person has died. An integral part of himself, of his image in terms of 'me and us' also disappears.
> 
> (Elias 1995a: 164; own translation)

The relationality of the affects is positioned in the interstices of subjectivity and intersubjectivity – which are assembled from the image of said bond – as more here of the social made body, expanding we could say, to the plane of a socially made body/emotion.

As an object of study, it is not enough to inquire into interpersonal or work relationships, but rather this concept of valences or affective ties occupies an important place within the framework, be it these small groups or larger communities, such as nations. In the latter case, emotional ties are expressed through symbolism (flags, shields, hymns, among others), accounting for a larger-scale I–us relationship. This assumes that the affective dimension – in accordance with his approach – is not something "internal" to the subject, but is embedded in the relational dynamics itself, in the network of interdependencies.

In this same sense, emotions are present and are socially configured within the webs of configurations, generating a dynamic that becomes more complex with the increase in interdependencies. Emotions have three components: a somatic component (involuntary physiological reactions such as the speed of digestion or the heartbeat), a behavioural component (a motor dimension, such as "fight or flight") and a feeling component. Combining non-learned forms with those learned human behaviours has displayed the greatest diversity according to previous situations and experiences. Life with others made it possible to mould the ways of expressing emotions, such as laughter (Elias, 1998).

When we review history, we notice that modifications in the psychic apparatus were possible due to the intensification of the division of functions, which accentuated the dependency among people. With this, the individuals had to adjust their modes of action in terms of greater regularity and stability, combining conscious self-constraints together with others that, instilled from childhood, became unconscious and automatic. This made it possible to achieve a level of behaviour that was considered to be socially correct.

The most visible place of orientation of the civilizing process lies in the habits and customs of human beings, not only in their way of reasoning and reflecting, but also in their feelings and passions, since changes in affective structures correspond to changes in the rationalization of consciousness.

In the framework of the civilizing process, where it is evident that the body is socially constructed, an emotional dimension is present, neither parallel nor superimposed, but intrinsic to the corporal. In other words,

> (…) an automatic, blindly functioning apparatus of self-control is firmly established. This seeks to prevent offences to socially acceptable behavior by a wall of deep-rooted fears.
>
> (Elías, 2000: 368)

Shame, along with scruples, are central components of this great transformation. For Elias:

> The feeling of shame is a specific excitation, a kind of anxiety which is automatically reproduced in the individual on certain occasions by force of habit.
>
> (Elias, 2000: 415)

From this analysis, shame can be seen in two ways. In the first place:

> (...) it is fear of social degradation or, more generally, of other people's gestures of superiority.
>
> (Elias, 2000: 415)

This means that shame can be equated to a feeling of inferiority or humiliation, which is inscribed in the interdependencies of a particular configuration and depends on the positions occupied within it. For this reason, it is activated from a superior gaze that reveals interdependent relationships crossed by subordination and submission. It is worth highlighting here the complex plot that is put together between bodies/emotions, between looks, social places and shame.

In this sense, it is understood that, for example in court society, the modesty linked to the presentation of the naked body depended on areas of subordination within the groups. Thus, the King could take off his clothes before his ministers or, the man in front of the woman – the superior before the inferior – while generating "(...) no feeling of inferiority or shame" (Elias, 2000: 417). It could even mean condescension and a benevolent attitude. On the contrary "Exposure by someone of lower rank before a superior, or even before people of equal rank, is banished more and more from social life as a sign of lack of respect" (Elias, 2000: 418), as a transgression of the norms that causes fear.

Second, at the level of the subjective body, shame for Elias reveals an internal conflict between the desire for self-defence and the emergence of socially incorporated prohibitions:

> But it is a form of displeasure or fear which arises characteristically on those occasions when a person who fears lapsing into inferiority can avert this danger neither by direct physical means nor by any other form of attack (...) this defencelessness results from the fact that the people whose superiority one fears are in accord with one's own super-ego, with the agency of self-constraint implanted in the individual by others on whom he was dependent, who possessed power and superiority over him.
>
> (Elías, 2000: 415)

In this sense, shame supposes a conflict that occurs, as we mentioned in the paragraphs above, in the interstices of subjectivity/intersubjectivity. It manifests itself in the internal world – so to speak – and at the same time, it is stressed within the framework of certain differential relations of authority, which is why, despite its intensity:

> (...) it is never directly expressed in noisy gestures. Shame takes on its particular coloration from the fact that the person feeling it has done or is about to do something through which he comes into contradiction with people to whom he is bound in one form or another, and with himself, with the sector of his consciousness by which he controls himself.
> (Elías, 2000: 415)

Paradoxically, the non-expression of shame has to do with the high level of self-constraint and regulation of affections, as we will see in the next section.

In relation to society, shame, as a fear of transgressing social rules, clearly reveals the passage that operates in subjects from being sanctioned by others – coercion – to making such provisions their own. In this way, when self-constraint increases, there is tensity in the face of the possible social sanction that could be received, but above all:

> it is a conflict within his own personality; he himself recognizes himself as inferior. He fears the loss of the love or respect of others, to which he attaches or has attached value. Their attitude has precipitated an attitude within him that he automatically adopts towards himself.
> (Elías, 2000: 415)

When the subjects embody the norms, the social prohibitions, they no longer need a strictly physical punishment or sanction. But on many occasions, punishment goes unnoticed in interpersonal relationships, in intersubjectivity. This can trigger a conflict between will and duty.

Civilization then, not only supposes a greater rationalization, but there are also changes in the emotional barriers in two directions:

> a reduction in the direct physical fear of other beings, and of a consolidation of the automatic inner anxieties, the constraints which the individual now exerts on himself.
> (Elías, 2000: 416)

In this sense, we see that both emotions are socially constituted and therefore, vary according to space and time. Shame is not the same in a class society as in the bourgeoisie. Therefore, Elias considers that the continuous increase in the differentiation of functions that occurs in society, corresponds to the same differentiation within the subject:

> Both – the intensification of shame like the increased rationalization – are different aspects of the growing split in the individual personality that occurs with the increasing division of functions; they are different aspects of the growing differentiation between drives and drive-controls, between "id" and "ego" or "superego" functions.
>
> (Elias, 2000: 416)

In parallel to social changes, internal functions begin to display a double function:

> (…) the conduct at the same time at domestic policy and a foreign policy – which moreover, are not always in harmony and quite often are contradictory. This explains the fact that in the same socio-historical period in which rationalization made perceptible advances, an advance in the shame and repugnance threshold is also to be observed.
>
> (Elias, 2000: 416)

As a counterpart of shame, "Embarrassment is displeasure or anxiety which arises when another person threatens to breach, or breaches, society's prohibitions represented by one's own super-ego" (Elias 2000: 418). This is clearly seen, in the decline of the warrior class, which supposes greater self-control and, with it, greater levels of shame and displeasure, which are complemented by a greater pleasure from the gaze, from the observation, while emotions are contained:

> Just as the latter [shame] arises when someone infringes the prohibitions of his own self and of society, the former [embarrassment] occurs when something outside the individual impinges on his danger zone, on forms of behavior, objects, inclinations which have early on been invested with fear by his surroundings until this fear – in the manner of a conditioned reflex – is reproduced automatically in him on similar occasions.
>
> (Elias, 2000: 418)

Shame and displeasure reinforce socially accepted behaviours. They are emotions that appear as regulators of social relationships, and replace the sanction of physical punishment. Rationalization as foreign policy models the superego, while shame constitutes the reverse as domestic policy.

Elias's gaze on emotions also extends in relation to learning and possibilities, even as a kind of survival based on socially constructed and transmitted knowledge. This allows him to affirm that in the case of children, the learning of a language is possible "through relationships that involve both affection and emotions as well as intellect, that is, a relationship of 'affect-learning'" (Elias, 1998: 306).

Emotions are an important dimension in the social life of subjects, from when they are babies and while they are adults. Emotions and cognitive abilities make it possible to become a social, bodily subject and this body is the "locus" where this process is possible. So, emotions are in an intrinsic relationship with the body, with thought, with networks of interdependencies. They change over time, forming part of social processes. And once again, Elias affirms the complex way of understanding the real world: far from dichotomies.

After what has been explained in this section, we notice how emotions are socially constructed, like the body, from properly human biological structures, which they assemble at the behest of particular circumstances inscribed in social structuring processes and which have a preponderant role for social learning itself. These three dimensions allow us to analyse how they can be regulated.

## 10.4 The social regulation of emotions

In this third section we will realize a connection between the previous two that allows us to stress the categories proposed by Elias, in order to problematize social processes that operate in and through the bodies/emotions.

As we saw at the beginning, the civilizing process was a concrete change in the behavioural structures of the subjects, which can be observed from the correlation and parallelism between the modifications in the way of establishing control in societies – fundamentally the monopoly of physical violence and the collection of taxes by the State – and changes in the behavioural structures of the subjects. In relation to this last aspect, Elias specifically refers to a growing individual self-control, that is, to a passage "from external interhuman coercion into an individual self-coercion makes many affective impulses unable to find a channel of expression" (Elias, 1993: 41).

The growing deployment of these self-constraints, which come to work automatically, lead individuals to experience the presence of a wall that separates them from the rest of the people; a barrier that makes the interior of the subject impenetrable, now becoming a *homo clausus*, given "the firmer, more universal and more regular containment of the affects" (Elias, 1993: 42).

This control of emotions, inscribed in the large-scale civilizing process, was also identified in a particular social configuration, the court society that had little room for the expression of affections:

> Just as each one is compelled to seek, after the controlled and disguised outward behavior of others, his true motives and impulses, and he is lost, if after the dispassionate appearance of those who compete with him for opportunities for prestige, he is not able to constantly discover

the affections and interests that drive them, thus he must know his own passions in depth in order to be able, in truth, to cover them up.

(Elias, 1996: 143; own translation)

The game of looks, interpretation and self-observation is based on a double plot of emotions and actions, both on the outside and inside that are permanently mixed, depending on the position occupied in the configuration. What is acceptable and permitted in this way is not only the behaviours or actions, but also the emotions and affections that must be regulated:

> The charismatic boss directs his central group in the ascent, by virtue of the need for promotion, covering the risk and the anguish of the ascent, which frequently produces dizziness.
>
> (Elias, 1996: 169; own translation)

Whether you are a leader or a nobleman, the recognition of the regulation of one's own emotions and those of others is part and parcel of social interactions. Not only are they regulated on an institutional scale, restraining (or eliciting) violence by the State, but the subjects themselves embody in a practical, daily, habitual way the recognition of the emotional dimension in interactions. For this reason, pay attention to the recognition that the subjects themselves inscribed in this web of interdependencies make of emotions:

> "You must," he said to his son, "distribute your trust among many. The envy of one serves as a spur to the ambitions of others. But even if they hate each other, they nevertheless also have common interests and can, therefore, agree to deceive their master."
>
> (Lavisse, 1905, p. 167 cited in Elias, 1996: 175; own translation)

The quote offers at least two reading possibilities. The first referred to the upbringing and socialization around one's own handling of emotions, for who governs, leads and makes decisions, since both the interests in dispute according to the social positions and the emotional work at the same time. The second is in respect of how emotions act in their own networks of interdependencies. Not only shame and displeasure come together in the civilizing process, envy also occupies a key place among the unstable balances in human groups. Therefore, emotions interfere, are part of and configure actions and behaviours, while they must be controlled, observed, and interpreted to avoid conflicts. This is because emotions can become part of the strategies of power and domination, affecting unequally according to the positions occupied in particular configurations. Therefore, this dimension that Elias describes in court society enables us to transcend this specific area to question ourselves about how emotions are/can be regulated in society, whose structuring axes continue to be the expropriation of energy from common goods and at work, as well as consumption.

## 10.5 Final considerations

We have revisited a part of Norbert Elias's work from three analytical topics, in which the place of the social in the construction of the body, the relevance of emotions in daily actions, and the imperative of regulation or control have been highlighted according to the positions they occupy and the figurations in question.

Both in the long-term empirical researches of the civilizing process, or in that of a particular figuration, such as court society, as in its abstract and conceptual developments, we find epistemological, theoretical and empirical elements that consolidate the relationship between bodies/emotions.

In this framework, we consider that the social construction of emotions and their relationship with the practices of social agents find a central place for sociological theory and for a sociology of bodies/emotions from Norbert Elias's works. From his socio-historical studies about the relationships between shame and displeasure in the unfolding of the civilizing process, as well as his postulates about social figurations, this theory illustrates that the relationship between emotions-practices-bodies are fundamental for understanding social processes in terms of social structuring. That is, practices located in a space/time are inscribed and account for processes of vast scope, in which the emotions that generate interstices between subjectivity/intersubjectivity participate in an inherent and inseparable way.

Now, at this point, and considering the multiple challenges that the twenty-first century society faces, it is worth asking ourselves with Elias and from the standpoint of a sociology of bodies/emotions:

> What biological peculiarities are premises of variability and particularly of the ability to development of human societies?
> (Elias, 1995a: 127; own translation)

The question does not displace us from the theme developed in this chapter, but rather seeks to deepen it further.

A sociology of the bodies/emotions, cannot consider the social construction of the body only in terms of the acquisition of habits, norms and customs. From a realistic place of the human body (and returning to the epigraph from the beginning), Elias takes advantage of biology itself to condense his sociological thought:

> The extended learning device, favored in man by the development of the brain, the musculature of the throat and face and hands therefore have

as a condition a reduction, a withdrawal, so to speak, of the blind, automatic and innate direction of behavior.

(Elias, 1995a: 129; own translation)

The biological body itself, from which emotions are configured, makes it possible for society to become a body. As in an ellipsis, without determinisms, generating new dispositions within the framework of technological developments that metamorphose the spatial/temporal experiences of bodies and their sensibilities.

Here, we could stop and from a critical look at twenty-first century capitalism, return to the regulation of emotions within the framework of unequal relationships. The differential levels at which brains can develop given the conditions of poverty and malnutrition, the metamorphosis of hands with the intensification of digital society (where touch implies a basic function to the hands and fingers), together with the faces and throats made invisible by exploitation, alert us to the challenges of the social sciences. The close connections between bodies/emotions and the possible mechanisms of regulation of the latter that the author proposes, can serve as a possible way for the interpretation of processes of social structuring articulated in inequality, domination and exploitation of all species, human and non-human alike.

## Note

1  In other places we have started this work Cf. Scribano and Vergara (2009); Vergara (2009; 2010a; 2010b; 2014).

## References

Béjar, H. (1994) Norbert Elias, retrato de un marginado. *Revista Reis* No 65. Enero-Marzo 1994. Madrid. Available at: www.reis.cis.es/REIS/PDF/REIS_065_04.pdf . Accessed 24 May 2021.

Elias, N. (1993) *El proceso de la civilización*. Buenos Aires: Fondo de Cultura Económica.

———— (1996) *La sociedad cortesana*. México: Fondo de Cultura Económica.

———— (1995a) *Sociología Fundamental*. Barcelona: Gedisa.

———— (1995b) *Mi trayectoria intelectual*. Barcelona: Península.

———— (1998) *La civilización de los padres y otros ensayos*. Bogotá: Norma.

Elias, N. (2000) *The Civilizing Process. Sociogenetic and Psychogenetic Investigations*. Oxford: Blackwell Publishing.

Morrow, R. A. (2009). Norbert Elias and Figurational Sociology: The Comeback of the Century. *Contemporary Sociology*, 38(3), 215–219. Available at: https://doi.org/10.1177/009430610903800301

Newton, T. (2006). The Sociology of Norbert Elias. *Contemporary Sociology*, 35(3), 311–312. Available at: https://doi.org/10.1177/009430610603500359

Scribano, A. and Vergara G. (2009) Feos, sucios y malos: la regulación de los cuerpos y las emociones en Norbert Elias. *Revista Caderno CRH*. Universidade Federal da Bahia. V.22 N°56. Maio/Agosto, 411–422.

Scribano, A. y Figari, C. (2009) Cuerpo(s), Subjetividad(es) y Conflicto(s) Hacia una sociología de los cuerpos y las emociones desde Latinoamérica. Buenos Aires: CLACSO – CICCUS.

Scribano, A. (2012) Sociología de los cuerpos/emociones. *RELACES*, núm.10, año 4, 93–113.

Scribano, A. (2018) *Politics and Emotions*. Studium Press LLC: Houston.

Smith, D. (1984). Review Article: Norbert Elias — Established or Outsider? *The Sociological Review*, 32(2), 367–389. Available at: https://doi.org/10.1111/j.1467-954X.1984.tb00820.x

Smith, D. (2009) Norbert Elias and The Court Society: from Gallapagos to Versailles via Quai des Orfèvres. Paper prepared for presentation to The Society for Court Studies in their meeting at the Château of Versailles: 'Les cours en Europe: bilan historiographique. Colloque international,' Centre de recherché du château de Versailles, Chateau de Versailles (France) 24–26 September 2009.

Vergara, G. (2009) Conflicto y emociones. Un retrato de la vergüenza en Simmel, Eliasy Giddens como excusa para interpretar prácticas en contextos de expulsión. In Figari, C. y Scribano, A. (eds). *Cuerpo(s), Subjetividad(es) y Conflicto(s). Hacia una sociología de los cuerpos y las emociones desde Latinoamérica*. Buenos Aires: Ciccus-Clacso, 35–52.

Vergara, G. (2010a) Norbert Elias: el cuerpo en los entramados o la lógica de lo procesual. *Revista Argentina de Sociología*. Año 8, No 14. Mayo–Junio 2010. CPS. Buenos Aires, 15–34.

Vergara, G. (2010b) Sociedad y corporeidades en relación: una lectura en paralelo de Marx y Elias. In Scribano, A. y Lisdero, P. (eds). *Sensibilidades en juego: miradas múltiples desde los estudios sociales de los cuerpos y las emociones*. Córdoba, Cea-Conicet, E-book, 69–98.

Vergara, G. (2014) Procesos, interdependencias y transformaciones (inter) subjetivas: miradas posibles desde y, en la recuperación de residuos. In *Prácticas de oficio*, IDES, ISSN: 1851-6076. No 14, pp 1–12. Available at: http://ides.org.ar/wp-content/uploads/2015/02/Vergara-texto.pdf

# Chapter 11

# Ibn Khaldun

*Adrian Scribano*

## 11.1 Introduction

Wali al-Din Abd al-Rahman Ibn Muhammad Ibn Khaldun al-Tunisi al-Hadrami, better known as Ibn Khaldun (1332–1406), was born in Tunisia in the fourteenth century, grew up in an intellectually and politically active family and was educated by the best Spanish and North African Muslim teachers. His education included Islamic jurisprudence, mysticism or Sufism, and rational or philosophical sciences such as astronomy, metaphysics, logic, mathematics, history, and with special emphasis also studied the traditional sacred sciences, including the Koran and the Hadith (tradition of the prophet Muhammad). Ibn Khaldun is generally regarded as the greatest Muslim historian and the father of modern social science and cultural history (Abdalla, 2016, Alatas 2006).

Ibn Khaldun founds and elaborates the "Umran science" (Laroussi, 2008) which involves the elaboration of a theory of social change that explains the successive transformations of social structuring processes aimed at building happy societies based on knowledge and faith. In this context Mahayudin Hj Yahaya states:

> According to Ibn Khaldun, the human society is not static but moving and growing from small groups to larger groups, from primitive society (Badawi) to a civilized society (hadari), from civilized society to a prosperous society (`Umrani). A prosperous society is enjoyed in every aspect of physical, mental and spiritual matters.
>
> (Yahaya, 2017:17)

Ibn Khaldun is considered a jurist, historian and "theologian" who elaborates a new vision of science and knowledge where various epistemes were put into play giving space to the place of bodies, spaces, climates, food and feelings. This kaleidoscope of knowledge produced a particular and novel epistemological outlook. Ahamad has written about it:

DOI: 10.4324/9781003088363-12

He continues to clarify the nature of intellect and how the process of thinking takes place. Thinking comes from perception (...). Perception is the consciousness of the perceiver (...) in the essence of the perceptions that are outside his essence. This (kind of perception) is peculiar to living beings. Therefore, living beings (in this category) can perceive things outside their essence through external senses that God gives them, i.e., hearing, vision, smell, taste and touch.

(Ahmad, 2003: 11)

The place of the senses in perception and of living beings in the landscape of knowledge clearly frame a particular epistemic perspective where sensibilities and emotions play a central role as objects to be revealed and understood.

From another perspective, our author, as a historian with a strategy of inquiry and novel argumentation, is the subject of various interpretations that bring him closer or further away from the current ways of writing history. In this sense, Mohammad Salama's presentation in this regard is interesting:

First, there are writers like M. Kamil 'Ayyād and E. Rosenthal who emphasize his secular thinking and modern ideas on history. A second group, represented by H.A.R. Gibb, Franz Rosenthal, Mustafā al-Shakʻa, and Saʻīd al-Ghānimī, study Ibn Khaldūn in a Muslim context, stressing his faith, historical setting, and judiciary career. A third group, notably H. Simon, M. Mahdi, and F. Gale, emphasizes the influence of ancient Greek philosophy on Ibn Khaldūn. A fourth one, represented by Wlad Godzich and Hayden White, deals with Ibn Khaldūn exclusionally, underscoring his difference from European modes of thought; and a fifth group, including Ḥasan Ḥanafī, Muḥammad Jābir al-Anṣārī, and Saʻīd al-Ghānimī, looks at Ibn Khaldūn with nationalistic eyes and regards him as an inspirational restorative figure of lost Arab glory and a memory of the future.

(Salama, 2011: 78)

As we have already argued, another way of understanding Ibn Khaldun's work is as the founder of a new science aimed at studying social change and institutional modifications, a view from which he can be seen to be developing a state theory, and in this regard Syed Farid Alatas argues:

This new science was necessitated by Ibn Khaldun's discovery of problems surrounding the nature of historical studies up to his time. An understanding of the relationships between the state and society, group feeling or solidarity, and the question of the development of society require an understanding of the nature of society which Ibn Khaldun approached by way of the study of the constituent elements of society, such as economic life and urban institutions, the organizing ability of the state, and solidarity or group feeling ('aṣabiyyah), the primary factor affecting societal change. The above can be said to be the elements of Ibn Khaldun's general sociology, applicable to all types of societies, nomadic or sedentary, feudal or prebendal, Muslim or non-Muslim.

(Alatas, 2014: 21)

Clearly, for Khaldun, emotions, institutions, power and the state are united in a whole where such emotions play the role of cement/union by imprinting their particular features at each space/time.

## 11.2 Underlying basic assumptions

From a contemporary perspective, the "Prolegomena" is a text of political ecology based on a sociology of emotions that considers human beings as part of a society/nature metabolism where bodies/emotions are the foundational starting point for achieving knowledge about the processes of social structuring.

Our author outlines six preparatory discussions so that he can then concentrate on social historical analyses that can be perfectly read as basic assumptions that underlie his analysis and makes it intelligible. All these assumptions are associated with what we might call a story of bodies and emotions that share a time/space where soil, water and food are the keys to their reading.

At the beginning of the book, Ibn Khaldun exposes six preliminary reflections that serve as analytical assumptions of the history which he will discuss further and which have become a set of fundamental axes to understand the idea of group feelings that he has. We summarize these below, pointing out how the beginnings of the sociology of sensibilities can be clearly seen.

1   "FIRST PREFATORY DISCUSSION. HUMAN SOCIAL ORGANIZATION is something necessary. The philosophers expressed this fact by saying: 'Man is 'political' by nature.' That is, he cannot do without the social organization for which the philosophers use the technical term 'town' (polis)'" (Khaldun, 2015: 87 capitals in original).

In the first preliminary reflection, our author makes clear the social constitution of the human being in terms of the relationship with nature and its intersubjective character; we could sustain that this imposing book begins with a theory of sensibilities. The human being is political insofar as he is social, and he is social insofar as he articulates his desire, the food he needs to produce, and the organization that this implies. Thus, a geometry of desire, need and social structuring is expressed, and from here we can visibly see the connection between sociability, experientiality and sensibilities in this first reflection by Ibn Khaldun. For our author, civilized life, life in the city, is the product of a geometry of the bodies and grammar of action articulated by the organization that human beings give themselves to provide themselves with food, the cooperation necessary for the elaboration of tools and special defence, the forms of authority to balance the aggressiveness between human beings, and the existence of a spiritual guide that produces prophecies and interprets dreams.

2   "FOOD AND DESIRE. SECOND PREFATORY DISCUSSION The parts of the earth where civilization is found. Some information about oceans, rivers, and zones" (Khaldun, 2015: 90 capitals in original).

In the second preliminary observation, Khaldun's proposal is to explore, as an analytical assumption, what we might call the ecological conditions of the existence of "civilized" social organizations according to his own definition. To achieve this objective, he makes a detailed synthesis of the geographical location, the climate and natural resources, especially those related to obtaining food. Thus, the second preliminary observation refers to the planet and connects air, water and land in such a way that it begins to make sense how the human being cannot be understood without understanding his place on the planet; without the time/space and the will to forge the sensibilities of the peoples. In this way, we could say that our author intuits and originates a political ecology of the sensibilities. In this context, it connects and divides different parts of the Earth with the possibility of cultivating plants; where there is cultivation there are cities and civilizations.

3   "THIRD PREFATORY DISCUSSION. The temperate and the intemperate zones. The infuence of the air upon the color of human beings and upon many (other) aspects of their condition" (Khaldun, 2015: 123 capitals in original).

The third preliminary observation reconstructs the connection between bodies, emotions and cultures. The conditions imposed by the climate on human beings impacts on their skin colour, the proportions of their body and the moderation of their character. Also, the construction of their houses, clothing and jewellery, and the trade of precious metals and minerals. Ibn Khaldun emphasizes the weight of the geographical on the body and on the possibilities that emerge, in certain contexts, as a civilization as he can imagine it as a criterion of validity in an organization. An overemphasis on the weight of geographies places one type of social organization over another, but also allows the possibility of thinking how Ibn Khaldun emphasizes the weight of the geographical on the body and on the possibilities that emerge, in certain contexts, as a type of civilization; he imagines the place and weight of geography as a criterion of validity of a social organization.

An overemphasis on the weight of geographies places one type of social organization over another but also allows the possibility of thinking how the human being rebuilds the planet and the planet is rebuilt in the human being. The third observation is, therefore, an emphatic continuity of the second where there is an "overdetermination" of the weight of ecology and geography to constitute superiority among peoples.

4   "FOURTH PREFATORY DISCUSSION. The influence of the air (climate) upon human character" (Khaldun, 2015: 127 capitals in original).

In the fourth preliminary explanation, the climate appears as a conditioning factor of human character and of the sociabilities, experiences and sensibilities of people. The prevailing emotions in a city and civilization condition its entire social organization. A very clear presentation is made of what the climate implies, as it is the air that is breathed, that induces and builds emotionalities and sociabilities that colour peoples', colour sensibilities and lead to joy. An ecological theory is elaborated, a theory of emotional climate from the geographical position of the air and food available. It could be said that people are what they breathe, and this clearly has to do with what they have at hand, so they can organize themselves by preparing and caring about the future. Being worried or carefree causes social organizations to change: it is sensibilities that shape them.

5   "FIFTH PREFATORY DISCUSSION Differences with regard to abundance and scarcity of food in the various inhabited regions ('umran) and how they affect the human body and character" (Khaldun, 2015: 129 capitals in original).

The fifth preliminary discussion is dedicated to connecting food, the body, emotion and social organization. The availability of food, the form of sensations and the social organization to satisfy those needs and structure those sensibilities, shapes the social. These sensations are combined with the emotionally expressed, with the emotionally experienced, or with the emotionally unexpressed and with emotional regulation. The differential and unequal distribution of nutrients impact the bodies, emotions and social organization. The distance and proximity between scarcity and abundance configure the character of a city.

6   "SIXTH PREFATORY DISCUSSION. The various types of human beings who have supernatural perception either through natural disposition or through exercise, preceded by a discussion of inspiration and dream visions" (Khaldun, 2015: 132 capitals in original).

The sixth preliminary discussion refers to the possibility that in the community there are subjects who can interpret dreams and who may have a more refined spiritual access to the structure of the present and the past, again the logic of the symbolic joins the logic of sensibilities. There is a connection between wisdom, prophecy and social organization.

> The first (inward sense) is the "common sense," that is, the power that simultaneously perceives all objects of sensual perception, whether they belong to hearing, seeing, touching, or anything else. In this respect, it differs from the power of external sense perception, as the objects of sensual perception do not all crowd upon external sense perception at one and the same time.
> 
> (Khaldun, 2015: 138)

The hexagon that makes up the preliminary discussions becomes a geometry of the connections thought by our author as the basis of his analysis of the social, and clearly places him as a classic of the sociology of emotions.

## 11.3 Asabiyyah

The Asabiyyah group feeling is one of the most interesting concepts coined to understand the connection between social structuration processes, emotion, and social cohesion. The sentiment of collective identity, interpersonal recognition, and the position and conditions of classes/ hierarchy are articulated in Ibn Khaldun's theory.

Asabiyyah appears over 500 times in Muqaddima. As "teased", the Arabic verbal root usually has a verb related to camels or a noun derived from it:

> Usub, derived from the same root as asabiyya, means a camel that will not give much milk unless its thigh is tied with a rope. What Ibn Khaldun called 'asabiyya' refers in the first instance to the harsh conditions of life in the desert in which tribal groups necessarily have to develop a special type of group solidarity. The root verb 'asaba means' he twisted [one thing] and 'usbah' means 'a group of men who unite to defend each other'. Bi Asabiyya was defined in medieval Arabic dictionaries as a strong attachment, which has several people closely united by the same interest or opinion.
> 
> (Irwin, 2018: 45)

According to another, but similar, interpretation, the term

> Asabiyyah point out the action of an individual who associates with others, of someone who protects others, also implies a strong association between people closely related based on the same interest and opinion.

> Along the same lines, it refers to the action of those who invite others to help their group, to combine or join with them to confront those who act hostilely towards them, Asabiyyah which refers to the action of those who help their people or their group against any aggressive action, the quality of a person who is angry for the good of their group and protect them.
>
> (Halim et al., 2012: 1233)

For us, the concept and hermeneutical device that constitutes Ibn Khaldun as a founding father of the sociology of emotions is that of "aṣabiyya". Like any unit of perception, neither the author nor his interpreters always assign the same "value" to the concept, transforming it into a sensitizing concept (*sensu* Giddens). The meaning of aṣabiyya, its content and extension as an "explanatory" term is controversial, and recently Abou-Tabickh has systematized these differences as follows:

> Al-'aṣabiyya or the solidarity of the group, according to another scholar, is constituted within the tribe itself by sheer power. It is generated by lineage affiliation and is maintained by a dominant 'aṣabiyya with a mandate to coerce. Therefore, it is the tribe as a power actor. This feeling of solidarity is generated by familial relations and is intensified by external hardships, common interests, and shared experiences. However, in the transition to political society, another suggests, the sentiment of al-'aṣabiyya turns into an efficient cause that seeks royal power by its nature, which is derived from the nature of man who seeks domination. Al-'aṣabiyya of the cohesive tribal group, according to others, is a socio-political structure that marks the transition from a classless to a class society. Its essential elements are tribal aristocracy and military democracy, and its cohesion is expressed in warlike activities, which foster the feeling of unity.
>
> (Abou-Tabickh, 2019: 19)

As we have seen, the proximity and distance between sentiment, emotion and a feeling of solidarity beyond the different interpretations they promote constitute a clear sign of how, for Khaldun, emotions are a set of practices that fulfil a fundamental place in the constitution of society.

In a similar direction, Douglas H. Garrison (2012) has indicated that religion, homogeneity and the stage of oppositional 'Asabiyya are the three "variables" that help to establish its consistency and "strength". In this context, it is easy to understand how, for our author, group feelings could be, at the same time, the nexus of constitution of the collective, as shared practices of feeling, and a hermeneutical key for understanding the processes of conflict and peace in that which he calls civilization.

The next section presents a selection of some examples of the use of the concept in Khaldun's narrative and his hermeneutics about history.

## 11.4 The use of emotion

Ibn Khaldun is a classic of the sociology of emotions because he is a pioneer of "using" emotions as traces and keys to understand society and the organizational and institutional transformations that these emotions, throughout history, make it possible to understand.

> IT SHOULD be known that history, in matter of fact, is information about human social organization, which itself is identical with world civilization. It deals with such conditions affecting the nature of civilization as, for instance, savagery and sociability, group feelings, and the different ways by which one group of human beings achieves superiority over another. It deals with royal authority and the dynasties that result (in this manner) and with the various ranks that exist within them.
> (Khaldun, 2015: 5 capitals in original)

In the first place, it is possible to notice how our author is thinking about a world systematic history that, as we have already seen, is based on the connection of climate, emotions and civilization. It is within this explanatory framework that group feelings become one of the three explanatory factors of that world history.

When our author begins to describe the life of the Bedouins, he argues that there is no tribe that can live in the desert without the shared experience of a group feeling:

> Nothing can be achieved in these matters without fighting for it, since man has the natural urge to offer resistance. And for fighting one can not do without group feeling, as we mentioned at the beginning. This should be taken as the guiding principle of our later exposition.
> (Khaldun, 2015: 171)

Inscribed on the surface of conflict, struggle and survival, group feelings become central to "common life" to such an extent that Khaldun designates such feelings as guiding principles of his subsequent analysis.

Now, what is the origin of these group feelings? The answer is clear: the ties of blood relatives. Once it is understood that "primarily" they are consanguineous connections it can then be understood that it involves all kinds of close contact.

> *"8. Group feeling results only from (blood) relationship or something corresponding to it.*

> (Respect for) blood ties is something natural among men, with the rarest exceptions. It leads to affection for one's relations and blood relatives, (the feeling that) no harm ought to befall them nor any destruction come upon them. One feels shame when one's relatives are treated unjustly or attacked, and one wishes to intervene between them and whatever peril or destruction threatens them. This is a natural urge in man, for as long as there have been human beings. If the direct relationship between persons who help each other is very close, so that it leads to close contact and unity, the ties are obvious and clearly require the (existence of a feeling of solidarity) without any outside (prodding).
>
> (Khaldun, 2015: 172 italics in original)

It is easy to observe how, for Khaldun, emotions are practices that move to action, they imply a reaction to what "the other" experiences, they are links of solidarity that act as motivation and are also the result of an emotion.

## 11.5 Group feelings as a theory of state

One of the factors that makes Ibn Khaldun a classic of sociology is his theory of social change and social structuration processes, and it is precisely this perspective that serves as conceptual tool for his social theory. In what follows it is shown (a) how Asabiyyah is a theory of power and change, and (b) it is a synthesis of some chapters of the Al-Muqaddimah and these are provided as an example.

### 11.5.1 State, power, social change and Asabiyyah

As the Masters' thesis of Douglas H. Garrison attests, what in this chapter we understand by "group feeling" is the backbone of Ibn Khaldun's theory of the state beyond the multiple hermeneutics that the translation of Asabiyyah into English can admit. Asabiyyah is a unifying force, it is a special political cement, it is a parameter of "modernization" that, when translated, in various ways, makes its plural meaning even clearer.

> Ibn Khaldun's greatest contribution to the study of politics—indeed, of human social action generally—is his concept of 'asabiyya. For Ibn Khaldun, 'asabiyya represents the principal driving force behind all collective, 'civilizing' social activity. More than simply an explanatory heuristic device, Ibn Khaldun describes 'asabiyya as simultaneously a shared human bond, an identifying social construct, and a force unto itself; it is a blind will to power and impetus for conscientious right action, a mobilizing process and, in the end, its own telos. It is, as Lenn Goodman argues, the substrate of political change and the engine of history. However,

before engaging in a lengthy hermeneutical discussion of 'asabiyya and its application to contemporary political theory, we must first deal with how both the word and the idea are and have been defined in translation by modern scholars.

(Garrison, 2012: 34)

Garrison systematizes four forms of translation of Asabiyyah: that of Franz Rosenthal, who was the first to make a complete translation of the Muqaddimah into English, as "group feeling"; Ernest Gellner takes a different approach to the interpretation of Asabiyyah, and tries to link it with Durkheim's theory of organic and mechanical solidarities, translating it as "social solidarity"; Allen J. Fromhertz similarly links Asabiyyah with Durkheim's concept of solidarity, translating the term as "tribal solidarity" and, in the same vein, Akbar S. Ahmed chooses to use "social cohesion" as an alternative translation.

Given the possibilities described in this chapter, beyond what has already been pointed out in the previous sections, Rosenthal's translation has been selected because, according to the criteria of the writer, "group feeling" implies the forms of solidarity to which Garrison refers.

What is clear is that Ibn Kaldun finds in the Asabiyyah an explanatory concept of the "rationalization" or not of the world, a parameter to explain social cohesion, and a collective practice to understand the connection between State and Power.

One of the possible meanings imputing to Asabiyyah is Ibn Khaldun's intention to connect through said explanatory concept, power and knowledge. As stated in the previous sections, our author is a founding father of the sociology of emotions, but it must be emphasized that this original gesture is produced based on an epistemic turn in the historiography and sciences available in the Islamic culture of his time. As stated by Mohammad Salama:

… Ibn Khaldūn's theory of history holds some grains of the connection between power and knowledge. In seeking to interrogate history within a broader epistemological framework, Ibn Khaldūn becomes the first historian to overtly criticize the Arab sense of 'aṣabiyya (feelings of blood solidarity) and to expose the Arabs' injustices. Ibn Khaldūn's Kitāb al-'Ibar is ostensibly an apology to the Berbers who, while still having their own 'aṣabiyya, had long suffered from the Arabs' degrading view of them. To Ibn Khaldūn, the Berbers are brave people worthy of glory because 'the strength that they have revealed throughout time makes them fearless; they are as brave and as powerful as the other nations and peoples of the world, such as the Arabs, the Persians, the Greeks, and the Romans.

(Salama, 2011: 1)

Group feelings, being a modality of identity in which the sanguine, the passionate, the familiar, but also authority, politics and order coexist, become traces of the reproduction and modifications of the valid, acceptable, and accepted forms of power.

A sense of the connection between authority, power and Asabiyyah is clearly pointed out by Gabriel Ramírez Acevedo in the context of his explanation of the different reaches of the impact of group feelings from a small community up to complex regional states:

> ... Thus, for example, speaking of this last form of asabiya, it is in it 'where the strength of the State resides and in its degradation its degradation'. For the author, then, there is a direct relationship between asabiya, power and sovereignty, since it is precisely this force that gives legitimacy to the ruler, as the leader of a group that recognizes itself as homogeneous. Leadership finds legitimacy in the spirit of the community and, therefore, the affinity relationship that the governed find with whoever governs them will be decisive when following their orders. It is precisely in the central role of the leader and his connection with the community that the traces can be found to indicate the modifications of times in the forms of power. Legitimacy, sovereignty, and leadership are united by the bonds of group feelings, their production, reproduction and "degradation".
> (Ramírez Acevedo, 2009: 6)

In a complementary sense, it is possible to understand the view from the Asabiyyah, as Muhammad Dhaouadi maintains, as a theory of social change, which provides a cyclical understanding based on the intensity of blood, religious and, obviously, emotional ties:

> Third, the Muqaddima is rich in sociological grand theories on Arab society in particular: How did it rise and fall? What were the roles of al-asabiyya and religion in its making and its disintegration? Why do the vanquished always tend to imitate their conquerors? How did the Arab State systematically follow the short-lived cycle patterns of growth and development? (...) Ibn Khaldun's sociology echoes deeply the moving forces at work in his time in the Arab world, both in its Western and Eastern parts: al-asabiyya, "Bedouinity", political instability, affluence (al-taraf), urbanization, etc.
> (Dhaouadi, 2006: 49)

For Dhaouadi, the testimony of Khaldun reflects the subsequent and continuous decline of the Arab–Muslim civilization that caused, among other things, stagnation, poverty and the demise of religious, philosophical and social thought.

## 11.5.2 Group feeling and social/political change[1]

In the first four chapters of Al-Muqaddimah, Ibn Khaldun explains some concepts related to different types of society: sedentary and nomadic society. He wants to explain how a society is stabilized and what are the consequences and the items that follow stabilization; in the index of the book, it is presented thus:

> Chapter I Human civilization in general; chapter II Bedouin civilization, savage nations and tribes and their conditions of life, including several basic and explanatory statements; chapter III On dynasties, royal authority, the caliphate, government ranks, and all that goes with these things. The chapter contains basic and supplementary propositions and; chapter IV Countries and cities, and all other forms of sedentary civilization. The conditions occurring there. Primary and secondary considerations in this connection.

In the first chapter our author, based on what was already developed in the preliminary course, lays the foundation for the notion of cooperation whose existence enables groups to acquire food or weapons to survive and defend themselves. He then introduces the concept of royal authority which has great importance in his thinking. Royal authority, which is necessary for human beings, is only possible through religious laws and family ties.

Before explaining how the royal authority is constituted, we draw an overview of the natural conditions that allow humans to survive, such as the influence of the climate or the abundance/scarcity of food that determines human character and their will to live in a group. It gives way to an understanding of how social organization is the only means through which people can produce convenience. He takes the Bedouin as an example; for him, they have created a better society compared to a sedentary people that are lazier because they are surrounded by walls that protect them from enemies, and they don't have to hunt to find food because they have an agricultural system that ensures they have easy access to food.

It is this second chapter, dedicated to the Bedouin and tribes living in the desert, that reintroduces the concept of group feeling as the only way to survive in these harsh conditions. People living in tribes that walk in open spaces have to defend each other and this defence is guaranteed only if they are close to each other with more conviction. If they are all related, they will be more willing to defend each other because compassion and affection for blood relatives is something that comes directly from God, so fighting is something that people only do if there is a group feeling that descends from being between relatives.

It is observed in this context how, for Ibn Khaldun, two elements are in particular necessary for the creation of group feeling: the purity of the lineage, therefore the genealogical consideration that allows determining where someone comes from and not their place of residence. This also brings us to the second element: the tribe is considered the best place for group feeling. The greater the luxury or the easier it is to enjoy life for people, the more the group feeling diminishes, so the nomadic conditions are the best condition to develop the group feeling.

Changes in authority/power are explained by Khaldun from group feeling:

> 21. As long as a nation retains its group feeling, royal authority that disappears in one branch will, of necessity, pass to some other branch of the same nation.
>
> The reason for this is that (the members of a particular nation) obtain royal authority only after (proving their) forcefulness and finding other nations obedient to them. (Only a few) are then singled out to become the actual rulers and to be directly connected with the throne. It can not be all of them, because there is not enough room for all to compete (for leadership), and because the existence of jealousy cuts short the aspirations of many of those who aspire to high office.
>
> (Khaldun 2015: 194)

So, we see that the group feeling derives from having a common descent and ensures mutual affection and help. The nobility and purity of a house is directly related to the degree of group feeling. The fact that the Bedouin are nomadic ensures that they do not mix their blood which can thus remain pure.

The group feeling is transmitted only from the masters of a family and not from their slaves or clients. Life in the harsh desert conditions, preserves the power of the group feeling by providing mutual protection and defence.

Ibn Khaldun also states that group feeling must lead to an authority, a person who must have superiority over others; this superiority is called royal authority (mulk, in Arabic). Royal authority – a very important concept for our author – is a way to hold the group together under someone, it is a goal of group feeling and belongs to someone who has qualities such as generosity, tolerance, hospitality, patience, and who faithfully fulfils their obligations.

In the third chapter he refers to "stable societies", but previously synthesizes the process leading to the group feeling: the defensive strength is obtained only by the group feeling that makes people willing to die for each other.

> 2. When a dynasty is, firmly established, it can dispense with group feeling.
>
> The reason for this is that people find it difficult to submit to large dynastic(power) at the beginning, unless they are forced into submission by strong superiority. (The new government) is something strange. People are not familiar with, or used to, its rule. But once leadership is

firmly vested in the members of the family qualified to exercise royal authority in the dynasty, and once (royal authority) has been passed on by inheritance over many generations and through successive dynasties, the beginnings are forgotten, and the members of that family are clearly marked as leaders.

(Khaldun, 2015: 206)

In the analysis of stabilized societies, Kaldun begins to speak of dynasties, and the royal authority is based on that. Dynasties unfold in five stages: by taking the royal authority from the previous dynasty and causing the opposition to fall, the ruler then gained complete control over the people; there is a quiet time that comes directly from the authority, the ruler is happy during this time; it is a time of peace and fun. The prestige of the dynasty is evident from its monuments and the gifts it makes to other dynasties.

We saw then that royal authority is necessary to dominate but is not present in all group feelings because each one is different and exercises its own authority. There are group feelings that cannot fulfil missions like protecting the border regions or gaining control over the feelings of other groups. Royal authority is a necessary form of organization for humanity, it requires superiority and strength, but also a system of political norms for which the caliphate exists: to give and stabilize political and religious rules.

The caliphate is God's substitute on earth, it manages its affairs and gives man the direction to follow. Royal authority is the natural goal of group feeling, but it also results from it through necessity and order of existence.

Everything that the masses are expected to do requires a group feeling that allows the community to fulfil what God expects of them.

Ibn Khaldun also explores the different ways in which the ruler manages his dynasty such as the way he manages money or laws, taxes or the army, and describes the way they are administered. It makes clear that the only way through which the dynasty can achieve power and domination is through a group feeling which has its main characteristics in desert life that is why sedentary civilization slowly collapses.

And finally, Chapter 4 explains how a dynasty shows power and stability through architecture such as buildings, walls and mosques. He also claims that the buildings in Islam are few compared to their power because the Arabs were firmly rooted in the desert and their sedentary culture did not fully develop. In the end, this explains the decline of the dynasty into a sedentary civilization, as opposed to nomadic societies where civilization has not declined.

It is very interesting to see how our author exemplifies the expression of group feelings in social organizations in light of the politics of sensibilities:

Crafts and labor also are expensive in cities with an abundant civilization. There are three reasons for this. First, there is much need (of them), because of the place luxury occupies in the city on account of the (city's) large civilization. Second, industrial workers place a high value on their services and employment, (for they do not have to work) since life is easy in a town because of the abundance of food there. Third, the number of people with money to waste is great, and these people have many needs for which they have to employ the services of others and have to use many workers and their skills. Therefore, they pay more for (the services of) workers than their labor is (ordinarily considered) worth, because there is competition for (their services) and the wish to have exclusive use of them. Thus, workers, craftsmen, and professional people become arrogant, their labor becomes expensive, and the expenditures of the inhabitants of the city for these things increase.

(Khaldun, 2015: 454)

In a city with a great civilization the need for food and crafts increases, so convenience, food and labour become expensive because there is high demand; however, the wealth tends to accumulate in the hands of the few people who can afford these goods, so poverty increases. The dynasties shine and then fall, the sedentary culture reaches a limit that it cannot cross. When civilization grows, sedentary culture becomes more perfect, but this development brings an increase in prices that cannot be shared among all people and the capital focuses on few people, then business decreases and the situation of the town deteriorates. Among the causes that ruin the sedentary culture is the disposition to pleasure and corruption. In the end, our author argues that royal authority is the basis of the dynasties that are the target of group feeling.

### 11.6 Some summarized conclusions

To explain the constitution of society, our author puts at stake the place and weight of bodies, spaces, climates, food, and feelings by developing a new vision of the sciences and knowledge of their time. This particular view revolves around a special consideration of the senses in terms of their influence on the elaboration of perceptions and social relationships. It is in this context that Khaldun, beyond inaugurating a "new" science of history, has constituted one of the first steps in the architecture of a sociology of emotions that finds, in the politics of sensibilities, a key element for understanding the social structuration process.

Within the framework of what has been stated so far, there are three features that allow us to synthesize the importance of our author for the sociology of emotions:

First, in Ibn Khaldun's writings there is a close relationship between geography, geopolitics and the geoculture of emotions as explanatory factors of social organization.

Second, his view of group feelings as a key to reading identities, disputes, and forms of organization of power clearly anticipate many of the current discussions of the sociology of emotions.

Third, the relationship between ethics, aesthetics, politics and emotions, from the perspective of our author, is an ample sample of the important and foundational place that he has in the subdiscipline.

## Note

1 I wish to express my gratitude to Alessandra Poladori who helped in the preparation of this section of the chapter.

## References

Abdalla, M. (2016) Ibn Khaldun (1332–1406). In *The Wiley Blackwell Encyclopedia of Race, Ethnicity, and Nationalism*, First Edition. Edited by John Stone, Rutledge M. Dennis, Polly S. Rizova, Anthony D. Smith, and Xiaoshuo Hou. Chichester, John Wiley.

Abou-Tabickh, L. (2019) Al-'Aṣabiyya in Context: Choice and Historical Continuity in Al-Muqaddima of Ibn Khaldūn Doctor of Philosophy Dissertation, Department of Political Science, University of Toronto.

Alatas, S. F. (2006) Ibn Khaldun and Contemporary Sociology. *International Sociology*, 21, 782–795.

Alatas, S.F. (2014) *Applying Ibn Khaldun: The Recovery of a Lost Tradition in Sociology*. Abingdon, Routledge.

Ahmad , Z. (2003) *The Epistemology of Ibn Khaldun*. London, Routledge.

Dhaouadi. M (2006) The Concept of Change in the Thought of Ibn Khaldun and Western Classical Sociologists. *Araþtýrmalarý Dergisi, Sayý*, 16, 43–87.

Garrison, D.H (2012) *Ibn Khaldun and the Modern Social Sciences: A Comparative Theoretical Inquiry into Society, the State, and Revolution*. Faculty of Josef Korbel School of International Studies University of Denver June 2012, USA.

Halim, A.A, et al. (2012) Ibn Khaldun's Theory of 'Asabiyyah and its Application in Modern Muslim Society. *Middle East Journal of Scientific Research*, 11(9), 1232–1237.

Irwin, R. (2018) *Ibn Khaldun. An Intellectual Biography*. Princeton NJ, Princeton University Press.

Khaldun, I. (1377) (2015) *The Muqaddimah: An Introduction to History – Abridged Edition*. Edited by N. J. Dawood Translated by Franz Rosenthal.

Laroussi, A. (2008) The Concept of 'Umran: The Heuristic Knot in Ibn Khaldun. *The Journal of North African Studies*, 13(3), 351–361. doi: 10.1080/13629380701844672.

Ramírez Acevedo, G. (2009) Los aportes teóricos socioculturales de Ibn Jaldún para la comprensión del fenómeno migratorio de musulmanes magrebíes a Francia entre 1990-2001 Universidad Colegio Mayor de Nuestra Señora del Rosario Facultad de Relaciones Internacionales Bogotá, Colombia. Available at: https://nanopdf.com/download/1020712371_pdf.

Salama, M. (2011) *Islam, Orientalism and Intellectual History. Modernity and the Politics of Exclusion since Ibn Khaldūn*. London and New York, I.B. Tauris.

Yahaya, M. H. (2017). The Science of 'Umran: Its Origin, Role, and Function. *The Journal of Middle East and North Africa Sciences*, 3(12), 17–22.

# Index

Abou-Tabickh, L. 174
affection 50
affective valences 158–159
Ahamad, Z. 168–169
Ahmed, Akbar S. 177
Alatas, Syed Farid 169–170
altruism: Cooley 119; Durkheim 59, 61
ambition 120
ambivalence: Simmel 87–89, 92–94; Tarde 50
*American Journal of Sociology* 109n4
anger: Cooley 122, 123, 130; Weber 71
anomie 59–60, 61, 62
anxiety 161, 162
Aron, Raymond 100
Asabiyyah 173–182

Babbage, Charles 6
behaviourism 136
beliefs: Durkheim 64; Tarde 42–47
benevolence 17
Berger, Brigitte 105–106
Besserer, Federico 57
Bierstedt, Robert 114, 128, 131
blasé attitude 82, 85
blood relatives 175–176, 179–180
Blumer, Herbert 134
Bobbio, Norberto 101
body: Elias 154–158, 160, 163, 165–166; Khaldun 170–172
Bongiorno, M. A. 109n4
Borkenau, F. 97
brain 25, 26, 28–30, 32
Brinton, Crane 98, 110n6
Burgess, Ernest 114

Calvinism 76–78
capitalism: Elias 166; Marx 24–37; Weber 75, 77, 78

Carlyle, Thomas 6
causality 6
charisma: Elias 164; Weber 72–75, 79
Chicago School 40, 98, 114, 136
children: Elias 162; Martineau 15–18; Marx 29, 33, 36
civilization: Cooley 126–131; Elias 155, 159, 161, 163–165; Khaldun 171–172, 174, 175, 181–182
classification systems 64–65
climate 172, 175, 179
coercion: Durkheim 56, 58, 60; Elias 161
combinations, instinct for 102, 109
communication: Cooley 115–117, 122, 127–128, 130; Habermas 134; Mead 134, 145–146, 149; Simmel 87; Tarde 40, 41
communism 37
compassion 117
Comte, Auguste 7, 42, 81; and Pareto 101, 104
consciousness: Elias 159; Mead 137–138, 139, 146–147, 148; Simmel 82–85
contagion: Pareto 104; Tarde 41
control of emotions: Durkheim 57, 62; Elias 154, 163–165
conversation 40
Cooley, Charles Horton 113–31; *Human Nature and The Social Order* 116, 122; micro–macro link 126–129; nature and culture 122–126; primary group, feelings and sentiment 119–121; self and society 114–115; sociability and sympathy 116–119; *Social Organization* 121
coquetry 89
cosmopolitanism: Simmel 81; Tarde 51
crowd 44, 47, 99

cruelty: Marx 24, 32–35, 36; Pareto 103
culture 122–126

Dante Alighieri 33
Darwin, Charles 96, 104, 122, 123
Deegan, Mary Jo 135, 144
Deleuze, Gilles 41
democracy 127, 128–129
depression 60
derivations 102, 104–105, 107–108, 110n11
desires: Durkheim 62; Khaldun 171; Tarde 42–47; Thomas 110n12
despair 74
determination 155–156
Dewey, John 136
Dhaouadi, Muhammad 178
disability 6
discipline 56
discontent 129
discretion 92
displeasure 154, 162, 164, 165
division of labour 58–60
domination: Elias 164, 166; Weber 72–73, 78–79
dreams 172–173
dualism of individuality 88
Durkheim, Émile 7, 54–65, 81, 113; and Cooley 130; *The Division of Labour in Society* 58–60; *Education and Sociology* 61; *The Elementary Forms of the Religious Life* 62–64, 102; emotional foundations of the normative world 55–58; *The Evolution of Educational Thought* 61–62; *Les formes élémentaires de la vie religieuse* 42; and Khaldun 177; modernity 58–62; *Moral Education* 62; and Pareto 96, 99, 108; *Pragmatism and Sociology* 65; religion 50, 61, 62–65; "The Religious Problem and the Dualism of Human Nature" 65; rituals 102; *The Rules of the Sociological Method* 10, 55–58; social integration 42, 46, 49–50, 54–64; social solidarity and Paretian residues 104; *Suicide* 60–61, 62; *sui generis* society 46; "Systems of Primitive Classification" 64–65; and Tarde 39, 41, 42, 47, 50

duty: Durkheim 56, 57–58, 62, 63; Elias 161; Weber 75
dynasties 180–182

education: Durkheim 61–62; Elias 162; Martineau 15–18, 20, 21; Marx 33
effervescence: emotional 79; social 50, 54, 63–65, 104
egoism: Cooley 118, 130; Durkheim 61, 62; Pareto 97, 103
Elias, Norbert 130, 131, 152–166; biography 153–154; "The court society" 153; emotions in interactions 158–163; social construction of the body 154–158; social regulation of emotions 163–165
embarrassment: Elias 162; Mead 142; Scheff 143
emotional: Cooley 113–114, 116–120, 125–126, 129; Durkheim 54–65; Elias 155, 158–159, 161, 164; Khaldun 172, 178; Martineau 14; Mead 143–148; Pareto 99–100, 103–109; Scheff 143; Shott 141; Simmel 81–83, 87–89, 91, 94; Tarde 41–51; Weber 68–79
emotional infection 43–46, 47, 51
empathy: Cooley 119; Martineau 12; Marx 35, 36, 37; Mead 142
Engdahl, Emma 115
enthusiasm 71, 74
envy 164
Erasmus 155
ethnocentrism 131
ethnography 8
evolution 129
experience 135, 140

failure 143
fairness 130
fatalism 61
fear: Cooley 121, 123; Elias 160, 161; Martineau 15, 16–17, 18, 21; Weber 71
feeling rules 141
feminism 8, 20
Feuerbach, Ludwig 41
flesh 30–32
flirtatiousness 89
food 170–171, 172, 179, 182
Fourier, Charles 27
Frankfurt School 153
freedom: Cooley 126; Elias 155–156, 157; Simmel 85–86, 91

French school 40
Freud, Sigmund 100, 101
friendship 90–92
Fromhertz, Allen J. 177

Garrison, Douglas H. 174, 176–177
Gehlen, Arnold 124
Gellner, Ernest 177
gender 152
generalized other 139, 141, 142
gestures 138
Giddens, Anthony 64, 174
Ginsberg, Morris 109n4
Good, the 57–58, 62
Goodman, Lenn 176
gratitude 89–90, 92
greed 120–121
group feeling, Asabiyyah 173–182
group-persistence 102
guilt 142

Habermas, Jürgen 134
habit: Cooley 123; Elias 159; Simmel 83–84, 86–87; Weber 71–73, 78–79
Halim, A.A. 173–174
happiness: Martineau 8, 18; Simmel 88
Harvard University, Pareto Circle and "cult" 98
hatred: Martineau 19; Weber 71
Henderson, Lewis 98, 110n6
heredity 122, 124
Hinkle, R. C. 116, 125
Hochschild, Arlie 57, 141
Homans, George 98
*homo oeconomicus* 97, 99
honour 130
hope: Martineau 15, 16, 18, 21; Weber 74
humanism 128
human nature 122–126
humiliation: Elias 160; Scheff 143
hunger 30, 33

ideals 61, 63–64
idolatry 17
Illouz, Eva 65
imitation: Tarde 44–45, 47–48, 49–50, 51; Weber 70
inadequacy 143
indignation 123
individualism: Cooley 131; Durkheim 59; Elias 155; Mead 137; Pareto 97, 103, 106; Simmel 88, 91–93

inequality: Elias 166; Martineau 18, 19; Marx 36
inferiority 160
influence 72
informed consent 56, 61
instincts: Cooley 122–125, 131; Mead 143–149; Pareto 102–104, 107, 109
interactions, emotions in 158–163
interest 147–149
interpretative sociology 69–71
intimate relationship: Cooley 119–120, 121, 127; Mead 135, 145; Simmel 89, 90, 93
Irwin, R. 173
Islam 181

James, William 116
Jaspers, K. 68
jealousy 71
Jones, Ernest 100
*Journal of Social Philosophy* 109n4
justice 126, 128–130

Kant, Immanuel 45, 57, 106
Khaldun, Ibn 168–183; Asabiyyah 173–182; biography 168–170; group feelings as a theory of state 176–182; Muqaddimah 173–183; "Prolegomena" 170; underlying basic assumptions 170–173; use of emotion 175–176
kindness 119, 128–130
Kropotkin, Peter 129–130

laughter 159
Lavisse, Ernest 164
Lazarsfeld, P.F. 40
leaders: Elias 164; Khaldun 178, 180–181; Tarde 43–46, 47–48, 50, 51; Weber 72–74
learning *see* education
Le Bon, Gustave 99
legitimation: Khaldun 178; Weber 72–74
liberalism 97, 99
lifestyle 86
linguistic turn 110n14
Livingston, Arthur 98
Locke, John 6
logico-experimental actions 99, 104, 105
Lombroso, Cesare 40
loneliness 87–88
looking-glass self 118–119

love: Cooley 120, 121, 123, 126, 130; Martineau 15, 17–18, 21; Simmel 81, 90, 91, 92–94; Weber 71
lust 120, 121, 125

Machiavelli, Niccolò 106
Madoo Lengermann, P. 5
Malthus, Thomas 6
Marshall, Thomas Humphrey 106
Martineau, Harriet 5–21; biography 6–8; *Deerbrook* 6; emotions, senses, and sensibilities 8–10; *The House and Man* 6; *Household Education* 8, 15–18; *How to Observe. Morals and Manners* 8, 9, 10–15, 21; *Illustrations of Political Economy* 6, 9, 18–20; "Letters on Mesmerism" 6; "Life in the Sick Room: Essays by an Invalid" 6; *The Rules of the Sociological Method* 7; *Society in America* 6, 8, 9–10
Marx, Karl 23–37; *Capital* 24–37; cruelty 24, 32–35, 36; Doctoral Thesis 23, 24; flesh 30–32; *The Grundrisse* 23, 24; *The Manuscripts* 23, 24, 26; muscles and brain 25, 26, 28–30, 32; senses 25–28, 32, 35–36
Marxism 98
Mayo, Elton 98
Mead, George Herbert 40, 134–149; and Cooley 114, 115; *Emotions and Instinct* 135, 144, 147–149; intellectual profile 135–137; *Mind, Self and Society* 109n3, 136–137, 138–139; *Movements of Thought in the Nineteenth Century* 136; *The Philosophy of the Act* 136; *The Philosophy of the Present* 136; role-taking 116–117; *The Social Character of Instinct* 135, 143–147, 148; social theory 137–140; sociology of emotions 140–143
meaningful gestures 138
Merton, Robert K. 98
metropolis: Marx 33; Mead 136; Simmel 82–87, 88
microsociology 41
Mill, John Stuart 6, 96
modernity: Cooley 127; Durkheim 58–62; Pareto 101; Simmel 50, 82, 87–88, 91–92, 94; Tarde 45–46, 50–51; Weber 68, 75–78
modesty 92
money 82, 85

monogamy 46–47
morality: Cooley 119–121, 125, 129–131; Durkheim 47, 54–63, 130; Kant 57; Martineau 5, 7–14, 18, 21; Marx 24, 29, 35; Parsons 57; Shott 142; Simmel 83; Tarde 46–48; Weber 76
Mornati, F. 97
Morris, Charles 109n3, 137
mortification 118, 119, 130
muscles 25, 26, 28–30, 32
Mutti, Antonio 108

nationalism 105
nature: Cooley 122–126; Elias 153
neophobia 103
nervousness 88
Niebrugge, G. 5
non-logico-experimental actions 99–108
non-rational choice 69–78

obedience 56, 61
oppression 35
Owen, Robert 6

pain 35, 36
Pareto, Raffaele 97
Pareto, Vilfredo 96–109; biography 96–98; derivations and social equilibrium 104–106; logico-experimental and non-logico-experimental actions 98–99; *Manual of Political Economy* 97; non-logical actions and rationalizations 100–101; residues 102–104; *Les Systèmes Socialistes* 97, 107; *Trattato di Sociologia Generale/The Mind and Society* 98–104, 108
Pareto Circle, Harvard 98
Park, Robert 40, 114
Parsons, Talcott 153; and Elias 154; morality 57; and Pareto 96, 98, 106–107, 109n2; societal community 128
passion 17
patience 15, 17, 18, 21
perception: Cooley 116, 118–120; Khaldun 169, 172–173, 174, 182; Martineau 10; Marx 24, 26; Mead 135, 142; Simmel 84
pity 81
plasticity 116, 122, 124–126
pleasure 85, 87

political economy: Martineau 5–7, 9, 14, 18–20, 21; Marx 24, 28, 34, 35; Pareto 97–98, 105
positivism: Comte 104; Pareto 97, 99, 101, 106, 108
power: Elias 164; Khaldun 180–182, 183; Weber 72–75
pragmatism 135, 136, 140, 149
predestination 76, 77, 78
pride: Cooley 118, 119; Mead 141, 142; Scheff 143
Priestley, Joseph 6
primary groups 119–121, 126–129
prisoners 19
Protestantism 76–78
Puritanism 77, 78

Radical Reform Movement 6
rage 121, 123
Ramírez Acevedo, Gabriel 178
Ramos, R. 57
rational choice 69–70
rationalizations 100–101, 104, 106
rationalization theory 100
reason 124–125, 129
recognition 103
Reddy, William 57
reflection: Mead 138, 143, 148; Scheff 143
reflexive emotions 142
Reinharz, Shulamit 8
religion: Cooley 129, 131; Durkheim 50, 61, 62–65; Khaldun 174, 179, 181; Martineau 14–15; Marx 33, 34; Pareto 99, 102–103, 107; Simmel 81, 87; Tarde 46, 47, 49–50; Weber 69, 70, 73, 75–78
repugnance 162
repulsion 43
research methodology 8, 10–15, 21
resentment 120, 121, 123
residues 102–104, 105, 107, 108
resilience 17
revenge 120
ritual: Durkheim 49–50, 63–65, 102; Weber 74
role-taking: Mead 116–117; Shott 140–141, 142, 143
Rosenthal, Franz 177
royal authority 179, 180–182

Sacks, Harvey 40
Salama, Mohammad 169, 177

salvation 76–77
Scheff, Thomas 142–143
Schlucter, W. 70
Schumpeter, Joseph 98
Schutz, Alfred 113
Scribano, A. 156
self: Cooley 114–116, 122, 129–131; Mead 137, 139–140, 143–145; Simmel 82–87
self-consciousness 138, 139
self-control 163
self-expression 102–103
self-feeling 116–119, 130
selfishness: Cooley 130, 131; Durkheim 61
self-pity 103
sensations: Elias 154; Khaldun 172; Martineau 10, 13, 16, 21; Marx 24, 27
senses: Elias 155–157; Feuerbach 41; Khaldun 169, 170–173, 182; Martineau 7–8, 11–12; Marx 24–28, 30, 32, 35–36; Mead 146; Simmel 83, 85
sensibilities: Durkheim 65n2; Elias 152, 155, 166; Khaldun 173, 181–182; Martineau 5, 8–10, 12–13, 15–17, 19–21; Marx 23–24, 29–36; Simmel 82
sex residue 103
sexual morality 46–47
sexuality: Elias 152, 158; Simmel 90
shame: Cooley 119, 131; Elias 154, 160–162, 164, 165; Khaldun 176; Mead 142–143, 148–149; Scheff 142–143
Shott, Susan 140–142, 143
shyness 143
Simmel, Georg 39, 42, 81–94, 113; emotions and daily life 87–92; formal sociology and Paretian residues 104; *Große Soziologie* 42; *Die Großstädte und das Geistesleben* 50; love 81, 90, 91, 92–94; metropolis and the image of the self 82–87; *The Metropolis and Mental Life* 82, 88; *The Philosophy of Fashion* 83; *The Philosophy of Money* 82–86; *Sociology* 82
slavery: Khaldun 180; Martineau 7, 20; Marx 30–31, 33, 35
Smith, Robertson 62
sociability 116–119
social behaviourism 136

social construction of emotions: Elias 165; Marx 36; Pareto 107; Scheff 143; Schott 143; Tarde 41, 48, 50
social control 140, 142
social effervescence 50, 54, 63–65, 104
social equilibrium 105–106
social facts 55–56
social integration: Durkheim 42, 46, 49–50, 54–64; Tarde 45–46, 48, 49–51
socialism 97, 98, 105
sociality, residues connected with 103
social logic 43, 45, 46–49
social order 59, 61
social psychology 135–136
social regulation of emotions *see* control of emotions
social teleology 43, 48
society: Cooley 114–115, 122, 126–131; Elias 153, 155, 161; Khaldun 169–170
*Sociological Review, The* 109n4
solidarity 119, 126
solitude 86
Sorokin, Pitrim 98, 109n5
Spencer, Herbert 44, 96, 101
suicide 60–61
symbolic interactionism 134, 140, 142
sympathy: Cooley 116–120, 123, 126–129, 130; Tarde 46, 49, 50

Tarde, Gabriel 39–51, 96, 99; biography 39–40; *Contes et poèmes* 40; emotional infection and leaders 43–46, 47–48, 50, 51; emotions as social glue 49–51; logic of social sphere, emotions and morals 46–49; *La logique sociale des sentiments* 40–43, 49; *Les lois de l'imitation* 39, 40, 45, 51; *Les lois sociales* 40, 42–43; *La morale sexuelle* 46–48; *L'opinion et la foule* 44
terror 121
theodicy 77
Thomas, William Isaac 110n12
Tocqueville, Alexis de 9
touch 92
truth 128

utilitarianism 96, 106, 107

vanity 142

Walras, Leo 97
war: Cooley 125; Tarde 46, 48; Weber 73
Ward, Lester Frank 114
waste: Martineau 19; Marx 27, 36
wealth 18
Weber, Max 42, 68–79, 81, 113; "Basic Sociological Terms" 69, 71; modernity as a child of non-rational choice 75–78; and Pareto 96, 99, 101, 104, 110n11; political power of non-rational choice 71–75; *Die protestantische Ethik und der Geist des Kapitalismus* 42; sociological dignity of non-rational choice 69–71; "Sociology of Domination" 69
Wiley, N. 116–117
will: Durkheim 56; Elias 161
women: Martineau 5, 6, 7, 10; Marx 29, 36
Wordsworth, William 6

Yahaya, Mahayudin Hj 168

Znaniecki, Florian 114